SHED

One woman's journey *from being her old-self to becoming her* God-self

Michelle Martin

ISBN 979-8-89130-665-3 (paperback)
ISBN 979-8-89130-666-0 (digital)

Copyright © 2024 by Michelle Martin

All rights reserved. No part of this publication may be reproduced, distributed, or transmitted in any form or by any means, including photocopying, recording, or other electronic or mechanical methods without the prior written permission of the publisher. For permission requests, solicit the publisher via the address below.

Christian Faith Publishing
832 Park Avenue
Meadville, PA 16335
www.christianfaithpublishing.com

Cover photo by Danielle Arcilesi

This is a true story. However, I have changed the names of all individuals mentioned in the book except for mine, the author. Some changes have also been made in the setting and the descriptions of some individuals.

All the above was done to protect the identity and privacy of the individuals involved. Any resemblance between fictional names and descriptions and the names and descriptions of real persons is strictly coincidental.

The sole purpose of this book is to tell my personal story to inspire and motivate other individuals to seek healing and truth. My greatest desire is that you know your worth through the love of the Lord and become best friends with the Holy Spirit.

Printed in the United States of America

The power to pursue this project until the very end was only possible by countless words, moments, peace, inspiration, and an unbelievable closeness with my dear friend, the Holy Spirit. This was a ride I never expected but cherish wholeheartedly.

This book is dedicated to my silver linings—my children. - The unconditional love and belief given of them, the forgiveness, and the knowing of my true heart all inspired me to keep getting up and moving forward.

Special thanks to my greatest cheerleader, Heather, for always lifting me up and selflessly typing these words! You are the best soul sister I could have been blessed with!

My life group girls and prayer warriors—Barbara, Christy, Jackie, and Rhonda. You each supported, pushed, and loved me in a way I desperately needed.

Jill, you became a friend when I needed you most. We have many treasured adventures.

My husband, always praying, believing, supporting, and speaking truth over me.

Last but never least, my parents for always having open arms.

1

Darkness. It's the only thing I can see. Nothing.
This room is so cold, my bed so comfy. I don't want to leave. I just want to stay here. Hide. Bury myself under the covers. I don't know how I made it to bed last night, or even got undressed.

Oh, what did you do, Michelle? I hope nothing stupid.

I have no idea where my phone is. What time is it? According to the beaming of infrared coming from my alarm clock, it's 7:00. Ugh, 7:00! I need to get up, get ready for work. I roll out of bed.

"Come on, my sweet Buttercup, you need to go out, go potty."

It's still really dark outside. There are not many people stirring. That's odd. I flip the TV on. Oh, what a relief! It's nighttime. Thank goodness I don't have to go to work yet. Since it's still nighttime, I may as well fix another drink. I won't be able to sleep if I don't. I'll just think. And I don't want to do that.

*****

My alarm blares so loudly I hear it vibrate through my head. And that's not a good thing. My stomach is swirling. How am I going to make it through this day? I stumble to the kitchen and pop open a beer, then head to the bathroom to get ready. I still have some of yesterday's makeup on. I'll just touch up a little, make it look fresh, throw on some scrubs and tennis shoes.

I make my salad for lunch, mix up my protein shake, add a few shots of vodka. That'll ease me out of this hangover. Okay, look in the mirror. Smile. I look fairly normal, ready to muddle through the day. I really love my job. I love helping people. The elderly are so sweet. I enjoy hearing their stories of the simple old days. They tell some great jokes, and I adore the hugs. I throw myself into caring for them, helping them get stronger and, some, even to walk again.

I hope none of them can see past skin deep. If anyone took a look inside, they'd only find remnants of a shattered life. No one would believe this woman that stands before them with a warm smile and a tender touch has really lost it all. This woman that wants to see them get strong and able enough to go home has no home left at all.

The kids, they live with their dad, one hundred miles away. She talks about them all the time and shows their pictures, tells how amazing they are, how much she loves them; but she never fills in the blanks. She only gives an incomplete story. I guess you can say she lives in an imaginary world ever since she ruined the last one. Sometimes she can't believe it herself. Who is this woman that stands here now? A wreck. That's her only answer.

*****

The day eases by. The occupational therapist and I, the physical therapy assistant, make therapy fun and enjoyable. We all laugh together and really have a good time. As soon as I'm done with work, I head straight to the gym. I go for my run, then meet my friend Rex to lift weights together. Tonight we're going to Cajun's to listen to live music. He's been wanting me to meet one of his friends. I told him I wasn't interested. Although I'm not sure how to fix it, I'm greatly aware my life is a disaster in high speed. I've been kind of seeing someone in my apartment complex anyways. He and I drink together and spend most nights at my place or his. He's going through a divorce too. It's kind of nice to have someone to fill the void.

Rex and I decide to leave around eight. He lives a building over, so I walk to his place, then we go. I have a friend meeting me tonight too. I told her Rex was fixing me up, so she's coming as my rescue.

Cajun's is packed. I had a few shots before leaving my apartment, so I'm already feeling relaxed. We find a table and order some drinks. My friend Marla is already there. We all sit, talk, and laugh. Rex's friend arrives, and he brings him over to meet me.

"Michelle, this is my friend Jared. He works with me on Post. He's a warrant officer and a pilot for the Army National Guard."

He shakes my hand, says a few pleasantries.

I'm totally irritated with Rex. Not my type at all. Not good-looking and very scrawny. I like a guy with some muscle. I cut my eyes to my friend Marla; and she comes over, grabs me, and says, "I have got to tell you something."

We go sit on the couch and talk.

"I can't believe Rex set me up with this guy."

"Me neither," says Marla. "I'm sure he's nice and all, but not your type in the least."

We slip off to the dance floor and enjoy ourselves. Rex cuts in to dance with Marla. I go back to the couch and sip on my drink. Jared comes to sit beside me and talk. I'm so not interested I actually start playing on my phone. He asks for my number, and I don't know how to politely say no, so I give it to him. He asks all kinds of questions about my kids, job, and hobbies.

"After my divorce from Everett, the only full-time position I could find was in Cobalt, one hundred miles from where I was living, also my hometown. The girls and I moved, my youngest son stayed to live with his dad, my oldest son was in college. The girls didn't like the schools, so they moved back with their dad. I haven't been able to find work close to where they live."

The actual truth was that I really couldn't find full-time employment anywhere close, but the other part was one of my fill-in-the-blank truths. The girls and I had moved over Christmas break. I had them both signed up for school. I had just bought my first-ever new car; and to celebrate, I had a few drinks, which I tried to keep hidden from the girls. You would think by this time I would have realized how impossible that was. They called their dad, and he came the next morning to get them. Somehow Ashlynn wanted to stay with me, and he agreed. I believe she feared for me if I didn't have anyone besides my little Buttercup. Ashlynn went to school for a week and hated it. She had come from a small-town school with a total of two hundred students K-12 to over six hundred per class. She desperately wanted to move back. I would have too.

Jared said he has two boys from his first wife (they live with him) and has a daughter from this marriage (she lives close by with her mom). Yikes. Two divorces. Kind of alarming. He'd been divorced for a year.

"How long have you been divorced?" he asks me.

"It's been a month," I tell him. "He remarried the day after. Yes. The. Day. After."

Boy, that was quite a shocker. I was on a road trip with my friend Alexis. We had gone down to Alabama to visit her friends and family. Her dad and stepmom had been killed in a tornado the year before. The town had fixed up a memorial, so we went down to see it. We had gone out with some of her friends that were playing in a band. I was pretty trashed. Ashlynn called me, bawling, because her dad had taken off and got married. He didn't talk it over with the kids, and they weren't even aware he was dating. I had only moved a month and a half earlier. He married my son's best friend's mom. We used to camp and go to the lake together. Talk about mind-blowing.

I actually didn't remember any of that conversation with Ashlynn. The next day, when Alexis and I were driving back to Tennessee, she asked if I remembered Ashlynn calling and telling me. I completely lost it. Our kids have just gone through hell with us splitting up, and he's bringing another woman and her two boys into the mix? So soon! My poor kids. And I, I could do nothing.

Marla and Rex come back, thank goodness. Jared is asking questions that require creative answers, and right now I just don't have them. The night rolls on with everyone laughing and talking. Jared asks me to dance. I love to dance, so we hit the floor. Oh my. He can't even dance. Not my type at all. I have no desire to see this guy ever again. And, Rex, you are in so much trouble, friend.

2

Within days, Jared was calling, and I was ignoring. I'm not attracted to him at all. I have something going with Eric anyway. He lives right here in the same apartment complex, and we spend most nights together drinking. When I left Everett, he had me put a breathalyzer in my vehicle to ensure the kids' safety. Rightfully so. That thing would pick up alcohol in my system even the next morning. After a few months of that, I bought a cheap car to drive so I wouldn't have to deal with that annoying thing. After a night of drinking with Eric, it was easy to get up and grab a beer to ease off the hangover.

On the weekends that I didn't have the kids, I made sure to have my time stocked with partying. I didn't want to be alone too much. I always had Eric at the apartment to fall back on. Jared persistently called and texted. Geez! Doesn't this guy get it? He was very flirtatious and gave me some really sweet compliments. He invited me to several events that sounded like my kind of fun. He was always asking. Weekends, during the week, he came up with some great ideas.

Several weeks of him sweet-talking, and I caved. He invited me to a downtown food-and-beer event. We met up with a good friend of his and his wife, a prominent photographer. I instantly loved them! They were both sweet, caring, and down-to-earth. Even if Jared wasn't my kind of guy, he had the right idea of fun and friends. When Jared dropped me off, I made it clear that I only wanted to be friends. I told him my divorce was too fresh and my kids were already having to see their dad with someone else, they didn't need that from me too. Unknown to him, I had already done enough damage. As soon as he left, I went in, changed clothes, and walked over to Eric's. He had even given me a key to his apartment. It was comforting to have someone to crawl in bed with whenever I wanted. He never asked questions when I went out. No strings attached, as we were both filling an empty space.

Every night was a party, either by myself, with a bunch of friends, or Eric and me. St. Patrick's Day, my friend Rachel and I had gone shopping for cute outfits and accessories. Alexis's band was playing, and a bunch of friends from high school were going. I hadn't seen many of them in years and years. Rachel and I spent hours getting ready and drinking. I was wasted by the time we got there. There's no telling what a fool I made of myself. Alexis was pretty irritated with me and tried taking care of me. Rachel and her boyfriend wanted me to leave with them. Alexis begged me not to go.

"Rachel's not a good influence, Michelle. Let's go to my house, you can sleep it off."

I hung out with Alexis and another friend of ours, Rick. I continued to party quite a bit over at Rachel's. We always had different guys over. Rex and I spend a lot of time together. We went to Cajun's almost every Thursday, ladies' night. Jared would meet us there some. He was pursuing me pretty hard. We had gone trail riding on bikes, and we met his best friend and his wife for dinner one night. Another nice couple. Jared said they loved me instantly and added, "What's not to love?"

Oh, if he only knew, I thought. No one could ever love me. The things that have happened, well, they destroyed the person I had once been. The person who is here now, she is the biggest ball of many intertwined levels of pain. Rejected, unloved, unwanted, worthless, destructive. There's a ginormous wall around this heart. It's permanent, strong stone protection.

3

Rex came up with an idea to take a trip with a group of friends to Vegas. I had never been, so it sounded great to me. He was always trying to get me to set him up with my single friends. I asked several, but none of them were able to go. He had asked many of his friends too. I told him to please not ask Jared! He'll try to be all over me, and I don't want that. I want to be free to explore. What do you know? He asked Jared, and Jared wanted to go. Great. So there we go. The trip to Vegas was set to be the three of us. I was so excited because, heck, it's Vegas; but I wasn't sure how to handle Jared being there. I'm not the kind to be straight-out rude. I really just wanted to let loose; have fun; and look for a good-looking, muscled-up guy to hang out with.

    I spent the week of our trip packing. My best friend Jade came over to help. We had clothes, shoes, and jewelry all over my bed. The trip was only three nights. I had eight outfits and six pairs of shoes. I've always been a terrible overpacker. How can I know ahead of time what I'll feel like wearing? Or what the weather will be like? What if we go somewhere casual or nice? And the right shoes are a must.

    Rex and I rode to the airport together. My suitcase was over the fifty-pound limit, so we started transferring stuff into Rex's bag. Jared met us there with little time left before takeoff. Those two must have planned the seating. Jared and I were seated together, and Rex was way in the back.

    The flight was actually fun. Jared and I sat by some guy from Chicago. We played the drinking game Never Have I Ever. It was very interesting, and by the time we arrived in Vegas, we all felt pretty good. We made it to our hotel by midnight, but my suitcase didn't! It was left on the transport van. Jared took over. A few calls and an hour later, we were changed and hit the strip.

It didn't take long for Rex to wander off, leaving me with Jared. No way around it. Just go with it. There was so much to see all around—lights, colors, activity, a variety of people from a variety of places. It was kind of magical. Abnormal. Lively. A different world. And I liked that. I for sure didn't want to be a part of the world I had created.

I closed my eyes and imagined who I could be. Here, I could be anyone. Tonight I was like the top sales rep for a million-dollar company. I won this trip, and my kids were all so proud of me. "You deserve it, Mom. Go have fun." That was a reality I could live with.

I relaxed and began to enjoy my surroundings. Jared was very attentive and complimented me over and over. He opened doors for me, pulled out my chair at the table, brought drinks to me, even bought a rose for me from a street vendor. I've never had anyone treat me with such admiration. He put his arm out for me to hold on to as we walked down the street. His jokes were funny, and he even gave me a piggyback ride since my heels were killing my feet. He was a lot of fun.

I woke up the next morning with Jared beside me. I couldn't remember the details, but it was obvious things had advanced between us. It didn't change my heart's position. It is still locked up and not to be given away again.

The three of us continued to take in the sights of Vegas. Jared continued to edge closer. Each step forward he took, I shimmied back. The trip was quick, busy, and a lot of fun. It was everything I imagined it would be. Vegas, the place where anything can happen, and when it does, it stays there. That's how I wanted things with Jared and me to be. The advancement of things between us was only a Vegas thing.

4

Only a few days back from Vegas, I get a call from Everett. He immediately begins to yell and cuss at me.

"Do you have any idea what people are saying about you, slut? I can't believe you'd take off to Vegas with two guys. How many did you sleep with while you were out there?"

"Whoa, you need to stop talking to me like that. This trip was not like that, and it's not any of your business."

"Well, the kids are my business, and they're too busy this weekend. You can't have them."

"You have no right to withhold the kids from me just because you don't approve of a trip I took on my free time. How can you hold that against me? You're the one that got married the day after our divorce!"

"I do have the right to not let the kids see you. And they won't!"

Helpless. Limp. Frozen. I have no rights. I have no power. I loved these babies before they were able to breathe, and now I can't reach them. There is no life. I reach for the bottle of vodka and sip until the pain is numb and then nonexistent. Like I wish I could be.

That entire week was a blur. I'm broken, bleeding, and I don't want to move. I answer a few texts. Marla asks what happened, so I fill her in. She tells me I need to fight for my rights. I tell her I don't have any and I don't deserve any anyway. She asks me to contact her lawyer and gives me his name and number. Rex stops by to check on me. He says Jared has been asking about me, says he's worried because I won't reply.

I tell him, "I really don't care. I'm not interested in him anyhow."

It takes me a few days to stew over everything. Marla calls and encourages me. I finally call the lawyer. I give him a quick overview of the last several months. He tells me that once something like that has been signed, there really isn't much I can do about it. Wow. This is really it. I've dug a pit, jumped in, and there is no chance of daylight. I just want to see my kids. I ask Everett if I can pick them up from school and take them to dinner. He won't even go for that.

5

There's one thing I am good at, and that is wallowing. I decide to wallow to the best of my ability. I desire distraction because the reality of the real circumstance is only a stabbing pain. Alcohol, parties, and sex. Distractions that are easy to come by and fill most of my days and all of my nights. Jared keeps pulling closer and closer. He's a smart guy. Does he not realize how much of a disaster he keeps trying to pry himself into? He calls and texts a lot.

One night he took me to dinner and somehow got me to talking. We had several drinks, which compounded with the ones I had before he came to pick me up, and it made it easier for me to start opening up. He asks when my marriage to Everett started having trouble. I haven't had too much to drink to not be coherent but enough that I allow myself to travel back.

I had started giving in at the very beginning of the marriage, the honeymoon, actually. Everett wanted to come back early so he could go to the races with the guys. I wanted him to be happy, so I agreed. That was the beginning of him pushing me aside. I got broken into disappointment quickly. When I would wake in the mornings, he was already gone. I'd get Lane ready and dropped off, then drive forty-five minutes to work at the hospital, my first job as a physical therapy assistant. I graduated, got married, and started a new job all in one month. I'd pick Lane up, go home, clean, and cook.

Everett would come in late, usually between eight and nine. He'd eat supper, shower, want sex, and then go to sleep. Every night, in that order. It was always very quick and never an attempt to offer me satisfaction. Even on the weekends, he'd be gone. On Sundays, he would leave, come in for church, then leave again after lunch.

6

Lane and I had been on our own for two and a half years, so I was used to that, but it wasn't what I hoped for after adding a husband. I had hoped the heartbreak from my first love would be my last. That was a devastation my young heart had barely survived. Lane was my saving grace.

I met his dad, Johnny, my senior year in high school. My romantic heart believed deeply in love, but I thought love at first sight was a myth beyond reach. Until Johnny. Something was created between us with only the gaze from our lovestruck eyes. He didn't have to speak a word or touch me; he was able to access my heart from a distance with the lock of our eyes.

Falling never felt more magical as when our hearts fell together. The power was so gentle, yet forceful, I couldn't stop it if I had wanted to. But I didn't want to. He was the first person I gave my heart to. I dove in with no thought to it. I immersed him in my love, holding nothing back for myself.

Just after graduation, I discovered I was pregnant. Johnny and I were madly in love. He had a ring picked out, and we were trying to decide on a wedding date. Telling my parents was terrifying. My dad was Marine Corps; Mom, strict in the church. And this wasn't something that was supposed to happen. But I knew I loved Johnny with my whole heart, and he loved me with his. We could overcome anything with our power of love.

I started college in the fall. I was due in February, so I could at least get one semester in. When Christmas rolled around, I looked as if I had swallowed the turkey at Thanksgiving. My parents had adjusted to the change of my life course and had come to accept Johnny.

Johnny spent Christmas break in Georgia with his family. While he was gone, I began to discover his unfaithfulness. I couldn't understand. He said he loved me. In my world, love is real and authentic. It's not shared out of the scope of two people. Truths began to unfold before me that shook the unexpected world I had come to accept. I could adjust my goals to an unplanned pregnancy; I could not adjust my heart to an unfaithful love.

When Johnny called to check on me one evening, I told him about the truths I had found while he had been gone. I told him I wanted him in our son's life but no longer in my heart. He was heartbroken and didn't return after Christmas break. I kept in touch with his mom and sister that still lived in the same town as me.

One evening in January, I got a call from Johnny's mom. Johnny had been shot in the head and was in critical condition. The bullet entered his skull behind his ear and exploded out of his jaw. I fell to the floor in total devastation. My love, the father to my unborn son, was lying in ICU; and I couldn't be there. Several hours later, I went into labor.

Although I had broken up with Johnny, the plan was for him to be in the delivery room. The ICU nurses ran a phone into Johnny's room so he could hear the birth of our son. He didn't come to see Lane until he was six months old. I had to grow up in that time and had become a dedicated mom. I still loved Johnny and wanted a complete family so badly. I just wasn't able to trust him. And he wasn't able to be a father. He left and went back to Georgia.

7

Everett was very strict with Lane, borderline mean. Well, he *was* mean. That didn't go over well with me in the slightest. When I would say something, Everett's temper would flare. I began to dislike him. My needs were being ignored in the bedroom. That's fine. It's not important. I can survive. I just wanted a family. Surely, Everett's heart would soon soften.

Lane was already four. I wanted more kids soon so they would grow up with a closeness. Everett said he wanted kids too, so we quit taking precautions. Only a few months of trying and my period was late. I remember the day so clearly. I was at work at the hospital, and our director of therapy was also over the lab. She told me she would do a blood test, and I'd know for sure in no time. What seemed like hours later, I had the results I'd hoped for. We were pregnant! I was beyond excited! My dreams of being a mom and sharing this intimate creation with my husband were finally being pieced together!

I had done the pregnancy thing alone with Lane. This time I was getting to share it with my husband, to dream together. To anticipate this human together. Who would the baby look like? My freckles and stubbornness or his jet-black hair and height? A mystery waiting to be born and loved already.

I couldn't wait to tell him. I called right away. His excitement blew me over with the force of a feather. Not the response I was looking for but it'll change. It has to. This is my dream. I loved being pregnant. I knew all the science behind it, but the details amazed me. Everett's lack of interest slowly began to pierce my bubble. I went to the doctor, alone. I listened to the heartbeat, alone. I found out the sex of the baby, alone. I watched her move in my belly, alone.

Ashlynn was beautiful the moment she made her debut. We had a waiting room full of family and friends wanting to meet her. Everett was a dad for the first time. I saw a look of love and pride in his eyes when his burly arms held this little treasure. He was in love at first sight too. Everett took us home from the hospital the next day. I couldn't wait for my little family to all be home, cozy and warm together. Everett unloaded me and the baby, our things, and then he left. He left.

I must have unconsciously sunk down in my seat so no one would see the tears leaking from my eyes. I had no idea they were there myself until I snapped out of it. I took several deep breaths and tried to push it aside like it was a lifetime-ago story that didn't still affect my present. Jared saw too much of me. He softly took my hand and gave me a smile that apologized for my pain.

Don't do that. That smile of understanding is prickling my heart. I don't want to feel.

I continued the evening in complete Michelle style. One drink after another until the pain transitioned into dancing and laughs. Jared stayed the night with me that night. I realized I had let him into an area of myself that was supposed to be barricaded. He must have overlooked the yellow caution tape and signs saying "Keep Out!" I tried acting like nothing was different between us. But I couldn't deny he had taken a glimpse of my soul, and I felt it.

8

Everett finally gave in and let the kids come stay the weekend with me again. I tried to keep our weekends filled with fun activities. I want the kids to enjoy being with me. Jared had several good ideas, and we started spending kid weekends together—as friends. And I repeatedly made sure the kids knew that's all it was. I love having my weekends with the kids, but at the same time, it stings. Nothing is normal about it. The fact that their dad is remarried and they have a new family, a new home without me, is one I can't grasp. I fought with Everett to get to be a stay-at-home mom because I didn't want to miss anything. Now all I get feels like only minutes every other weekend. I try to come to their games when I know about them and can. Everett didn't communicate with me when we were under the same roof; it was a hundred times worse now.

I remember one Sunday a few months after the divorce when we met to swap kids, I confronted Everett. Josie was only nine and had a bra for the first time. I told him to please let me do the mom-daughter stuff with her like that. He looked at me with disgust burning in his eyes and said, "You should've known you'd be replaced." That summed up every single bit of what I felt. So insignificant. So replaceable. That became my scarlet letter. A big roaring *R*, not just on my forehead but stamped on my chest and seeped into my heart. I'd been through hell to earn it. Now I own it.

I really began to live it. Replaced. When I called the kids to see how school was, it blazed in my ears. Replaced. When I had to let them go back with their dad, it slapped me in the face. Replaced. Knowing they were living without me was the worst prickling pain. I didn't call as much because it hurt to hear the things they were doing without me. I gave that pain the right to not care what happened to me. They were better off.

I continued to nurse my gaping wounds with alcohol and busyness. Jared and I went out a lot, but I kept him at arm's length. I continued to go to Eric's. I didn't care about much of anything at this point, except not feeling.

Memorial Day weekend Jared and I had planned to go to the concerts at Riverfest and a pool party at some of his friend's. Rex had told me Jared was getting irritated with me. He'd pick me up, we'd go out, and, when he'd take me home, I'd say goodbye and jump out. No smooches. I wanted to keep it casual. After all, he wasn't my type.

So this night, instead of him picking me up, we were to meet in Nashville. I did my usual drinking while getting ready. I didn't make it far. Only as far as the police station via the back of a police car. Another "first" I didn't want to add to my list. But there was no chance of pulling it back. I was booked for a DWI with a refusal. When they decided to release me, both Jared and Eric were there to pick me up. Talk about awkwardness! I told Eric I had plans with Jared and I'd be fine. We had missed the concert, so Jared took me home with him. We went to the pool party the next day. He had more cool friends, and we had a great weekend together.

Monday being Memorial Day, Eric was off work. I only had to work a part of a day. We spent the rest of the day hiking and picnicking. It was a beautiful day. I was able to escape the thoughts of the DWI mess for a little bit. I had made emotional escaping an art form. If you don't want to feel or think of the horrible, awful of any part of your life, just push it down and cram your mind and time with distractions. Yeah, I should have a master's in that.

According to Rex, Jared was really upset with me for spending time with Eric after Jared and I had such a nice time together that same weekend. Well, that irritated me because I had made it clear so many times that I wasn't interested in him. That Thursday night Rex and I met up with Jared and some girl he brought to Cajun's, trying to make me jealous. She was cool and a lot of fun. She and I danced together on the floor and enjoyed talking. I also met a guy named

Kyle that night. We hung out, danced, and he ended up coming home with me.

Rex and I would take turns cooking for each other. We were both into working out and healthy eating, so it worked. He stayed at my place some, and I stayed at his. We were both on the same page as far as friends only, which allowed him to be open with me about certain things. He told me he thought Jared was falling in love with me. He tried telling me he's a good guy and would take good care of me, to give him a chance. Well, that sounds all fine and good for a girl looking for that, but I'm not one of those girls. I'm only looking for meaningless, emotionless, not-developing-into-anything distractions. Which is so odd, because my entire life, my biggest fantasy was to be deeply, madly, intimately in love with one man and be the loving mother to our beautiful babies. Happily ever after, "The End."

When that fairy tale crashed onto the island of hopeless dreams, it left me planted inside the tale of the complete opposite, hopeless destruction. Funny how your intended destination can be on the other side of the world of where you land. But whatever, I'm here, it sucks, and I'm stranded with no knowledge or map of how to get out.

9

My time was now occupied with Eric, Jared, and a sprinkle here and there of Kyle. Things were different with Jared though. He wasn't only concerned about having a good time; he wanted to know me. I suppose that's why I tried so hard to avoid him. I'm not worth knowing. How could he not see that? Me pushing him away was for his own good. The lack of avoiding poison has never been considered brave, only stupid.

Jared's ability to get me to start opening up surprised me and totally pissed me off. I shared with him how after having my third baby, Brock, I fought to be a stay-at-home mom. Everett was so against it. I knew it would be difficult financially, but I was willing to do without. My marriage was lacking for anything I had hoped it would be. The chance to be a mom was all I had. I wanted all of it.

Everett was rarely home. We didn't talk much, never had since the day we were married. He was a hard worker and provider, yes. He farmed. Sunup to sundown. That was his life. I guess for him I completed the missing piece he needed—housekeeper, cook, baby momma, bed warmer. He was emotionally absent. The long talks lying in bed I longed for was replaced with quick sex and sleep. I got used to expecting nothing more.

I did all the housework, laundry, cooking, yard work, bathing kids, homework, putting them to bed, nursing them when they were sick, middle-of-the-night feedings, diaper changes. Anything that took place inside our house and surrounding yard, I did. All the school functions and kids' activities, I attended alone. Family get-togethers, alone. Even Christmas Eve, it was my sister Leah that helped me put toys together and wrap presents. I was exhausted. I was lonely and emotionally starving.

He was difficult to talk to. He didn't like to listen, and his usual response was to fly off the handle. I couldn't control his lack of interest or participation in my emotional needs, but my kids needed me. So I bit my lip, shut my eyes, and presented my request to him about me quitting work.

He did his usual fussing and griping at me for weeks. I don't know if it was the look of desperation in my eyes or if somewhere deep inside he located the love he had for me, but he agreed to let me stay home. Good thing because I felt as though I couldn't continue it all anymore. Being a stay-at-home mom was literally a dream come true for me. I didn't want to miss anything my kids did. Rolling over, cooing, first steps, learning the alphabet, silly songs, puzzles, little helping hands in the kitchen, riding in the little red wagon, swinging on the swing set—I wanted them to have it all and me to soak up every second of it.

As I shared these moments with Jared, I told him in a spaced-out monotone voice, "I was living my biggest dream but watching it be stolen at the same time." My eyes clicked back to the present, and I caught the questioning in his eyes. It was difficult to explain the feeling of having part of your biggest dream a reality but the other half of it so far out of your grasp. These were all the moments I never wanted to miss, but they were also the moments I never intended to keep to myself. Imbedded in my deep desire to be a mom was the deep desire to share these magical events. To share them with the man that helped create the little beings creating the magic. The intimacy of watching it all unfold together. I had always imagined it to be a bonding of epic capacity. That was a huge missing piece beyond my ability to create by myself. Everything else I could do on my own.

Jared had secretly snuck his way up on top of the wall I had built around my heart. He wasn't getting my creative fill in the blank answers anymore. He was getting truth. I still didn't like it, but somewhere, something inside of me did. I started spending less time with Eric and Kyle, more time with Jared and his kids. I adored his kids and enjoyed being with all of them. We did a lot together—dinner, movies, took my jet skis to the lake, played games. As much as I enjoyed our time together, it deepened the already painful longing for my own kids.

It's strange how my life continued in a pattern of opposite extremes. He was the involved dad to his kids that I had once believed existed and ever so desired. I still longed for a piece of that a lifetime ago. The lifetime that was gone. I allowed myself to venture into their world, but when I met with my true reality, I boomeranged back to my present emptiness. And there was my ever-faithful alcohol. Always reliable to numb me into nothingness.

10

One evening as Jared and I lay on my bed, my wounds continued to bleed in front of him, but he wasn't afraid of them. He listened. I told him how I always felt like an outsider. How could a girl from the city ever expect to fit in the country? And what was I thinking? It goes back to that dream. The country is the safest place to raise kids, right? I suppose I didn't truly understand how different this would be.

Johnny was nowhere close to stable and reliable. He had a very hard life. His mom had been married five or six times when I had met him. Everett filled in the gaps where he lacked. His parents were still married, he went to church, he was a hard worker. Reliable. All the things Lane and I needed. I couldn't have known that moving to this place that was so beautiful would be the place where I would lose myself.

The loneliness began to eat away the parts of me that had once been good until they were nonexistent.

I lay there on my stomach with my hands holding up my chin, bleeding out these pains to Jared. He took my hands and looked deep into my eyes, all the way into my soul.

He said, "Michelle, you're still in there. I see you. I see how loving you are with your kids and mine. I want to be here for you, with you. I'm falling in love with you. I can't continue to be here for you as a friend and watch you go out with Eric and Kyle. It hurts too much. I want us to be together, or I'm going to have to step away."

I was somewhat stunned by that. I knew he had been developing feelings for me, but I had hoped somehow I could avoid this.

I had hoped we could just keep being friends and not get feelings involved. I had even told him countless times I was too much of a mess to get involved with. I warned him, but here we were.

"Jared, I care for you, but I am nowhere close to where I need to be for a relationship. I don't even want one. My kids have been thrown into a new family only five months ago with their dad. They don't need another. I'm only a bunch of trouble. You don't want that."

"I know all that, but I don't care. I can be good to you. I can help you."

"I don't know, Jared. I feel like I keep making one bad decision after another. I don't want to keep doing that."

He gave me a hug and kiss, then left.

I don't understand why he would want me. I never thought anyone would ever want me again. He doesn't even know my whole story. I've been rejected and replaced. I'm not good enough to be loved. I figured he would have found that out by now.

About an hour after he left, he sent me a song, "Somebody That I Used to Know" by Gotye.

"I don't want that to be you," he says.

I have several drinks and go to bed.

About three o'clock, I'm wide awake. This is usually when I would call him. He never minded. He was just happy to hear my voice. I've never had someone that didn't mind sharing my sleepless nights with me. I know I don't want Jared out of my life, but I don't know if I can be in his the way he needs.

Despite my best efforts, Jared started taking up more space in my heart. He asked again for me to make a commitment to him. I knew I didn't want to be without him, so I agreed. I cut ties with Eric and Kyle. Jared had become aware of my drinking problem and tried to help.

"Don't drink alone," he requested.

I would do great for periods of time. Jared and I took several trips together but as a couple now.

The days following my kid weekends were the worst. Jared still had his boys and also got his daughter every Wednesday night. When those reminders of what I didn't have piled up, I would drink the screaming pain level down. I let the alcohol drown the feelings I wanted to bury them, as if it would stop them from coming back.

I was back and forth between Jared's house and my apartment. Jared had a deck with a hot tub that overlooked the Tennessee River. It became one of my favorite places to be. Either in the hot tub with him or on the swing watching the thousands of stars twinkle. This porch seemed to have mystical powers of reaching into the memories that continually swirled in my head and slipping them across my lips. I ignored the vulnerability it gave me. He listened. His touch always seemed to soak up some of the hurt. One of the most difficult sections of my past to reveal was when it all completely spiraled beyond saving.

11

As the kids grew, so did the loss of my dream, the dream of not doing this alone. I went to Everett countless times begging him to spend time with the kids and me. He would toss us a Saturday afternoon from time to time, then it was right back to the same routine. I shared with my best friend, my sister-in-law, and a cousin my despair, asking for advice. One of them suggested marriage counseling. It took quite the effort of convincing Everett, but I knew he could feel the unhappiness under our roof. I had no idea how grueling counseling was going to be.

When I had married and moved to the farm, I had left all my friends behind. Contact with them was rare, which only grew my feelings of isolation. Here, in counseling, was an actual person to listen and offer help. I shared how I needed time and connection with Everett, but he was always gone. Everett's stance was that he was busy making a living. The counselor asked Everett to make time to spend with the kids and me, and for me to tell Everett my appreciation for his hard work.

We continued in therapy several weeks, uncovering the less desired parts of our marriage. It was painful, exhausting, and frustrating. I told the counselor about the hidden camera I had found in our bathroom. I was on our computer one day and came across a set of photos I wasn't familiar with. They were photos of me undressing to shower. I had an enormous feeling of invasion of privacy. When I confronted Everett with it, he said, "You're my wife, I can do what I want." And so he did in many ways. The counselor told Everett he needed to respect me as a person. That being his wife didn't mean

I wasn't allowed privacy. It didn't make me his property. When the time came for our next appointment, Everett said he was too busy and didn't like it anyway. There, my scarlet letter that I would one day own made a deep claw mark on my heart. Rejected.

The greatest joys in my life were my children. This was one area I actually got right. I put my all into my kids. They were the diamonds that sparkled in my darkness. Three beautiful children but I longed for another. Everett wasn't onboard with it, so I continued on the pill. I started to accept it and got rid of my maternity clothes and baby items that Brock had now outgrown. Life loves irony. Not long after getting rid of all the baby stuff, I found out I was pregnant again. I had been on the pill; but during a sickness, I had taken antibiotics, undoing its effectiveness. I actually cried not knowing how to accept what I had already let go of. I knew Everett wouldn't be happy with me, and how were we going to afford this now?

I always loved the magic of being pregnant. This time I did have someone to share it with. Lane was able to understand what was going on. Ashlynn, at four, was not completely able to understand, but she was a big, sweet help. Brock totally swallowed up into the terrible twos and ever so adorable at the same time. The doctor's visits were the usual, on my own or with a kid or two. My sister Leah was the one with me when I found out I was having another girl. That's about as perfect as you can get—two boys, two girls.

I had made many attempts over the years to make my marriage work, to get Everett to do things with me, spend time with me and talk. We must have been two people with polar opposite definitions of marriage. His the more old fashioned—man works, is waited on hand and foot, what I say goes, wife is property type. Mine was shaped with love story, fairytale, happily ever after, hearts beating as one, best friend, do everything together, we are intertwined, romanticism. Those two extremes obviously don't mesh well. I'm not saying mine is right and his is wrong, but his wasn't right for me.

I had been raised in the church, and divorce is very frowned upon. It's wrong, not acceptable. I didn't want to be divorced. Everett didn't pay much attention to the kids now. The thought of him having to care for them without me was scary. Not that he didn't love them, he did. But he was never hands on with their care or safety. I made another attempt to pull this family together. A few months before Josie was born, we bought a camper. There were about six to seven families that would spend a week together at the lake every summer. Everett was onboard with this, and we had many enjoyable summers at the lake.

Not even two weeks after the first lake trip, very hot, mid-July, I had been mowing and weed eating. Alice, Everett's mom, was inside playing with the kids. She was one of my favorite people and had become a best friend to me. I got cleaned up and was relaxing on the couch, the kids in their usual state of entertaining. The contractions began. Alice called Everett, and it wasn't too long until he made it home. He had hurt his ankle and was limping. We loaded up the van, three kids, Alice, Everett, and me driving while in full-on labor. Once settled in, Everett went to the ER and ended up on crutches. I don't even remember what was wrong. Josie made her appearance that evening, the shortest labor of all four.

Josie had a head full of jet-black thick hair. She was a little darling. The final piece to the family I had always longed for. I dressed her in the same outfit I brought Ashlynn home in. My mom was waiting at the house with the other kids to welcome us home. We pulled into the garage; and Everett unloaded me, the baby, and our things. The kids were so excited to have their new sister home. I settled in on the couch so they could love on her with sloppy kisses. Everett had gone to change and was about to leave when my mom stopped him.

"You can't just leave. Michelle and the baby just got home."

Arguing ensued between them, as did my tears. Then like the other times, he left.

He left.

12

Jared always held me as I revealed my scars. I kept expecting him to get enough and leave too. He'd have to soon. The more deeply he looked inside me, surely, he'd see it. I don't deserve anything good. Something was broken within me. All that is left is tainted worthlessness. Johnny didn't want me. He left. Everett didn't want me. He left many times. Jared is going to dig deep enough and find my scarlet letter. He'll reject me too. I know this. I kept a section of my heart secluded. Not to be touched. It held my realities. They were painful, but they were mine.

As messed up as I was and as hard as I tried running from my feelings, having someone to listen felt good. I tried to escape that fact, but like a rubber band, it kept pulling me back. The final collapse of my marriage and the undoing of myself, I shared in pieces with Jared. He could've handled the truth in one dose. It was my revisiting of the events that needed to be shared like a slow-dripping infusion. Drip by drip, he'd get the whole picture.

13

My fondest memories come from my years as a stay-at-home mom. Each one of my kids from birth until late toddler years were rocked into naps with my singing or humming "Amazing Grace." We did project after project from bean art to finger painting. I liked to play games and do puzzles with the kids for intellectual stimulation. Our days were full of activity. The kids were involved in tee-ball and basketball. My parents, Everett's mom, and my sister-in-law were usually there. Everett made an appearance occasionally.

Four kids is a lot to handle. Lane was in school by the time Josie was born. She was up every two to three hours to nurse and be changed, so I basically slept an hour at a time. By the time actual morning came and it was time to get Lane ready for school, I entered zombie mode. I was busy twenty-four hours a day. The kids didn't nap much or rarely at all. I tried my hardest to do it all—wife and mom. I didn't realize it at the time, but when you continue to use something that's broken, it only breaks more. Even the best-built machine or car can't get far with a flat tire.

I always made sure supper was on the table and tried to have dinner as a family. Many, many times that meant just me and the kids. Everett wouldn't help with anything in or around the house. When he came in from work, it was shower, supper, then either bed or TV. I remember playing in the floor one night with the kids, trying to get his attention. He was kicked back in the recliner watching TV. I finally picked up the baby and sat her on his belly, trying to lure him to see the beauty of our family.

My loneliness continued to grow, but I'm not a quitter. I was raised in church and believed in marriage. My vows were serious to me. The merry-go-round spun relentlessly. I spoke to Everett countless times about the need for him to be involved. Over time, slowly, like air seeping out of a tire, I felt my love for Everett slipping away. But even worse than that were the feelings that began to take up the empty space. Feelings of anger, hurt, dissatisfaction, and even dislike, started to brew in love's place. This didn't so much scare me as it did break my heart. If I had known what was to come, there would have been fear.

I pleaded again for us to start marriage counseling. It was wintertime, and Everett wasn't as busy. There was about a four-month window of a not-so-busy season. Luckily, the counselor we had been to before was still on staff. We were able to continue without having to unload our full history. We updated the changes that had taken place and revisited the hurts that continued. The counselor's assessment was basically the same. Everett needed to try to spend more time with the kids and I. I needed to show appreciation for his hard work. I told the counselor that most of the time I was exhausted and frustrated that Everett wouldn't help with anything, and I didn't feel like showing appreciation for that. He spoke about how biblically we are supposed to honor each other. He said do these things out of duty and, eventually, the feelings will be restored.

You should've seen the sword fight I took on with my stubbornness! I did not feel like continuing to bend over backward while my needs kept being shoved aside like a pile of manure! The desire to keep my family together won over, and once again, I soldiered on. I didn't want my kids to have a broken home. I didn't want them to have two houses and separate holidays. I continued to do all the things around the house and with the kids. I waited on Everett when he got home, as usual, but with a smile instead of rolling my eyes. I went to the bedroom when he was ready, as usual, but nothing changed.

We were about a month back into counseling, and I told the counselor what was going on. I had made changes with my attitude and had made more of a point to make Everett feel appreciated. He continued with his same behavior and ignored my needs. The counselor gave Everett specific ideas on what he wanted him to do. Help with the kids some, not work on Sundays, and implement date nights. He told him it is God's plan for him to honor me as well. That final suggestion was all Everett needed. He was done with counseling. "He didn't have time for this" was his justification. I looked at my scarlet letter and rolled my eyes at another layer of red.

A few days after that last session, Everett stopped in for lunch. He did that from time to time if he was working cows close by. It was the normal come in, eat, leave the mess on the table, and leave. No thank-you and most of the time not even a goodbye. I felt like a cook and his maid. I remember the day so clearly. I can still see his truck driving off down the driveway. That's when I changed. I stood there in the kitchen and let all my feelings drain.

I'm done. I will not do this anymore. I'm staying in this marriage for the sole purpose of my kids having a home. I will only go through the motions with Everett to keep the peace.

Like pulling a plug, I disconnected my heart.

14

My older sister and I decided to take a trip to Washington, DC, to visit my little sister. Josie was three. This was my first trip away from all the kids and was much needed. I was always so focused on everyone else's needs and basically lived in a shell. I missed the kids terribly, but the time away was so nice. Our cousin lived in DC too, and all of us went out to a gay bar. That was a very unique experience! It was so much fun dancing and drinking wine together. It was a world I had never lived in. The following evening we went to dinner at my cousin's friend's condo. His place was amazing, and the food was top notch. We also had delicious wine. On my way back from the bathroom, I stopped and sat down in the study. I guess I've always been a dreamer, but somehow along the way, I forgot how. I imagined a different life, here in the city, where there's life and excitement. People and activity. Vibrance! I wanted that. I wanted to live. I wanted to be noticed, not tucked away on a farm. Unloved and nonexistent. I wanted to be loved, held, treasured.

Day in and day out continued like a well-oiled machine. That's what it became, motions of effectiveness. I concentrated on my kids. I don't think Everett even noticed my disconnected heart. Our ten-year anniversary was coming up soon. My best friend Jade asked what we were going to do to celebrate. At this point, my heart didn't care. I had built up so much resentment and dislike for Everett there wasn't anything to celebrate. She suggested it might be a good thing.

"Time alone may help bring back some of the things you two have lost," she said.

Ten years and we had never gotten away together. We weren't even doing date nights, ever.

Josie had started preschool a few days a week, so she had been adjusted to being without me some. Everett and I decided to go to Branson. It was only a few hours away. We made reservations at a beautiful lodge and got a private cabin, hot tub included.

You know how sometimes you meet someone and at first you don't think they're very attractive? But after getting to know them, your affections for them grow and, along with it, your attraction to them does too? The same happens in reverse order when you receive rejection and pain from someone. You begin to dislike everything about them. Tack onto that the fact that not once did Everett ever take the time to meet any of my needs physically or emotionally. At this point, you could say I was like a car trying to run on four flat tires.

I had hoped getting away would make things different. I thought he would want to give me time and attention. He didn't have the excuse of work. But it was exactly the same as usual. He got what he needed, then he went to sleep.

I made the best of our trip to Branson. We ended up buying a timeshare. My thought was that maybe occasional trips would make this marriage tolerable. If I wasn't able to enjoy Everett, at least I could enjoy things we did. And so it was at home—for a little while.

I suppose the pain, rejection, loneliness, frustration, and resentment began to stack up like Legos. Everyone knows what happens to Legos—they fall. With all the ickiness building up, it became more difficult for me to just go along with everything. I began to refuse going to the bedroom. It is impossible to understand someone when you don't spend time together. All I knew is that Everett started getting angry with me. And that rallied more resentment from within me.

We continued our lake trips every summer, and even bought a jet ski. I loved being on the water. It was freeing. It took several years to get Josie to even stick her toes in the water! Those first several years I stayed in the camper or on the beach under an umbrella with her. Everett did his own thing, not caring to leave me behind. It was those summer nights at the lake that the drinking began. We'd gather several friends at someone's campsite and karaoke. All the kids would camper hop and play games or watch movies. It felt good to be carefree and relax. I never drank much before. I had my moments in high school but had Lane not long after. When I was in therapy school, we had some good times, but that was short lived.

We started camping with several people that drank pretty heavily, and for a while, it remained at the lake. After some time, we started hanging out with them back home. Eventually, the alcohol came into our house. That's where it slowly began to seep into my existence. The first few sips would course through my veins and trickle its way throughout my body. My mind would ease. The anger I felt toward Everett drifted away. The pain and loneliness ceased to exist and transferred into momentary giggles and happiness. Life was masked with an altered reality. This one didn't hurt. The pain was numb. The hurtful memories distant. I could live here. This escape melted away layers of heartache. It erased broken dreams. It erased everything. Eventually, even me.

I didn't care about anything when I drank. I'm not sure I could've counted to ten; I really didn't care to. Those nights when I slipped into alcohol's grasp, I slipped out of myself. My once owned detest of Everett even disappeared. I went to the bedroom with him without hesitation or knowledge of anything beyond the first drink.

We didn't speak of it, but alcohol became the duct tape to what was broken in our marriage. It made things tolerable. For the first time in years, I felt as though I could survive life with him. Isn't that ironic? I could only survive it by not living it.

15

Time came around for our week to use the Branson timeshare. I've always loved the beach and suggested we exchange for a beach resort. They had one in St. Maarten that looked like a tropical paradise. Everett had never flown and was terrified, but he agreed. Getting him on the plane and through the flight was quite the comical experience.

The island was beyond expectations. As soon as we got to the room and unloaded, Everett fixed us a drink, and we started to unwind. We met a couple at the airport and made dinner plans with them. They visited the island often and offered to show us around. After dinner, we went to an open-air karaoke bar. We met with an older couple that lived on the island and invited us all to go sailing. Everett was a cutup and fun to be around in a group. That was part of what drew me to him in the beginning. I tried to let everything else go and reconnect to those feelings.

We were really having a good time. We rented a car and drove all over the island, went on a few excursions, and spent a lot of time with the other couples. Everett and I found this restaurant just down from our resort, walking distance. It was delicious authentic island food. We went several times. We only had a few nights left on our trip and wanted to get all of it we could. This one particular night, I wasn't having drinks. That had become very unusual for me. I was still enjoying the moment, but I was also lost in my head, dreading the way things would be when we got home.

We met several people and were hanging out at the restaurant. Island time, there's nothing like it. My asthma had started bothering me, and I hadn't brought my inhaler. I told Everett I was going back to the room. I requested he stay and have fun. I wanted some time alone anyway. I know it's horrible, but I remember walking back and wishing he'd get lost on the island and stay. I felt so bad for thinking like that, but every part of me desired the same.

It was maybe an hour later when Everett came in. He got ready for bed and lay beside me. He wanted his usual, but this night I hadn't been drinking. I wasn't putty in his hands. He continued to proceed as I repeatedly said, "No. Stop. Please stop." My voice had been ignored by him for so long, I'm not sure he even heard me. I pounded his chest with my fists several times. Maybe he was numb to all of me. He didn't even slow down. When he was finished, he rolled over and went to sleep. I lay there sobbing, and as I released my tears, I released myself with them. The only thought that cycled in my head: *You no longer own any part of yourself.*

I never looked at him the same after that. Hatred for him burned in every glance and every touch he gave me. His voice sent shockwaves of disgust through my stomach. I began to hate myself. A war raged inside me. I was weak and defeated already; I didn't require much more undoing.

16

Jared held me tighter than ever before that night as I unveiled my shame. Tighter, but with a gentleness that eased my heart, his fingers inched across my skin. I could see his touch by the moonlight. I began to feel it deep within as it started piercing that secret, locked-away space. It frightened me. But more than the fear tugging at me, the feeling of being wanted held on tighter.

We filled that summer up with lake trips, pool parties, and cookouts. I was letting Jared in more and more, but I still held onto my torment. I didn't want to let it go. I didn't ask for the things that happened to me, and it wasn't right. But more than anything, I needed to punish myself. I made so many terrible choices, and anyone that chooses to do the things I did never deserves anything good.

I wasn't settling into this new life without the kids very well. I didn't like anything about it, but I felt powerless to change any of it. Anytime I had to deal with Everett, he was angry and authoritative. It had a way of putting me right back under his thumb. I found myself turning to Jared more and more. He felt like a safety net. In the six months I had known him, we had spent more time together than Everett and I did in fifteen years of marriage. Not literally but in a connective way. He treated me like a princess. He made me feel beautiful and important. He was always surprising me with little gifts and taking me places. I ate it up like a piece of chocolate.

It made no sense to me why he continued to invest in me. There were so many times he made late-or middle-of-the-night trips to my apartment just to find me passed out or utterly incoherent. Many times he left work to check on me when he had that feeling in his gut. His gut was always right. Of course, he would get upset with me but in a way so foreign to what I'd ever known. He would still love on me and hold me. The way he loved me despite my destruction drew me to give him more of my locked-away self.

It broke my heart to see the hurt and disappointment on his face. I will never forget those hurt eyes. I had tried to get him to understand the war raging within me, but he refused to heed my warning. He always liked a challenge, his whole life, from the stories he had told me. I'm sure I was the greatest challenge he'd ever seen. Maybe he saw a victory looming in the future. All I could see was the war that had broken loose years ago and continued.

Defeat after defeat doesn't just knock you to the ground; it eventually puts you in it.

17

My time with the kids was very precious to me. I never drank around them again after that last December. I liked adventure and doing new things with them. To finish off the summer, I took the kids on a seven-day cruise, a first for all of us. All four kids were only together when they were with me. When Everett divorced me, he divorced Lane too. He made no attempt to have anything to do with him. Lane had seen too much and really didn't want to have anything to do with him either, but he had been the only man he ever called Dad. I can't imagine the hurt and rejection he took on as well. The way he disowned Lane added fuel to my hatred of Everett and, in my eyes, justified it as well.

We had so much fun on that cruise. We still laugh at the things that happened on that trip. It was fun and exciting. I took the kids to Atlantis, and we went parasailing. It was full-out adventurous. We were about eight months into the divorce and the family disassembling. Lane and Ashlynn had seen and understood more of what had happened in the undoing of me. Josie was too little to grasp much of it. Brock, he had always been his dad's sidekick. I think all he could see was what I had become in those final years. I don't know if he was unaware or just didn't want to accept his dad's part in anything. Brock had also picked up his dad's language and disrespect toward me. Regardless of why, I felt it. I felt his blame toward me. I wasn't innocent in the situation; my actions hurt a lot of people. I had to accept all of his blame whether it was rightly put or not. It existed.

I wish I could have been stronger then. The war continued to rage inside me. The only thing left in my ownership was my scarlet letter. It offered no protection, no defense. But it was mine. I lifted it high. It was all I knew. Rejection. So I clung to it. Like the alcohol that always saved me from my torment, they were always there. An enticing poison that allowed me to stay safely tucked away in my own personal hell.

I had been living two lives. One when the kids were around—soaking them up; denying the pain, disappointments, and regrets. The other when they were gone, letting it all exploded from the inside out. After getting back from the cruise, it erupted again.

I barely managed to make it to work, and I couldn't wait to get home and douse my brain with alcohol. The kids were starting a new school year. I asked Everett if I could take them to school that first day. That was denied. So was my request to pick them up.

Jared saw what I was doing, shutting down again. At this point, I couldn't hide much at all from him. He asked me to move in with him so it would be easier for him to keep an eye on me. As much as I had come to rely on him, he was also smothering me. He was interrupting my war of destruction. And even though I hadn't set foot in a church since Everett and I divorced, I still held onto some of my Christian roots. Right. That coming from a girl that has no rights to her kids and a DWI on her record. Weird, I know.

I reluctantly agreed to "stay at his place" the majority of the time. I loved his deck already. It was one of my most comforting places to escape my reality and unravel my past to Jared. He opened up to me too. He told about his experiences growing up in a small town. When he was about twelve, he discovered his parents' open marriage. They had lived a hippy lifestyle. They always had people over and played music around a campfire. He never thought much of it until he walked in on a most undesirable situation. He was completely enraged and chased after the guy he saw his mom with. He said his parents promised nothing of that sort would ever happen again. I felt so sorry for him having experienced that. I couldn't even begin to imagine. That would have shaken my entire belief system. It did throw up several red flags for me. If this was their lifestyle, what were his morals and beliefs?

Infidelity had already cut me to the core twice in my past. I didn't have trust issues. I had trust mountains! I voiced my concerns about it to Jared. He assured me that it made him swing the other way. That what he saw in his parents' lifestyle made him want complete commitment. It is rare and very difficult to break the chains of our upbringing, but I also knew it was possible. I wanted it to be possible. I had seen so many wonderful and endearing qualities in Jared.

I still held parts of myself back, but I had also let him in more than anyone before. And he wanted in, even with everything he had already discovered about me. I'm sure he had to have made assumptions about why my kids weren't living with me, despite those half-truths I unloaded on him. This guy is intelligent. He's good at piecing things together. I mean, he trained for the special forces. He was a people watcher and noticed detail about his surroundings. His reflexes were abnormally fast. He claimed to have superior senses, and him and his kids teased that he was secretly a superhero. Yeah, I rolled my eyes at that one, but it also seemed strangely true.

He would wait for the last minute for everything, but magically, it all fell into place. Five minutes late to the movies, he'd pull into the parking lot and a front row space would be opening up. Ten minutes until boarding the airplane, and the line for security would clear out. We'd go out to eat because he was craving prime rib. He'd order, and they'd say, "You're just in time, sir. That's the last one." Driving down the road, he'd say, "Oh, that skunk smells terrible." Five minutes later, everyone else would be choking from the smell.

He knew something about everything. He could fix anything. He was always prepared. Need a carabiner or Band-Aid? He had one. He was good at volleyball, tennis, water sports, board games, card games—everything except dancing. And he knew how to compliment people in just the right way. He could morph into any setting, a chameleon. I had never met anyone like him. He definitely had me captivated. His charm could bypass the many walls of security I had built.

How surprising. He didn't need a chisel or wrecking ball to crush my walls. It was his charm, time, and attention. My heart had been like a desert for many, many years. It was thirsting to the very core.

SHED

The drought created several veins of damage throughout the space of me. He never pushed. He allowed me to navigate him through those veins in my own time. It took several eruptions of my internal war and a little time before I could take Jared back to my past again, but in the safety of his arms, I allowed myself to slip back.

18

After that night on the island, I became disenchanted with my former dreams, but mostly with myself. Why did I ever think I deserved a happy life? How could I have been so stupid to think I could be worthy of anything good? It was clear I wasn't worth having anything of my own, not even a say in what happens to my own body. Everett took my choices away. My voice didn't matter. My hope crumbled. My existence vanished.

I became a shell. I looked the same on the outside, but everything inside imploded. I swore to myself that Everett would never have another piece of me. I had already disconnected my heart, not allowing love to flow between us anymore. I hadn't realized I left my self-respect unguarded, completely wide open for him to slash. The work he started that night on the island became mine. I built a wall of hatred around my heart so he could never break it again. I finished off the little self-esteem I had left. That scarlet letter of rejection became my identification, and I clung to it. It created other veins of pain—shame, disappointment, unworthiness, distrust, unwantedness, not being enough, ugly, unlovable, unimportant, hate. They each dug in, planted roots, and sprouted. I thought I could corral all those feelings into one space and not let them impact my entire being. These monsters of pain have no limits. Once they are bred, they take on a heartbeat of their own if you don't kill the source.

The last of my little ones started school, and I really didn't know what to do with myself. I had come to realize my dream of an intimate, cohesive marriage died the day I said, "I do." I started working part-time. My hope was to enjoy working part-time and focus on being a mom. I had thrown myself into caring for everyone, and with no babies left at home, I was lost.

I got along fine for some time. I made sure the house was spotless and meals were planned. Laundry was always done and put away. I tried to stay busy, but the emptiness of the house began to echo the emptiness of my soul.

I thought, *If alcohol made life tolerable with Everett, then alcohol would make life tolerable with my emptiness.*

I began to drink in the daytime. Just a little, to ease off the heartache. It seemed effective. It quieted my discontent. The more it quieted my monsters, the more I wanted.

I tried so hard to ignore the war that broke inside me, but it raged against my desire. I thought I had been building a wall of protection around my heart. I thought those monsters of pain were fighting for me, protecting me from being hurt again. I was too far gone to see that they had turned on me. They were silently slaying me on the inside, unknown to anyone…until one summer day.

Lane was helping farm, not to his liking, but it was the family business. Ashlynn and Brock were at friends' houses. Josie and I were home alone. I didn't drink every day, and I'm still not sure what made the loneliness beckon more some days than others, but it had been screaming at me that day. Once I'm a few sips in, I stop counting.

My sister-in-law invited Josie and I over to swim. There were several of them there, including my new little great nephew, whom we all adored. They didn't live too far away, and I hadn't had too much to drink, I thought. I've always been cautious and overprotective of my kids. I made sure Josie was strapped in, and we took off. Fifteen minutes later, we get there, by the grace of God. I get Josie out, and we go to join everyone. I'm my usual happy, goofy self. All is fine and wonderful. I'm not good at playing sober when I'm wasted. It didn't take them all long to realize something was very wrong. My brother-in-law, in a confused voice, finally put it together. "She's drunk!" That was the first time people outside of our home realized there was an issue, but they had no idea just how inflamed it was. While I was not talented at playing sober, I had become very talented at playing happy. I guess they were all surprised.

Lane and Ashlynn, being the oldest, were more aware of what was happening in our home, although I didn't know Ashlynn knew until after our divorce and I had gone to counseling with her. It was in that session that she told me she had walked in my bedroom one night and saw her dad with his hands around my throat. She also said she knew he liked to drink with me and then take me to the bedroom. I had thought she was completely unaware and tucked in her bed at night. I knew Lane was more clued in. The nights I wasn't drinking, I wouldn't go to the bedroom with Everett. The nights I did, he had seen Everett fix me several drinks, then easily guide me to the bedroom.

Those last few years were like a mudslide on acid. I had confided in my best friend and my younger sister about what happened on the island and my growing unhappiness, but I felt stuck. Stranded with no way out, yet moving further into destruction. The merry-go-round between Everett and I spun faster and faster. He would send me to the liquor store but tell me not to tell anyone he was drinking with me. He would even call my dad and complain to him about my drinking. I'm not sure when my parents began to see what was really going on.

One day, the kids and I had loaded up to stay with my parents at the lake. Before we left, I took the kids to the field to say bye to their dad. We all got out of the vehicle. He got off the tractor. He started yelling, walking toward me. I had no idea what about. He grabbed both of my arms and started shaking and squeezing me. I told the kids to get back in the truck. He nearly had me pushed into the dirt when I slipped out of his grasp and ran. I didn't say a word the whole trip. I silently wept as I drove.

I wasn't going to tell my parents; I knew they'd worry. It was all of ten minutes after we got to the lake that my dad asked what happened. I looked at him puzzled. He pointed to the fingerprint bruises that had already formed on my arms. I told him it was nothing, that Everett was a little angry the kids and I were going to the lake and he just grabbed my arms to get my attention.

He never slapped or punched me. And I suppose not being physically hurt allowed me to justify the other things that happened.

SHED

He forced himself in bed, but like he said, I was his wife. That's part of it, right? He ignored my emotional needs, even after years of my begging, but that doesn't leave physical scars. So if there's no visible scars, there's no damage. Right?

Wrong! So wrong! No amount of my acting happy or locking up my heart could stop the monsters of pain that had begun to war within me, against me. The more you ignore them, the bigger they get. They grow in darkness. They thrive.

So the pain, rejection, unworthiness, and shame took over. I began to drink most days. There were times the kids would come home from school and I'd be passed out. Me. The mom who always brought homemade treats to the parties, coached peewee basketball, and attended everything they did. The alcohol had drowned her.

One day, while the kids were with my parents, I decided to take advantage of the free time and get the mowing done. I also decided to take advantage of the bottle. My parents pulled up the driveway to find me passed out in the yard. They thought I had a heat stroke and called 911. That was the first ER visit my drinking led me to.

Another one happened when Josie and I were at a pageant in Nashville. Everyone thought I was having an asthma attack. See, alcohol became my go-to to celebrate or to escape. It overshadowed anything good or bad in my life. My dad came to pick me up from this one. Everett had gone from not giving time and attention to not caring at all. My dad asked me if he'd pay for outpatient treatment if I would go. I said yes. Everett told him he'd have to pay for gas too because he wouldn't do it. Spinning the merry-go-round, his cold half-heartedness only fed the monsters of torment growing inside me.

I can't imagine how impossible I was to deal with in those final months. I hope one day my kids will remember the good things about me over these bad parts. Everett got so frustrated with the kids coming home to a drunk mom that he set up the camper at his parents' house for all of them to stay. I truly don't blame him and am thankful he was trying to protect them. It still makes my heart bleed with sadness to think I was so lost that even my most desired dreams were being forgotten. I let the destruction outweigh how important they were to me. I didn't know how to stop. I couldn't find my way out. I didn't feel worthy enough to get out.

In one of my final counseling sessions at treatment, the counselor told me, "If you continue to stay in the same environment, you will continue to stay in the same activity." I knew she was right. I had never been one to stand up for myself, and I didn't know how to at this severely low point. Everett and I had talked divorce many times. He had been relying on Lilith, Brock's best friend's mom, pretty heavily for advice at this point. I didn't think anything of it since she was a family friend. She put him in contact with her divorce lawyer. Everett had papers drawn up and presented them to me.

I remember exactly where I was sitting when he handed them to me. I read them over and immediately disagreed. They gave him full custody.

"No. I will not sign these!"

"Michelle, I've talked to the lawyer about everything. You don't deserve to have the kids. If we go to court, they'll take them from you, and you won't see them again. I don't want that to happen. I won't keep them from you."

"No. This still isn't right. I can't sign away my rights. I need to talk to a lawyer. I can't do this."

I was bawling profusely. What should I do?

"Look, I've talked to them about everything. You know you can't take care of them. You're so messed up, you're not what they need."

He's right. I am so messed up. I've been a terrible mom. They deserve so much better. They deserve the me I used to be, but I don't even know how to find her.

"I just can't sign this. This isn't what I want."

He replied, "This is what they need for now. It's for the best, and I won't keep them from you. Do it for them. There's no other way."

The tears were so thick I'm not sure I signed anywhere close to the line. Within two seconds, my loveliest, lifelong dream became a terrifying real-life nightmare. The biggest mistake of my entire existence. Then I collapsed into misery.

19

Lying there in the dark, shaking with tears, I was no longer alone. I allowed Jared to enter into the nightmare with me. For the first time, I had someone who wanted to ease my pain and hold my hand in the darkness I created. It had been a haunting world. Finally, I wasn't alone.

As good as it felt to have Jared there with me, at the same time, I didn't want him to be. I was slowly opening up my heart and handing him pieces of it. Broken pieces. Pulling out those broken pieces cut on their way out like shards of glass. My heart wasn't even stitched together; it was shattered, still holding pain in each and every beat. Trust had vanished beyond the horizon. At any moment, he would see the less-desired parts of me and run.

Run! I want you to run, but hold me first.

It was a dangerously beautiful dance.

I'm not sure how we managed. We would talk and get lost in intimacy until the early morning hours. We were happily exhausted. He explored parts of me that no one had dared to go before. How I think, how I feel, what I want, what I lost. There wasn't an inch of my skin that he didn't caress and no dream he didn't dive into.

I journeyed into his past too. He told me how his first wife cheated on him constantly and blew their money. For the first time, I felt pain that wasn't mine, and that felt lively. I hurt for him, with him. It laced my emotions into his and me into his life.

I had met Jared's parents at dinner one night, but this time Jared wanted to take me to their place for the weekend. They had built a cabin up on Mount Magdalene and had several hundred acres. The cabin was simple but cozy. His dad had been a pilot like Jared. They even had a landing strip on the mountain. He and his dad were interesting storytellers. They captivated everyone. They had been to a lot of places and experienced a lot of things. Their family was different and very open. I was intrigued and curious. It seemed no matter what we did, it was fun. I wanted to be there. I wanted to spend more time at the cabin. It was a place of seclusion that felt like worlds away, back in time. It melted away the present chaos.

We built a fire in the designated pit in the yard. The stars must have migrated to the mountain. My eyes had never seen such a collection in one space. They twinkled like they were in a beautiful rhythm with the breeze and flames of fire. They created an orchestra of relaxation, love, and peace. I felt the tantalizing rhythm from head to toe. Jared and I slept in what was an added-on room with windows all around. The bed was a twin daybed with a pop-up twin side by side. The hand-stitched quilts were perfectly worn and tenderly soft. We cracked a few windows and let the breeze blow across us. It swept away some of the heartache I had recently shared with Jared. I lay over his chest as he brushed my back with his fingertips. He continued to ease closer to me than anyone had dared before.

Jared and his parents had shared stories earlier around the campfire about days gone by. His mom said Jared ran around naked as a little boy, had a fit when they made him wear pants to school. She said he was as stubborn as they come. He'd get a spanking for something but wouldn't shed a tear, just look at her and grin. I could see that. Jared never lost an argument, even when he was clearly in the wrong. He would leave you apologizing for something he did. He was a master at twisting details. His parents didn't think he'd live to see his twenties. He was a daredevil and always pushing the limits. In the end, it was his brother they lost as a teen. I think Jared lost part of himself with him too. There was a sense of a hollow spot he carried with him, although he would never say. He was busy fixing everything and everyone around him. I wanted to heal that hollow spot for him. Lying in that room, on top of the mountain with the breeze blowing across our bodies, I rubbed his hand, his cheek, his forehead. I unlocked the wall I had built around my heart and gently led him in.

Jared's mom had a garden and all kinds of flower beds. I piddled in them with her. She was so easy to talk to and made me feel like family immediately. She asked about my kids but didn't pry too much. My life was a complicated explanation. She was a neat person. She knew a lot about plants and vegetables. She kept busy.

Jared and his dad worked on building another barn. They were back and forth to the shop and all over. They had made this place self-sufficient. Even caught the rainwater in a bucket system to use. Jared's dad was very intelligent. He had built all kinds of workable gadgets. He demanded respect.

Jared's parents were crazy about each other. It made it so hard to see them having an open marriage. I could never do something like that. I want the man I love to be all mine and every part of me to be his in an intricate, passionate masterpiece. I still kept those dreams alive deep inside my broken heart. My first trip to the mountain was wonderful.

*****

It's difficult to hide from a past that has left its etchings inside you. I had seen a part of Jared that weekend on the mountain that made me want more of him but also made me guarded. I wanted my kids. I wasn't sure how to have both. I continued to look for a job closer to where they were but was never able to find anything. I started looking for a house in Cobalt, hoping if I made us a home, they would want to be with me. I was afraid if I gave into Jared completely, I would lose the ability to choose.

I was continually being replaced in my kids' lives. Josie was chosen to be in homecoming, and without even giving me a chance, Lilith took her dress shopping. That's a moment I'll never get back. Lilith was a force to be reckoned with. She took over everything. Her reign had begun before Everett and I divorced. She knew exactly how to nudge me out. She even distanced Everett and the kids from his family. It floored me that Everett let her take over. She also treated Ashlynn unfairly. I had stayed in touch with my sister-in-law, Misti. It sickened her to see it happening too.

I tried to keep my footing with the kids. That's hard to do when most of their influence is against you. Everett didn't respect my relationship with them in the slightest. He repeatedly called and yelled at me. He was so angry! I know I was difficult to deal with the last years of our marriage, but he was still trying to bark orders at me about things that were none of his business. There were several times when Jared took the phone from me and asked Everett to stop yelling and cussing at me. His response was to hang up. I had been so defeated for so long that I let it all pull me down further.

During the last five years of our marriage, when things were in high-speed demolition, I had asked Everett if we could move. I felt so isolated and lonely where we were. The church we were going to was barely thriving, and I wanted the kids to go to a bigger school, more opportunities. Everett agreed, and several times we would put our house up for sale. Then he'd change his mind, and we'd take it down. He said he wouldn't move and drive to the farm. We had even picked out some land in a neighborhood. A neighborhood! That was so exciting to me, the thought of not being so far out. But like all the times before, with everything in our marriage, he changed his mind. So when Everett and Lilith moved to the very town, in the very neighborhood I tried to get Everett to move to, with my kids, it felt like nails in my coffin. It added more than layers of red to my scarlet *R*. It put neon lights on my rejection. It burned so deep it reached back to when I was a girl and inflamed those dreams of love and family.

20

Jared had a front-row seat to my broken heart. He watched me crumble with every defeat. He tried to step in and fill in the gaps. He tried making me a part of his kids' world. I loved them and wanted to be in their lives. But there again, I straddled my two worlds. The most crippling pain is having no power. I had no power in anything that affected my kids. My hatred of myself deepened. So many times I just wanted to not exist anymore or disappear.

I never thought love and hate could coexist, but in my heart, they both declared space. My love for Jared and his kids grew, as did the hate for my life and everything I had become. In our starlight talks, Jared told me how he hated that my heart had been taken advantage of. We talked about how special it would have been to have had a child together. He would have been there. He would have marveled at my jumping belly with me. I wouldn't have been alone in the doctor's office. The thought made me mourn the possibilities, but we both knew we were well past the time for that.

We talked about what we could be for each other. He saw the way I tenderly cared for our kids. I gave him affection that he wasn't used to having. He returned that. I wasn't used to having that either. He told me he wanted to take care of me. Did he really have a clue how much of an undertaking that was? I carried my torment close to my heart.

I began to enter new dreams—dreams of a life with him. He liked traveling and adventure like me. I enjoyed doing everything and nothing with him. Was it possible that he could actually love me? I didn't love me. We had so much fun together! He even let me dress him up for Halloween. I love dressing up. We went to a super-fun party. We did lots of dancing and drinking. I tend to get pretty wild when I drink. I lose all control. He stayed right by my side and protected me.

My two worlds continued to collide. Jared tried so hard to keep me in line. He knew my past haunted me day and night because he walked in it with me many times. Sometimes we stayed up all night talking, loving, holding each other. It was common for him to cook me a steak and cut up pineapple or avocado at 2:00 a.m. He didn't mind. He only wanted me to be happy and healthy. He wasn't able to get inside my head and fix any of that though.

He mentioned marriage several times. He wanted me to have health care. I didn't have insurance and wouldn't go to a doctor for professional help. Being military, he had the best health care. It was hard to imagine a marriage where we would actually spend time together. I tried for fifteen years to get that to happen. I was terrified of being stuck again. I thought about taking on being a mom to his kids. They were raised so differently from mine. I was strict on my kids, with cleaning up after themselves and even the movies they watched. Jared's house was pretty messy. The boys rarely cleaned up after themselves. They were allowed to watch all kinds of movies even with nudity. That really concerned me. I was also alarmed at Jared having *Playboy* magazines in his bedroom. I felt strongly that my man needed to have eyes only for me. Anything else was an invasion of our intimacy. I wanted to be his muse, his treasure.

Jared listened to me and boxed up his *Playboy*s. Wait a minute. He heard me? He really heard my concern and listened. I couldn't believe it! He told me numerous times a day how beautiful I was. He cooked dinner quite often, even gave me massages. We spent all our time together. I began to feel loved. My heart started beating again. One night when we were lying in bed, as he drifted off to sleep, Jared whispered, "I want to marry you." I waited for him to fall asleep then I whispered back, "I want to marry you too."

I'm not sure if I would call it intuition or just plain nosey, but I found out Jared had been looking at diamonds. I was excited, but I thought he was crazy! I loved him and didn't want to be without him, but I was far from stable or ready. How could he not be exhausted from my shenanigans? There were many weekends when he had to work and I'd get into his liquor stash. Why would he want to chain himself to such a mess?

He made me feel so loved and special, but I felt so unworthy. How do you stop a war that rages inside you? How do you stop feeling rejected and replaced when it's not only what you've known for the last twenty plus years, but it's in your face every day? It's there when you wake up, and you don't have your kids to get up and get ready for school, but someone else does. It's there when someone at work asks how your kids are, and you make up something because you don't want to have to admit that you don't know because their home isn't the same as yours now. It's there when the what-ifs, whys, and regrets churn so loudly in your head they vibrate. It's there when you go home and the only faces looking at you are behind picture frames.

So you die inside a little more. The tears flow, and you can't stop them. Your heart cuts as it beats because it remains broken. You want it all to stop, but he told you, you were worthless and replaced, and it pounds into your belief. So you meet the standard. You are nothing. You live empty. Being empty, I knew I couldn't be enough for Jared and his kids. I wanted to be with him but didn't want him to be with me.

"Why don't you just leave me, Jared? Go before it's too late. But make love to me before you go because I need you."

That dangerously beautiful dance I knew so well.

21

Everett monopolized the kids the whole Thanksgiving weekend, so Jared invited me to go to his parents'. Then he wanted to take me to this beautiful lodge at Mt. Magdalene. I knew what he was up to. I text Jade and told her I thought this was it—he's going to ask me! His family had a big get-together on the mountain. Jared's mom was an amazing cook, and his dad smoked all kinds of meat. His family was a lively group. Everyone was very nice. They all cut up and made lots of jokes. Some I wasn't sure about. They referred to how Jared's dad always enjoyed having all the younger girls over, and they made references to their open marriage. Pretty odd.

Jared and I left to go to the lodge. It was maybe an hour away. It was stunning. A cedar lodge high in the mountains. Everything about it was perfect. We changed to go hiking and explore. Jared packed a backpack. He didn't know that I knew what he was doing. I had even seen the picture of the ring he had shown his mom. It was sunset as we hiked over to a bluff.

"Michelle, I have fallen so in love with you, and I don't want a life without you in it. I see how much you love your kids and my kids and enjoy doing things with them. You give me so much love and attention, and I don't ever want to be without that. Will you marry me?"

"Yes. I don't want to be without you either."

The ring was exquisite!

We got dressed up and went to dinner at their top-rated restaurant. We had delicious wine and perfect steaks. I was so in love with him yet remained scared. Over time, we could figure out the details.

*****

Trying to live in two worlds is difficult, especially when there is space between them. I needed Jared. He gave me strength where I had none. He loved me although I couldn't love me. He wanted me safe when I was working to constantly destroy myself. I needed him, but I didn't want him to have all of me. As disastrous as I was, I didn't want to inflict my disaster on Jared and his kids. I fought to not give myself fully to him.

I had high hopes of Ashlynn coming to live with me, so she and I started looking at houses. She was very unhappy living with Everett and Lilith. She wasn't treated fairly by Lilith, and many nights she called me crying. The powerlessness ached beyond my heart and into my entire body. I wanted to save her.

She pressed hard and may have been difficult to deal with. Whatever the reason, Everett let her come live with me. It was over Christmas break, so it was between semesters, a good time to transition. I thought Jared had put me together enough that I could handle this. But I've since learned, you can't save someone; they have to save themselves.

Ashlynn was with me for two weeks. The school was overwhelming, but she was willing to take it on. The weekend she went to her dad's, I got trashed. I was supposed to meet Everett that Sunday to pick her up. I was so hungover, I couldn't find my phone and was completely out of it. By the time I came to and took off to meet them, I was late. They weren't there. I didn't have my phone with me. I drove back to my apartment. When I got back, there was Ashlynn, Everett, and Jared.

I tried explaining that I had lost my phone and wasn't able to let them know I was late. I'm sure the stench of alcohol was seeping out of my pores, and they all knew. Once again, I let everyone down. I remember before Ashlynn left, she cried and hugged Jared, begging him to take care of me. There are few things more saddening than seeing hurt and disappointment in your child's eyes and knowing it was caused by you—the one that had been so cautious during the pregnancy to not drink caffeine, the one who stayed up all night listening to her breathe when she was sick and rubbing Vicks on her chest when her cough woke her, the one that carefully planned her birthday parties and took time to detail every speckle perfectly on her birthday cake, the one that sat with her for hours helping her understand her homework because she struggled but gave her your patience, the one that tucked her in bed and guided her prayers because you wanted to raise her right. That was the mom she needed. That was the mom she desperately searched for.

I cry excruciating tears as I think about and write this. My poor child had to endure such pain and disappointment. It is only by God's grace and under his hand that she was able to see my true heart and love me, forgive me.

22

Jared wanted to give up on me then, but he knew he was all I had. I pushed against him, but his stubborn pride fought back. He wanted to set a date to get married. I told him I wanted to wait a few years. He wanted to get married right away. I told him I wasn't ready. I was afraid to try to be a mom to his boys when I couldn't be one to my kids. I knew I couldn't deal with that. I was also terrified that he would leave me or not be faithful. I still didn't have the ability to fully trust. I asked him to wait, but he pursued even harder.

He's the type to get what he wants. I'm the type to give in. We set the date for May 13. We decided to do a destination wedding in St. Lucia. It was a place I had dreamed about. How can you not be excited about a place like that? We also began to look for houses together. Without him knowing, I continued looking for a job closer to my kids but found nothing. I was out of options. I had a fairly large sum of money from my divorce settlement with Everett. We had built a very large business that I walked away from and in turn got the money from the sale of our house. I gifted that money to Jared to put as a down payment on our house. We put it in his name since we weren't married yet.

We found a very large house right outside of town. Our kids were so excited. They all got along. The boys called me Mommachelle. Their mom lived in Colorado, and they didn't see her much. They were starving for a mom figure. Jared's second wife filled the spot for a little while, but they said she was moody and difficult to get along with. When Jared's daughter was born, the boys were pushed aside. I feared disaster on its way. Like a head-on collision, even the breaks couldn't stop it from happening. Jared didn't heed my warnings.

Jared was so intelligent and a success in the military. He was able to juggle many things at once. He was promoted quickly and highly respected, a warrant officer. He had to go to Alabama for training for about a month. He would get back about a week before we would leave to get married. Being without him scared me. He had become my everything. I was afraid to breathe without him. He was my comfort, my protector, my joy. He kept me safe. He gave me value and made me feel loved and needed. He literally worshiped the ground I walked on. I had built my world around him.

While he was gone, he arranged for the boys to stay with friends some and me to stay with the boys some. They wouldn't move schools and houses until after we were married. I approached the undesired situation in my typical manner, leaning on alcohol to get me though. Luckily, the boys were old enough to take care of themselves.

One morning, I was still wasted with a hangover on its way. I knew how to fix that. I guzzled down a bottle of wine as I got ready for work. I made the forty-five-minute drive from Jared's house to work with no issues, but when I got there, I realized how messed up I was. I made up an excuse to go home. The house Jared and I had bought was only three-fourth mile from where I worked. Not long after, I left I was pulled over, taken to jail, and charged with a DWI. Jared sent Rex to bail me out since he was out of state. He asked Rex to keep an eye on me as he had done many times.

Jared still didn't leave me. I went to Alabama to see him the following weekend. He was frustrated with me but still loved me and wanted to marry me. I couldn't understand him.

"Jared, why don't you leave me? I keep messing up. I don't want to, but I do."

"Michelle, I love you. When we get married and get insurance, you can get help. And I will help you too."

He amazed me. Despite his frustration, he still managed to love me and treat me like a princess. It was far more than what I deserved. At that moment, I no longer had doubts about marrying him. He loved me unconditionally and wanted to help me. I had hope for the first time.

23

For our wedding, Jared and I had chosen to stay at a secluded resort in St. Lucia. It had private cabins scattered out in the hills of the property. We wanted seclusion. I wanted to wrap myself up in nothing but him and the sunshine. It took three hours on a bus ride from the airport to get to the resort. Driving in the gates of the property was like driving into Fantasy Island. This was the most beautiful place my eyes had ever seen. It was so lush and green with vibrant flowers sprinkled in the perfect locations. The staff was so friendly, and when they found out we were to be married in a few days, the joy visibly spread across their faces. They all addressed us by name from then on.

We were escorted to our private cottage by an overly excited local. When he opened the double glass-paned doors, he opened the door to our fairy tale. Before us was a dark-stained wooden bed draped with linen hanging from the canopy. Colorful, exotic flower petals dripped across the bedding. The windows were open with the Caribbean breeze drifting through the room. The bathroom was tastefully decorated and adorned with more amazing flowers. It opened up to an outdoor shower area that was exotic and erotic wrapped up together. Off that was our very own private pool and back around to the front, a porch stretched out overlooking the Caribbean waters. It hosted a hammock and rocking chair. Paradise does exist!

This was a place I visited in my dreams. My heart was bursting with complete joy and excitement. I was no longer holding back. I gave Jared every single part of me—my broken areas, my broken love, my insecurities, my hope of a future being loved and adored in return, not being taken for granted but cherished. It amazed me how much love flowed through me for him once I took down the barriers. It was quite overwhelming. I had only had this kind of gaga love with Johnny. It was a feeling I desperately missed, one I never thought I would experience again. He was my knight. He didn't need to ride in on a white horse. He was enough just the way he was, and I couldn't wait to become his wife!

The entire place was exquisite. We had a four-star dinner at the open-deck restaurant overlooking the beach. We enjoyed flavorful wine. Although Jared disagreed at first, I convinced him my days of getting out of hand were over and I would never drink without him again. A promise I meant with all my being.

We walked the beach hand in hand by the moonlight. God sculpted perfection in this very place. The beauty was intense and impossible to deny. Everything inside me was alive again. One more day and I would marry this man that saved me from myself. He saw the scraps of goodness that remained deep inside me and had fought hard to revive them. I thought I would never be worthy of being embraced with love ever again. This was more than I deserved.

We met with our wedding planner the next morning. We were to be married at sunset the next day right on the beach. I had two ladies that would come help me get into my dress. The photographer would get photos of us separately before the ceremony. Everything was set!

We had signed up to take a sunset cruise that evening before the wedding. It was more beautiful than a dream could ever be. We met several couples on the boat. We all went to the bar to hang out after we docked. We shared our excitement about the wedding and made plans to rent a car and explore the island with one of the couples.

I woke up with the grandest smile and intense anticipation for my wedding day. It didn't seem real. A beach wedding was always my dream, but this—this was paradise. Although the photos in the brochure were gorgeous, it didn't do justice to the true beauty of the island. I literally pinched myself. Twice! After letting all my guards down with Jared, my love for him grew stronger minute by minute. I had tried so hard to push him away. I was adamant that I would not marry him. "He's not my type," I said countless times. So to be here now not only marrying him, but so hopelessly in love with him was a shock to me. I couldn't wait to solidify my commitment to him and take his name. This guy that I didn't plan for, see coming, or want had become the answer to my hopeless heart. He captivated me in every way. I wanted to be the anchor to his heart too. I wanted to heal his brokenness and be the love he deserved.

Jared and I went to breakfast together and were greeted by name from every staff member we encountered, along with, "Happy wedding day!" They all had the excitement of family awaiting our big moment. We went for a walk on the beach. The sound of waves and seagulls will forever ignite my soul. So life-giving. Each moment that passed, every wave that hit the rocks, each breeze that graced my lungs swept more perfection in with its arrival. I floated across that beach more than walked across it. We sat on the deck of the beach bar and talked about how excited we were. Jared had no idea what I brought to wear for the ceremony. He was in for a treat!

As we talked, I realized I didn't have a bouquet. Jared told me not to worry. While I got ready, he would take care of it. We walked back to our cottage so I could start getting ready. Jared left telling me he'd be back with my bouquet. I had learned not to question him. Jared always knew how to fix things. He grabbed some ribbon I had brought and went out the door.

Forty-five minutes later, there was a tap on the door. I pulled back the covering to open the door, and there stood Jared with his hands behind his back and that mischievous grin across his face.

"I got you something," he said, and held out the most perfect bouquet any bride could have requested. He spoke to the groundskeeper, which allowed him to pick the flowers of his choosing. He arranged each flower into the perfect location and wrapped them with turquoise and fuchsia ribbon. It was a breathtaking, exotic island bouquet.

Jared showered, changed, and went down to the beach bar to meet the photographer. I ordered some rum punch and continued working on my hair and makeup. A little rain shower came and left. The quick drink of water made the lush greenery perk up and glisten.

The flowers blushed even more radiant than before. I pinched myself again. Twice.

The ladies showed up to help me into my dress, followed by the photographer. My rum punch kicked in just in time to ease my nerves. The staff had a jeep waiting to drive me down to the beach. There waiting for me was Jared, facing the water. Standing beside him was our officiant. I stepped out of the jeep, kicked off my flip-flops, and walked over the wooden bridge ready to give myself to Jared.

The officiant told Jared to turn around. I lifted my gown and, with my bare feet in the sand, began walking toward him. Our eyes locked the entire way. His expression was my exact intent. My choice of a strapless, sweetheart wedding dress and bare feet seemed to be the right pick. I fixed my hair to the side with curls flowing down and adorned with flowers that matched my bouquet. The glow on my face radiated from within. He held that grin I had come to love. When I reached him, he took my hands and kissed me.

"This is it," he said.

"Yes," I could barely whisper.

The punch had calmed my nerves, but the butterflies were swirling in my stomach.

Our officiant had a beautiful Caribbean accent and began our ceremony. He guided us through our vows fairly well. Jared looked deep into my eyes as he vowed his love and faithfulness to me. My emotions erupted and took over. I bit my lip and turned my head. A tear graced my cheek. He squeezed my hands and winked at me. Oh, that wink! My insides gave way to crumbling. I couldn't pinch myself again because Jared was holding my hands.

How? How is it possible for this man to stand here and willingly accept me? He fought for me, despite my fighting against him. The wall I built was not strong enough or big enough to block him from saving me. His sacrifice was so overwhelming my heart ached. I will never be deserving of this powerful, unconditional love. I put him through so much pain. I let him down so many times I lost track. How many times did he lift me up from a drunken stupor? How many times did I disappointment him and he opened his arms up and held me? I could never love him enough to repay him. I am so unworthy of such an intense love, but here he is, freely giving it to me. How could such a broken woman not melt with complete gratitude? The tears of pain I used to cry were now, at this moment, tears of disbelief and thankfulness.

"I do, Jared." I give you my lost dreams, the pieces of my heart, the inner twinings of my soul and every step of my future.

24

We had little crowds that had gathered during the ceremony. One guy rowed up in a worn-out, turquoise-colored canoe and docked on the sand to participate in our moment. The sun must have received a timeline to complete its glorious dance across the waters. It released beams of yellow, red, orange, and purple all throughout the sky, slowly dipping into the ocean. We took photos as the sunset completed its descent. We were even gifted with a rainbow. I didn't try to pinch myself this time. I wanted to live in this dream, wide awake.

We continued our photos in the historic wine cellar and dancing at the main house. The day was even more astounding than I had planned. I couldn't contain my smile, and I couldn't keep my hands off my husband. We were both starving and definitely looking forward to the rest of the night. We happily sauntered back to our cottage with moonlight sparkling above us. Jared scooped me up and carried me inside. We changed for dinner quickly. The night was just the beginning!

We strolled across the grounds from our cottage to the open-air restaurant, hand in hand, giving each other grins of excitement, waiting to share our passions as husband and wife. The staff was so joyous in greeting "Mr. and Mrs. Martin," as if each had partaken in our ceremony with us. We enjoyed an authentic island-infused meal that quenched the inner hunger of our stomachs. The maître d' gifted us with one of the top wines from their extensive collection. Moment-by-moment perfection continued. The sun had been replaced by the moon, which glistened across the waters. The waves crashed beautifully against the rocks in chime with the beating of my heart.

The Caribbean breeze was once again life-giving to my lungs. The symphony of it all made my spirit soar in complete harmony with the earth. All was at peace within me. My head swam with a type of euphoric stroke. My entire being became whole and light with the trance of perfection, as if I could float away with the breeze. The entire experience poured healing into the cracks of me. I felt connected, no longer broken. Life has been restored to these dry, broken bones. I wanted to live. I felt worthy of living.

After every last drop of wine and every morsel of food had entered our bodies, we were more than ready to continue our evening in our cottage. I had given myself to Jared many times, but things were different now. Saying my vows out loud to him, but more so, hearing his to me, changed everything. He had broken down my walls, and I opened all the doors to my hidden places, but now the key had been tossed. There was no place closed or hidden to him. I gave him access to all of me.

All shields were down. With every touch and every stroke, I drank him into all the spaces of me. He trickled through every vein, and I welcomed the invasion. As he entered, it drove out all monsters that had claimed ownership in my inner being. The absorption of him even began to wash my scarlet letter. No longer did I feel rejected and replaced but received and restored. Renewed. I am cherished. I am wanted. I am loved.

Jared knew every part of me internally and externally. He had explored all areas of who I am, studied them, and knew the workings of my entirety. He was able to elicit satisfaction in me from head to toe with severe ease. I had never in my life experienced such deep, enthralling passion, and I wanted more. The intimacy entangled our souls into knots of quivering fire. *Don't stop. Never stop.* This was the dangerously beautiful dance my soul had waited a lifetime to experience.

The moonlight highlighted our dance as I watched the outline of our bodies become one. I slowly melted into him time and time again. The more I released myself into him, the more my heart felt complete, beating with the intense pounding it had lost years ago. We had loved so long, the moonlight transitioned onto sunbeams.

We were able to catch a few hours rest before starting a day of exploring with the friends we had made a few days earlier.

We had a rental service deliver us a Jeep. How perfect for exploring a tropical island? The road bumped and winded up and down a few mountains to the rest of civilization. We toured a botanical garden, drove into a volcano, and spent time walking the streets of a little beach town. It was another spectacular day. We returned to the resort with enough time to enjoy a nap before having dinner with several couples we had met.

We had dinner at the cozy little beach bar right on the water. The food was as amazing as expected. Our waiter tempted us with local shots that sounded dangerous but erotic, known to have an aphrodisiac effect. We all cheered on the arrival of a few sets of those. We decided to move our gathering to the bar, located halfway up the cliff of our resort. Everyone was drinking, singing, dancing, having a good time. I lose all sensibility when I drink and become very flirtatious, even without an aphrodisiac Caribbean shot. Apparently, I started getting too friendly with some fella at the bar, so Jared took me back to our cottage. He told me about it the next morning. I had no memory of it at all. I apologized over and over. I would never knowingly act that way. I was head over heels in love with my husband.

I promised Jared I would behave. The last thing I wanted to do was hurt him. We enjoyed the rest of our wedding-moon relaxing, canoeing, snorkeling, hanging out with other couples, and taking advantage of our private cottage. This place had certainly earned the title of Fantasy Island in my eyes.

25

Getting back home and into the swing of things is never easy after an amazing vacation but such is reality. We were back and forth between the new house in one town and Jared's house in another town, waiting for the boys to finish school. We spent our time doing repairs to get the house ready to sell. Jared's parents came to help us some, and my kids helped on the weekends we had them. We were also transitioning into the new house. That was difficult because my kids weren't there as much as Jared's boys, but they still needed space. We also had his daughter one night a week.

Luckily, Jared's house sold quickly. The deck overlooking the river would be so missed by us all. Everyone adjusted well over the summer. Our two youngest girls were like peas in a pod. They always stayed busy and entertained themselves. I had high hopes that the kids would want to move in with me now that we had a home. I knew it'd be a stretch for Brock and Josie, but Ashlynn had expressed interest. I felt she was more forgiving of me, having known more about the circumstances. I set my heart on it that she would. That I could regain a portion of what I had lost, although I would always mourn the loss of it all.

There were many lake trips made that summer with my jet skis, and Rex let us borrow his boat several times. My parents invited us to the lake with them for a weekend. They rented us a little cottage, and my nephews came too. Something happened that weekend, and I will probably never know what. I have several assumptions. I didn't find out until months later, but my nephew had some kind of encounter with Jared. He saw or heard something, and it frightened him enough to never tell nor would he come to my house after that weekend.

The Southern summer days slowly eased by as they seemed to have done when I was a child. I was happy with Jared. We spent most of our time together. I prepared Ashlynn's room in high hopes she would be moving in. I didn't pressure her but let her know she was wanted and welcome.

As summer came to a close, so did my hopes of her coming back. All three of my kids started back to school one hundred miles away. I made the request to Everett for me to either take them or pick them up that first day. The request was quickly denied.

Those feelings of rejection that had fluttered away in the Caribbean breeze months earlier found their way back to me. They didn't return alone. Along with it came all the monsters I thought had been subdued. I was unworthy again. Disappointment, hate, regret, rage, resentment—they all began to swirl inside of me. I didn't give permission for them to take over me, but they did anyway.

I tried to fight the war I could feel breaking loose. I just wanted to wrap myself in Jared. He knew I was hurting. It felt like my world was crumbling piece by piece. All the things I feared about getting married began to happen. I would get home from work before Jared, and the boys would have the house in a disaster. I didn't want to deal with those things! The boys were almost grown and didn't want to listen to me. I talked to Jared about it, and he would get on to them but not enforce anything. I started to avoid coming home. I would go to the gym or just drive around, that way Jared would have to deal with the mess when he got home.

His days, for some reason, started getting longer. Most evenings I would end up home before him. I ran out of ways to waste my time. He asked me to take on more responsibilities with the boys: conferences, appointments, and such. I don't think he realized how difficult that was. I didn't want to be there as a mom for his kids when I couldn't be there for mine. The pang of heartache began to throb louder, deeper. My military health benefits hadn't kicked in yet. I self-medicated the only way I knew how. I started to drink the pain away.

26

When core issues aren't addressed, they spiral out of control with an intensity and speed you can't catch a glimpse of. That's the only way I know how to describe our collapse. I had no idea what Jared was experiencing. I knew my war was launched, and my weapon of choice was alcohol. I reached for Jared too; but he had become so distant, not wanting to spend time together, Indian giving the crown he placed on my head. He had promised to be there for me. I had told him so many times I wasn't ready to get married. Countless times he assured me with his calm, exact, authoritative voice that it would all be okay. I trusted him more than I trusted myself, so I ignored my feelings and believed in him, but now he was pushing me away. He threatened several times to move out.

I never thought I would face the day when I couldn't count on him. But those days increased week by week. I know I made it worse with my drinking. The pain was so intense I couldn't take it. Every single thing I had feared happening and tried to avoid was upon me now. I didn't know how to fix any of it. Jared had been my "fixer" for the last year and a half. There were a few nights here and there he didn't come home. He claimed he stayed at Rex's place.

Even through our crazy arguments, we loved each other. We never had trouble expressing our passion. That was the dangerous part of our dance. The strong intimacy mirrored intense, almost rage. Like that type of fiery passion could only exist in extremely opposite parallels. We would love each other with the fiercest intensity of entering another world only to hurt one another with the stabbing of the soul. I loved Jared with a force that ran deeper than my creation.

I also felt his pain with the potency that surpassed every moment I had ever lived.

It all came to a head on the night of my birthday, November 5. I had cooked dinner and had Jade and her husband, Mark, over. We also had a friend from Jared's work join us. The evening was nice. We played cards, and Jared was once again playful with me, giving me that wink that stirred my butterflies. I thought we might be able to salvage us, although something left me questioning.

After everyone left, Jared and I got ready for bed and decided to watch a movie. The movie he wanted was in the playroom, so he went up to get it. I had never been inclined to check his phone, but the unsettling feeling in my stomach urged me to. I grabbed his phone from the bedside table and started to scroll his text messages.

I opened up the conversation between him and his ex-wife, Ellie. A few lines down, he asked her, "How are my girls?" implying her and his daughter. His girls? That sat with me about as easy as a ton of bricks. Further into the conversation, he was talking about fixing her garage light. He implied that the extra work would cost her and added several winky faces. Shock took over my ability to process. I heard Jared coming and quickly put his phone back. Vomit eased up into my throat, and I could barely breathe. Trembling took over my body, and I wasn't able to control it. I jumped up and ran into the bathroom. The one request I gave Jared was to never, ever cheat on me. A sickness ran through my veins as my biggest fear eased closer and closer.

I didn't want to ask Jared about it because I knew I wouldn't get the truth. The tears trickled one after another as Jared called for me from the bedroom. I had to fight against my desire to crumble.

Come on, Michelle, pull it together. You can investigate tomorrow.

Good thing the bedroom lights were out. Pain was written all over my face. My Jared would never hurt me like that. I was in complete bewilderment. He was my protector. This can't be happening. I climbed into bed lost in a daze that was shadowed by the darkness of the room. Just sleep. Don't think.

Some moments make an imprint into your memory like a scar, never to be forgotten. These are some of those moments. I can recall nearly every movement made, every word spoken, and the feelings still cut like a sword when allowed to linger. I needed answers. Answers can only be found at the source. Jared had become someone I no longer trusted. That left Ellie, his ex-wife. She and I had talked and texted several times regarding kids. I had spent a lot of time with her daughter, and our paths had crossed often. I took half the day debating what to say, but I knew I had to move.

I sent her a message telling her I had seen the text conversation between her and Jared. I told her how unsettling it was to me that he referred to her and his daughter as "his girls." I also asked about him fixing her garage light, the teasing, and the winky faces. I told her I hadn't asked Jared about it because I wanted the truth. I told her I needed the truth. I pleaded with her woman to woman.

She said Jared had always been the flirtatious type; she didn't think anything of it. Huh? How did I miss that? He made me feel like the only woman on the planet. Her answers didn't set well with me, and I did more probing. She told me that he had been coming to her house and had expressed his frustration with my drinking, that he wanted to leave me but was afraid I'd hurt myself. I confirmed to her that yes, I was having drinking issues and that we had talked about separating. But that he was making love to me every night and every morning and telling me how much he loved me. That sent her into a frenzy, and she started spilling out more than I expected.

"Oh, okay. Well, he's been telling me how he's still in love with me and wants me back. He said he made a huge mistake with you and wants out but isn't sure the best way to do that."

My mind was still in shock from last night's messages. My body froze as my mind tried to soak in what it was being given. Process. I can't make sense of this. The pieces don't fit. She's not talking about Jared. She's confused. He loves me.

He understood the depths of my disaster but walked in face forward like a warrior battling to win. He's my protector. He's held me and told me it would all be okay, that he'd help me. I begged him to leave, but he refused. He chose me. He held my hands, glared deeply into my eyes, told me to trust him and promised he'd never leave.

"No," I told her. "I'm sure you misunderstood. I know Jared will always love you because you have a daughter together and are still friends. He can't be in love with you. He tells me every day how much he loves me, but he is frustrated with my drinking and not sure what to do."

That makes sense. I can understand his frustration with me. The way he loves me so passionately tells me he wants me.

She goes on to tell me he's been to her house several times. He told her he's buying a camper to move into. Then she polishes it off by saying, "He even stayed the night one night. He slept in Lucy's room all night. It really bothered me when he told Lucy not to tell you. Maybe he's confused because he keeps asking me to get back with him. I've thought about telling you because it's not right."

She isn't describing my husband. All the times he's loved on me, showered me with compliments and gifts, went out of his way to fix my screwups, noticed my desires, and has quenched my lonely hunger. I'm the only woman in the world to him. He has given me that feeling without a shadow of a doubt.

"I don't believe you. This doesn't sound like Jared at all. I don't know you very well, and I'm not sure who I can trust. Do you have proof?"

"I have text messages I can show you."

"Please. I need the truth."

"I can meet to show you but not tonight. I have plans."

I plead with the woman that holds the evidence to the truth I am desperately in search of.

"Please send them to me. I have been through so much heartache in my past. I don't want to be deceived and hurt anymore. I need answers. Please!"

She sends me screenshots of their messages. Messages of him declaring his love for her, how much he misses her, begging for the chance to make her his princess again. I'm seeing this right in front of me, but it still can't be true. Maybe these are old messages. That's the answer. That's what's going on. She is trying to break us up.

"Do you have any with the date on them?"

Now this will all go away. I can go back to believing my husband holds me on a pedestal and I'm the only woman on earth in his eyes. His love for me is real, and I haven't been played a fool. I live in that explanation all of twenty minutes until I can no longer validate these lies. I received the messages with the dates. She says she's tired of the lies and feeling like she's a backup plan. He's been playing us both.

Have you ever seen a person lock into stillness every ability of their physical body? Like a mannequin. The body is there, but it is washed in silence. There is no breath, no life. Even the pulse ceases to perform its natural pumping. Life drained from every inch of my inner and outer self. All I could do was not exist.

I woke up from this lifeless trance completely unaware of how much time had passed by me. I wasn't sure how to breathe. I felt as though I had been stolen from one universe and dropped into an unfamiliar world. The foundation I relied on didn't really exist. Jared wasn't who he appeared to be. So who am I?

I stared at the messages Ellie had sent. I wished them to disappear, but there they remained. I had to remind myself to breathe. Breathe in. Breathe out. Everything was moving in slow motion around me. My heart, I couldn't feel it beating in my chest anymore. But my head was spinning. I wanted to run to Jared for comfort. The Jared I knew yesterday, before the unveiling of these lies. I had given him all my secrets. He owned the key to my heart.

I'm so confused. Who is this? Snapshots replay through my mind the man as I have known and felt him to be versus the man that is beginning to appear. He didn't take anything from me. He softly guided me into trusting him deeply enough until I couldn't resist giving him my heart. I felt his desire to know me and that enticed me to allow him access to parts of me that no one had ever been allowed to venture. He revealed my ability to love and trust again. I don't know how to exist in this world, the world where he isn't my everything.

Another text from Ellie interrupts the disagreements of my thoughts. She said she told Jared I had been asking questions, and she told me the truth. She asked me not to do anything crazy because

Jared was getting Lucy. What? They seem to be more connected than what is normal.

I made plans to stay at my sister's that night but needed to go by the house. Jared sent me a text as if he knew nothing about me knowing, asking what time I would be home. When I got to the house, he was in the bedroom changing.

"Hey, baby! You look beautiful."

Really? Since when did a mascaraed-up face become attractive?

He comes to hug me.

I put my hand up to stop him.

"Jared, I know you know that I'm aware of the texts between you and Ellie. I'm staying at my sister's tonight. We need to talk, but you have Lucy, and I'm too hurt and upset to be normal around her right now."

"Michelle, Ellie tends to exaggerate. There's nothing going on between us."

That line rolls off his tongue with the smoothness of silk.

I want more than anything for that to be true. He has no idea how shaken my foundation is. When I vowed myself to him only months ago, those were not only words from my lips. I bound myself to him. I gifted him my love with no intention of ever asking for it back. I knew my heart was broken and bruised, but it remained a love-giving heart through all its tattering journeys. It only desired the same love and care in return. It desperately and exhaustingly longed for such.

Sleepless nights are miserable. How can a brain reach severe exhaustion yet refuse to slumber? Not only refuse to be still but attack you with thoughts and memories, make you relive decisions and play out what-ifs and if-onlys, returning you to the very nightmare you thought you had been rescued from. I had an entire night of my brain being active, but I was still empty-handed for answers.

I needed answers from Jared, but my heart dreaded hearing them. When we were finally able to get together, he said when I started drinking again after the kids started school, he was lost as to what to do. He turned to Ellie as a friend for advice. Her dad had been an alcoholic, and he thought she may have some solutions.

He promised me there was nothing more to it. I told him she had sent me messages where he told her he was in love with her and wanted her back. He said there were a few moments he was confused and said things to her he shouldn't have. He held me and assured me that he loved me with all his heart, but the drinking was pushing him away. He thought it would all stop as I had said it would. He was so hurt that I turned to alcohol again a few months ago and was tired of dealing with it.

I asked why he hadn't told me he bought a camper to move into but Ellie knew. He said he had to drop some things off at her office and happened to mention it. He said he wasn't sure what he needed to do.

"Michelle, I love you more than I have ever loved anyone my entire life, but you have also hurt me deeper than I've ever been hurt. I want to be with you, I want to help you. You promise the drinking is over, then I turn my back and you do it again."

I felt the heavy weight of the world compressing my chest. Failure. I'll never be more than a failure. I longed for time and attention for fifteen years. To be loved, held, cherished, noticed. Jared gave me that, and now it's slipping through my fingertips. My heart cried with regret. I begged Jared for his forgiveness. I disgusted myself. I reeked of guilt, shame, and inadequacy. I wanted another chance to be his everything.

We danced that dangerously beautiful dance all night, as though no other soul had crossed into our territory of intimacy. I craved his touch deeper than ever before. I ached to be his muse again, the only one his heart ever sought, the first one to draw his thoughts and the last to kiss his lips, the one he breathed air for, and the one that walked through his dreams.

27

Over the next few weeks, Jared remained distant. It was the evening of homecoming when he told me he had decided to go forward with moving out. I pleaded with him until I was sure blood was pouring out of my eyes. My legs were unable to support the weight of my body. I sunk to the floor as he walked out. Utter devastation took over every ability I formerly had. My scarlet *R* that had been washed white made its reappearance in dark, screaming crimson. Rejected and replaced in one sweeping motion. I couldn't even roll my eyes at it anymore. I deserved that roaring *R*.

My best friend, Jade, is quite the trooper. She had ridden the ups and downs with me over the years and remained one of the few reliable constants in my life. She came to me that night and lifted me out of the floor as I was unable to command my legs to do so. She held me as I continued to unfold and wiped my tears that refused to cease.

Adjusting to Jared not being home was a painful task. He had been my rock the last year and a half. He was my answer to everything. He filled in every gap I created in myself, or at least attempted to. Now there was no one. Jared moved into solitude in the camper. He left his oldest son at the house with me. Our 3,200-square-foot house felt five times the size. Emptiness echoed into every corner. Loneliness illuminated every room. My guilt and shame grew day by day. I didn't want to experience another failed marriage. All I could focus on was getting Jared to want us again. Everything else faded into unacknowledgment.

Jared came to the house anytime he wanted and gave me scraps of his time and attention. I soaked up anything he would toss my way. He invited me to Thanksgiving on the mountain with his family. The magic of the mountain still had its power to melt away reality and heartache. We felt like us again. The us before the seeds of doubt were pressed into my mind. I tried not to water those seeds. I tried to focus on the many times Jared had been there for me and the many ways he rescued me. I couldn't understand how he was always so forgiving of me. Even still, he held me and told me how much he loved me.

I couldn't resist when the opportunity presented itself as I found Jared's phone unguarded. I scanned the conversation between Jared and Ellie back to the beginning of November when I discovered the secrets between them. It sat in the pit of my stomach, him asking what all she told me. Her replying, "Just that you stayed the night and slept in Lucy's room." Followed up with, "She said you've been sleeping with her every night, and that just pisses me off."

The mind is such a fool. I made up a handful of scenarios to validate why his ex-wife would be pissed off that I was sleeping with my husband. Seeing that conversation watered those seeds of doubt. It still wasn't enough to suppress the ache I carried for him to want me. The taste he gave me of being relentlessly pursued held on tighter than the feeling of being unwanted. Like the heroin addict continually searching for that virgin high, I searched through the scraps he gave me, remembering that euphoric entanglement.

The dynamics of our relationship as we had known them took a 180-degree shift. I went into a full-on pursuit of his heart. He gave me morsels of satisfaction with glimpses of him returning to my everything. It was enough crumbs to leave me begging for more. I continually choked on my guilt and shame, not able to completely swallow it.

Jared came and went as he pleased. Some weeks he would spend the night with me at the house more than he would in the camper. He asked me to stay many nights in the camper too. I took what I could get. I just wanted him to want us enough to come back. The intensity of our intimacy couldn't be denied. He never failed to tell me how much he loved me. It didn't make sense to me. He explained that he was exhausted. Two failed marriages and now on his third. He wasn't sure he even wanted to be married anymore. Maybe he should just be alone. He said he tried to fix me. Maybe leaving was the best he could give me.

I despised finding myself alone again. Jared knew all my defects but had refused to walk away from me. He knew them but chased me anyway and fought for me. Until now. My heart should have come with a return-to-sender label. It had been rejected so many times and abandoned as to find its way home. I was left with a gaping hole in my chest, unsure of my future and bewildered by my past. Jared had lifted me so high that when he let go, I plummeted into extreme desperation.

I clawed the air to hang on and tried to fight my demons on my own. Many nights they would take me over. I disappeared into the bottle, hoping to drown the hurt and rejection. It always came through until the next morning when all my heartache found me again. It seemed as though Jared's radar always alerted him. He would make his appearance in the height of my demise. His frustration grew, but so did mine. For fifteen years, I had lain beside a man and felt severe loneliness, followed by complete physical lonesomeness. Jared filled not only the space beside me but also the space inside me, against my attempts to avoid him. He created wanting and needing him within me, only now to dangle in front of me what had become my drug—him. Slipping me doses at his whim but denying the craving when I requested. He was the puppet master, and I the dummy at the end of the string.

I became angry with him. Day in and day out I had to deal with his son and his oddball antics while Jared enjoyed his freedom. It felt like I was standing dead center in the middle of a canyon yelling at the top of my lungs only for the sound to echo back to my own ear. The sound of loneliness vibrated in every crevice until it was all-consuming, causing a chain reaction: an earthquake loosening all my wounds to the surface. My rejection emerged stronger than when I had buried it. It had grown more layers since my last encounter, weakening me, leaving me stranded in its shadows.

28

Jared continued to toss me scraps. We took all the kids to a Christmas tree farm like one big happy family. We spent the day doing my favorite things, decorating while listening to Christmas music and baking. Togetherness, like I had always wanted. The house was beautiful with its Christmas lights and fragrances of the holiday. Jared even stayed Christmas Eve, and we all had Christmas morning together. The kids played and cutup with one another. Jared gave me the affection my body was screaming for and quieted my craving, and then everyone left.

The joyous noise of a happy holiday softened into screeching emptiness, so soft I could nearly hear the lights blink. I circled through the house looking for signs of life, but there were none. Jared, his kids, and my kids had gone on their way to spend time with other loved ones. Closing out my favorite holiday, I slipped into bed. Loneliness crept in with me, reminding me of my unwantedness.

I refused to sit at home on NYE alone, nursing the growing rejection I was carrying. This is Jared's favorite holiday, and I wanted to spend it with him. No invitation had arrived, so I made plans with friends. Thirty minutes out from meeting up with my friends, Jared calls asking me to his best friend's party. Of course, I make a detour in my plans. My friends, understanding my desire to save my marriage, wished me well.

You could have mistaken us for a happily married couple. Jared held my hand, kissed on me, introduced me as his wife. We had all the makings except wedding rings. Jared took his off when he moved out. Out of stubbornness, so did I. The only drink I had that night was the champagne Jared brought me for the midnight toast. I drove us to his camper to spend the night, just knowing he would soon come home.

*****

January marched on with the same rhythm as November and December. More and more I felt like Jared's rotating door. Access to the house, my body, my heart, my dreams, my hopes were pressed open and closed—all at this control. The future I could see with him became like a desert mirage, so vivid I could reach out and grasp it just to see it slip through my fingers like sand in the wind.

My heart was feeling sick and deprived, lacking for something. Alexis had invited me several times to go to church with her. She had been singing on the worship team of some church I wasn't familiar with. Church, ha. That hadn't been a part of my life for two years now. I wasn't fit enough to even be worthy of church. I loved Alexis and was proud of her, so I went in support.

I was not prepared for what happened that Sunday. The pastor spoke about surrender.

"It's a new year. Let God move into your heart. Lay your troubles down to his cross. Surrender your ways and let him heal your heart. Accept the Holy Spirit as your guide. Begin anew."

Softly, the song "I Surrender All" began to fill the room. My entire body started to tremble, and my brokenness poured out to the pastor's call and the old familiar hymn. He requested those wanting to surrender raise their hands to be prayed over. It seemed like such an insignificant gesture, but my hand lifted desperately, seeking the healing he spoke of.

Never in my life have I ever caved in such a manner. I knew my life was a mess, and my heart was broken and heavy. The tears flowed with such force I quivered from the inside out. "All to Jesus" gently touched my ears as I crumbled under the weight I carried. I felt the familiar tenderness of being somewhere I'd been before. A calm comfort softened and lifted my heart. Something that had gone missing was being returned, something I didn't realize I missed—home. It felt like returning home.

The music continued to stir and release pieces of me like a whirlwind of tranquility and torture all at the same time. I had felt a similar stirring before but never of this magnitude. I was more than heart sick; I was soul sick. My wounds gushed incessantly, not understanding how or what, but knowing it had sampled the remedy. I wanted to be undone. I wanted to unravel and fray the rope binding me to my destruction. Freedom appeared on the horizon; and with my hand stretched up, reaching as high as I could, freedom touched me back.

I was a massive, blubbering mess, but my heart had been ignited with a fire that was familiar and new. I was drawn to the feeling it sparked deep inside me. Hope, comfort, relief, intrigue, excitement—so many emotions were coming alive. I felt something new blooming inside me. For so many years all the emotions I had felt were painful and exhausting, cutting with sharpness. They only offered destruction and emptiness. This one little spark was powerful. It offered life.

Alexis looked at me with concern. I had completely melted during the service.

"Are you okay?" she asked.

There was so much to release I was still trembling and sobbing. Unable to find the words to explain the encounter I had just experienced, I simply nodded. She gave me a smile and told me to call if I needed anything.

My life was in shambles, and I had no answers concerning my future. One thing I was certain of: When I reached up to God, he reached back. I felt him. He wanted me. There was so much I didn't understand, but I knew I would never be the same. I knew I wanted more, and it was good.

29

My excitement could not be contained when Jared sent me a dozen roses to work on Valentine's Day. Validation. He was finally starting to want us again. "With all my love," read the card. My heart fluttered, and tingles zipped throughout my body. I couldn't wait to hold him and confirm our hearts as one again.

Nothing with him ever went as I expected. I called to make plans for a romantic Valentine's Day weekend with him. The thrill of my excitement was quickly extinguished as he revealed his plans to spend the day helping rearrange his daughter's furniture—at her house. His ex-wife's house. On Valentine's Day.

I'm sure my heart made a loud thud that echoed at least five miles. I bellowed throughout the canyon so loudly the screeching pierced my ears with its sharpness. Tears flowed as though they were offering nourishment, not wanting to cease. Each broken crevice deepened with surrender to ever be whole again, as all my hope followed. I stood there, dead center of the canyon, feeling the implosion prick my soul with each shift of its foundation, powerless to do anything but be encompassed by its masses.

When I was able to find my voice again, after another heartbreaking jolt, I told him I was done.

"File for the divorce you've been threatening for months. I'm sick of being your puppet."

My anger and frustration cushioned the falling pieces of my heart.

*****

Alexis invited me over and listened as I spilled my hurt out to her. It would have been so much easier had he let me go months ago. The cycle of being wanted, then unwanted, left me feeling tattered and confused and drastically unwanted. Like I was desired for a few fleeting moments, then discarded because I wasn't enough.

I just wanted to be loved, to be enough, for the one who loves me to keep their promises and hold on. Like letting go was to stop breathing. My fairy-tale-believing heart began to question if something so beautiful, raw, and true could ever exist. Like a unicorn. The idea is lovely, and you can capture the breathtaking image in your mind, but will you ever lay hands on one?

Alexis encouraged me to let go and move on. She had recently met someone online and was getting seriously involved. Maybe I should give it a try. I liked the idea. I needed to feel wanted by somebody and not just my heart, all of me. I felt like a black hole of emptiness. Nothingness.

I needed someone to fill the void that stood in Jared's place. In someone's eyes, I wanted to be beautiful. I opened an online dating account and started browsing. To my delight, there were many singles my age and appealing. That gave me hope for my broken heart. Maybe my chance for love hadn't completely eluded me.

Not even a week after I told Jared I was done and to file for divorce, he dropped the papers by the house. I made sure he understood he was not welcome to stay the night. He had drawn up the papers and outlined the property settlement to his liking. The only paragraph I didn't agree with stated after the sale of the house, his credit cards would be paid off and I'd get what remained. He had four or five credit cards, and I had no clue what was on them. Since it was my $89,000 down on the house, I disagreed with this portion. I put an X through that paragraph and signed the bottom and stated I was not in agreement with that portion, then returned the papers to him.

*****

I had conversations going with several different men that fit what I was looking for—good looking and adventurous. That was the main two qualifications. The distraction was nice, and I began picturing my life without Jared. I loved getting compliments. It felt good to have interest in me instead of constant discarding.

As much as I was enjoying the attention of the dating site, I longed for something more. Something deep and real to satisfy the emptiness that plagued my heart and soul. The spark that had ignited weeks ago continued to smolder and burn for my awareness. I attended church every Sunday and loved it. I needed connection. They announced a life group launch where you could come and sign up for a variety of smaller, intimate, interest-based groups. I asked Alexis to join me, but she worked late hours and declined.

I dreaded walking in by myself, but my hunger for more pushed me forward. I didn't even know what I was looking for, but I knew something more was calling for me. The very first table I came to was a women's Bible study group doing a book study. *Totally not my thing*, I thought. The lady hosting the table was very friendly and excited, but I walked on. I found several groups that sounded cool and put my name down. Pinterest ladies group, stage production—fun! I circled back around to leave and stopped again at the first table. Another lady was there and introduced herself. She said she has been leading the group in her home for several years. She was very excited about the new study. She encouraged me to put my name down, so I did.

Pain pushes a person to their jumping point. You can allow the pain to fester and scrape you into a deep, dark pit, or you can allow it to be a stepping stone to arise to be better. A reference of where you were, fighting your way up to where you want to be. You either give your pain permission, or you give it a voice. I had wallowed so long in my pit I had started believing it was where I belonged. The encounter I experienced in church lifted my face, and I began to look up.

Again, I found myself alone, approaching the address given for the women's Bible study. I had only met Christy once, the night of the launch. There was something so loving and pure about her; her joy was real and contagious. I was anxious as I approached her front door but so hopeful to find more of the remedy I had sampled.

Her house was beautiful and immaculate, in one of the best neighborhoods in town. I feared I wouldn't fit in. These ladies probably all have their lives together. Maybe every group needs a black sheep? The door was cracked open. I knocked and walked on in.

I followed the noise of happy chatter into the kitchen. Christy saw me come in and gave me an intense hug and said how happy she was I came. We talked a little, and she introduced me to some of the ladies. To make things easier, we all wore name tags. This first night was for introductions and getting our study book, *Your Beautiful Purpose.*

There was at least thirty women sitting around this living room. Christy asked that we tell our names, occupation, and if we had family. This is where things got sticky. Maybe I shouldn't be here. How do I explain the mess that has become me and is sitting here trying to look normal? I can't start unloading my imaginary life in a church group.

I searched the ladies, looking for someone bearing scars like mine. *Is anyone here messed up like me?* I begged for someone to reveal they had a drinking problem, drug addiction, DWI, or any form of arrest. Not that I longed for someone else to hurt. I longed to know someone else had walked this path and they were still able to stand. I longed to be accepted although I bore lashings of decisions I regretted but could not reverse. I wanted someone to recognize my pain and tell me there was a way out, that I was worthy of rescuing. I wanted to know it was possible to bear these wounds but not be rejected. I needed to be quenched with hope.

Simple. Just keep it simple, Michelle. Spilling my story would be like admitting I have the black plague, quarantined with a do-not-return stipulation. I needed connection, not to be shunned. I gave my name, told that I'm a PTA working at the nursing home. I'm married, and I have four kids and three stepkids. Done! I sounded fairly normal. I was able to keep my scarlet letter under wraps for the moment. The introductions continued around, simple for the most part. There were several other therapists in the group. Thankfully, I connected with someone on some level!

A little over halfway around, one lady introduced herself and then explained that her husband recently left her out of the blue. Tears flowed from her eyes as she spoke. I felt her hurt and cried with her, for us both. She was young and beautiful, but pain was owning her right now. I was so moved and impressed with Christy. She knew exactly what to do. She asked that we all gather around to lay hands and pray. That was something unfamiliar to me, but I moved to her and placed a hand on her shoulder.

Christy began praying, and emotions began to rise up inside of me. The stirring was back. I breathed in the words as they poured out of Christy's mouth. I spoke them with my heart and mind as though they were mine. I felt them pulse through me as they lifted up to heaven, and I cried out for God to take them and press them into his ear. In the moments of that prayer, I wasn't just laying my hand on this woman's shoulder; I was holding her hand, feeling her pain, and helping her carry it. It was intense, intimate, foreign, and wonderful. Connection. I felt connection, and it was good.

I don't believe there was one single eye that didn't cry for this woman. This point in time took its care to weave us all together. I instantly felt bonded to these ladies as I felt a part of something bigger than myself. I had a deep comfort that I was in the right place. Although I wasn't hearing my chains fall, each step I took was leading me closer to finding the key to unlock my destruction. I felt the assurance of that.

After the group ended, I went to speak with the woman we prayed over and to give her a hug. I told her I was in the same situation and would be praying for her. It surprised me that that came out of my mouth. I hadn't prayed since I don't know when. It seemed like a good time to start.

30

I quit pursuing anything with Jared. I was no longer sending messages begging him back. My conversations with some of the men I had met online deepened. One in particular had my interest. We texted every day, spoke on the phone, and planned to meet soon. One of the guys that contacted me through the dating site said he recognized my photo. He had been dating Ellie when Jared and I left to get married. He said he was with her when Jared called on his way to meet me to leave for our trip. Jared had called her one last time asking if there was any chance for something between them. Apparently, she turned him down, so he left to marry me.

That aligned with what Ellie had told me months ago. With one huge douse of water, those seeds of doubt of who Jared was sprouted, and the blooms were not beautiful. They were painful, loaded with thorns. I don't know how my heart continued to beat. I asked it so many times to stop. A heart is supposed to bring life, but mine was defective. Each beat pulsated unworthiness and rejection. As if my scarlet letter wasn't layered with enough coats of red, each revelation added another stroke. I was certain it would fall out of my chest from heaviness.

Battling the desire to not exist, something compelled me to pick up and read the Bible study book. In the first few pages, the author called to me.

"In case you are wondering if this book is for you: I'm thinking of the woman who's been so beat down by life, had so many heartfelt desires pushed aside, that she's barely alive, hardly passionate. The light has gone out of her eyes, life is mostly a duty, and she's quite sure it'll always be this way. She's afraid to dream because she'd rather not be disappointed."

I couldn't remember meeting this author, but she was speaking to me as though she knew me. She enticed me with hope.

Church and women's life group continued to open my eyes to possibilities I thought had passed me up. I assumed being so rejected and filthy with scabs of my life's mistakes made me undesirable everywhere. Especially to God. I had run so far from him I wasn't sure he'd still remember me. I knew something had been tugging on me and calling me closer. I felt him fluttering in my heart and wanting me, but my mind didn't understand. Why? Why would he want me when no one else did? He of all beings knew the entire scope of my damage. Like an EF5 tornado, I didn't leave anything undamaged in my path.

My life group leaders spoke of how much God loves each of us and is eagerly waiting for us to respond to his pleading. The study book explained how God has a call on our lives. He has a path of divine and appointed purpose and direction for even me. I liked the thought of that, but believing it was a struggle. I opened up to the group about my separation and asked for prayers. Many others in the group started opening up, and our life group drew tighter and tighter.

*****

The direction facing away from Jared began to look more appealing, still terrifying as I had placed my foundation in him. It had been nearly a month of text and phone conversations, and things moved forward with dinner plans to meet the guy that was really starting to draw my attention.

It felt odd planning to meet with someone else. Jared had made it clear he didn't want me, so I went with my plans. I had a lot in common with this guy, and conversation was easy. I was excited but also burdened.

He lived out of town and was heavy into motocross and was staying in Nashville for a race. We met at a nice restaurant for dinner.

He was so good-looking from head to toe. Exactly my type. Dark hair, blue eyes, incredible build. We were both into CrossFit, hiking, camping. It was like he was designed for me. I should have been swept away. As we enjoyed nice dinner conversation, my mind wondered, *This isn't Jared.* I wanted to look across the table and see the grin I had fallen in love with. I kept pushing those thoughts aside.

After dinner, he invited me to his hotel room. Trying to step away from Jared, I accepted. My desire to be wanted continued to burn. I was lacking in physical connection and begging to be embraced. When he took me into his arms and kissed me, I expected butterflies, but feelings of disgust bubbled up inside me. I knew I was in the wrong place and not sure how to explain myself.

I lay in torture all night trying to wash away my feelings of filth and explain the mistake I had made. Not knowing a better way, I sent him a text first thing in the morning, then headed to church.

Tossed back into confusion and still with no direction for my life, I slipped into a drinking daze to escape the mind torture again. Evan, Jared's son, got ahold of my phone and skimmed my texts. He immediately told his dad about my conversations, and Jared discovered I had joined the dating site. Jared came to the house that night and put me to bed. He rolled me over the coals for my behavior. Little did he know I had already taken my profile off the site and was whipping myself with guilt.

Being in the embrace of another man made me realize Jared still had my heart. I wasn't ready to give up on us. I had told my life group about me finding texts between Jared and his ex-wife, our separating, but I hadn't told them the whole story. I had said I was horrible to him but didn't define that as my drinking problem. I was riddled with conviction and wanted to set my life on the right path. I asked Christy if she would meet with me. I could no longer hide the full truth.

Christy invited me to her home as she had many times for life group. This time we were one-on- one. I was nervous to spill out the horribleness of my life. At the same time, I had the comfort of knowing I was safe with her. I just didn't know how she would react. Has she ever met anyone as destructive and filthy as me? I could see in her eyes that she listened with her heart, and to my surprise she didn't gasp at my revelation. She spoke a beautiful prayer over me. She told me to keep seeking God's will. I would have peace when I was on the right path.

I developed healthy relationships with many godly women in that life group. Two very impactful souls, Rhonda and Jackie, were an amazing pair. Longtime friends, they were die-hard biker chicks. Jackie with an unshakable faith, so strong and grounded, being in her presence radiated belief. Rhonda had the charisma of point-blank down to an irresistible art form. Her rendition of putting on the armor of God is forever ingrained in my heart. Barbara, a true Mississippi lady able to tell you how it is with the deepest, sweetest Southern accent that ever graced your ears, topped off with Southern sass that would make your eyes pop and belly giggle. God was gently leading support into my life for the upcoming storm.

31

Jared stopped by the house several times a week checking on Evan. I invited him to church, telling him how wonderful it was. Evan had been going and was dating a very sweet girl that was a member. I wanted so badly for Jared to feel the irresistible stirring like I was. I was ready to set my life straight, right my wrongs, and discover more of his presence sparking inside of me. I wanted to fight for my marriage. Easter! Everybody is usually open to coming to church on Easter. Jared, however, declined my invitation.

I received another heartbreaking jolt when I found out he went to church with Ellie. Jared poured his sweet, slick words all over me, telling me it was for his daughter's sake. He had a mesmerizing tone and explanations that fit together like puzzle pieces. By the end of the conversation, I was apologizing for being upset and thankful he didn't sit beside her but that his daughter was between them.

*****

The search for my path and purpose trudged on. I buried myself in the study book, prayer, scripture, reading anything my life-group girls recommended; and I even changed my hip-hop station to praise-and-worship music. I was a lost soul, still wandering, trying to find my way; but my eyes were focused on hope.

The outward activity I was participating in began changing me on the inside. Studying the characteristics of God started to build my trust in him. Everything I discovered about the Holy Spirit left me in awe. I felt gypped never having been taught about the enormous power of the Holy Spirit! The more I learned, it felt like Christmas. One gift after another. A hunger was born inside me. The more I learned, the more I wanted. Prayer became a new language that captivated me. Prayer brought unity. A beautiful language guided by the Holy Spirit, ushered through Jesus, and delivered to God's ear. Hands joined in a unison prayer multiplied the movement of the Holy Spirit in me.

My first of many revelations by the Holy Spirit came to me softly but with a knowing it wasn't of me. I was sitting in our big, empty house studying *Your Beautiful Purpose*. The Holy Spirit revealed to me three things that would take place in my life: (1) mission work, (2) Celebrate Recovery, (3) that through me, God would reveal himself to Jared. I began to ponder details of this gift I received. I had dreamed of mission work when I was a little girl. I had been a stay-at-home mom for some time and never pursued it. Am I supposed to start a Celebrate Recovery at our church? There isn't currently one. I pondered longer on the third revelation. My heart was deeply tied to this one. God would reveal himself through my ability to achieve what obviously was not capabilities of my own. Jared would know it was the work of God, knowing I did not possess the strength myself. I assumed that meant he would see God give me the strength to overcome alcohol. Where I was thinking small, God was preparing for much bigger.

May 13, our first wedding anniversary, approached quickly. I dreaded being alone, not how I envisioned the supposed to be celebration. Jade took pity on me, and we made plans for dinner and a movie. Jared texted me late afternoon asking if we could spend the evening together, celebrating our anniversary.

Wait. What? You want to celebrate our anniversary? I'm so ticked off and quite confused! We are separated. I have made many attempts to reconcile, at which you put me off. The times I was convenient for you, you took advantage. You have spun this rotating door off its axis! I grumbled in my head.

I simply replied, "Separation isn't anything I want to celebrate. I have already made plans with Jade because I didn't want to be alone."

I tried to ignore my aching heart and tuck the images of our beautiful beach wedding behind the realities of the lies and deception I had uncovered. Against my approval, my body burned for Jared's touch. The facade I had known before November beckoned me to reach for him. If only I could cut out chunks of time and bad choices, his perfect love would meet me there, in the pieces. My deprived heart struggled to release its deepest desire. Its ability was consumed by memories of the passions that had once given life to all the dry, decrepit, used, tossed aside crevices, now left to attempt beating as it looked up from the canyon again. How is it that the mind can succumb to feelings? Feelings are born of the heart, yet they transcend into the mind and override logic. That's power, the power of love.

All evening Jared sent messages and photos of us together. He had studied me inside and out. He knew all my weaknesses and how to play them to his advantage. He used my gift of a loving heart against me. My need for physical connection wrestled against his deception that was lodged in my brain. He towered over the lies that replayed like scenes of a movie flashing across my mind, overshadowing them with all he knew I desired. I craved another dose of him. He was responding to me with wanting. I had been praying and focused on getting him to want us again. I couldn't ignore this opportunity.

Jade knew my struggle and understood my wanting to rush home after the movie. Jared had a gift of sugarcoating bad situations under layers of everything I longed for. He greeted me at home as though he lived there, and the thoughts of his words to Ellie were erased from my mind. His facade was so powerful it sucked me right in, not even leaving skid marks as I fell under his spell. I met him there, in the picture-perfect world he had painted. It was the world I remembered stepping into on the beach, in my bare feet, looking into the eyes of my everything. Once again, he rekindled that spark and ignited my euphoric high.

32

My spiritual quest was filling me with a peace and joy I hadn't known before. Jared was intrigued, and our relationship started changing. He came to the house more often, and I stayed at the camper more. As odd as it was, my failed attempt at replacing him gave me the assurance that I needed to give my all to saving our marriage.

He asked me to join him for dinner at one of our favorite local places. I had gained so much hope that he'd be moving home soon. He approached the conversation with that sly, captivating smile.

"I don't want to lose you, Michelle. I've seen the changes you have made. I want us to put the past behind us and be together."

I had waited so long, prayed so hard, and hoped with intensity for him to want us again. I expected him to move back the next day. He said that part would take a little longer. Ellie was aware of my drinking problem, and he was afraid to move too quickly. He didn't want her to compromise his time with Lucy. I cringed with disappointment, but I accepted the fact that I was responsible for the situation.

I found him beside me most nights. There was no rhythm or schedule. He stayed when he wanted. He poured his sweet words all over me, and I drank them in. He said just the right phrases to satisfy my heart. My mind pulled the rug out from under me. His words to Ellie moved from text messages I saw to words echoing through a megaphone on repeat. They screeched through me nonstop.

I was engulfed with his plans for her to take him back. I became the outsider looking into the love story that interrupted mine. So many doubts pinched the assurances he kept giving me.

"Michelle, you are the only woman I ever want to make love to for the rest of my life."

The turmoil blindsided me as once again I found myself straddling two realities. I had been so devastated with him leaving and filled with shame for my behavior that his actions escaped any of my awareness. He had finally answered the screaming plea of my heart, but as he stepped closer to me, he removed the shadow covering my doubts until they were now magnified.

The feelings of suspicion and distrust settled into my stomach like digesting a ton of wasp-infested bricks. I questioned everything he said and everything he did. I've never been one to trust easily. My lack of ability had been warped by Johnny, Everett, and now Jared. Can I do this? How?

I plagued Jared with questions for details, searching for the confidence and reassurance I needed to ease the ache in my gut. He swore to me there had been no intimacy between them. Even the night he stayed at her house, it only went as far as a hug, his thanking her for her advice on how to deal with me and my drinking. Somehow my inquiries always left the finger-pointing at me. Jared had believed in me so many times, I felt I had to do the same for him, if only my gut would participate.

33

I was told that our church had started to offer Freedom Prayer. I was quick to join as my quest for internal healing beckoned to be found. This was a series of sessions with someone trained in the program and used the guidance of the Holy Spirit to heal inner hurts. I had felt the power of the Holy Spirit move through me that Sunday when I crumbled to his call. He spoke to my heart, revealing three purposes. I knew he was real, and he was reaching for me. I hoped his remedy would be stronger than the liquid poison I had been swallowing.

Prior to my Freedom Prayer session, I had to fill out a very detailed questionnaire. There were pages of possible hurts to check off, hurts from the entire scope of my past. That's a lot of ink. It required me to revisit situations I had buried and never wanted to resume because they still had pain attached to them. Digging up old hurts was no party; it was painful. But I wanted real healing, so I dug in. I needed to be fixed. I felt the weight of my marriage hinged on fixing me. My baggage had plundered me into the bottle and pushed Jared into the comfort of another.

Approaching the church, I was filled with hope and anxiety. Entering into the unknown is always scary. Natalie greeted me with a warm smile and a hug, giving me comfort that I was in good hands. She began with a prayer and invited in the Holy Spirit. I was immediately encompassed into his arms. Natalie journeyed into my past with me, holding me with her compassion. We dove into the pains of my being molested in childhood; a date rape in high school; an attempted suicide; and rejection for being different: short, redheaded, freckled. I had placed these hurts deep inside me and covered them with more recent hurts. These were places I never wanted to return to.

As we gently unburied the anchor, a root system of pain began to emerge. The old hurts were being lifted up. In its grasp, it held a connective system of destruction linked, twisted, and bound into a heap of darkness. My gut convulsed through the memories that flashed before me. Natalie took hold of me in my pain and asked for truth to be revealed among the terror. God didn't offer me answers at this time. He simply opened his arms and gestured for me to lay these hurts into him, to which I responded in complete collapse.

Natalie and I met weekly, uncovering and conquering old hurts until I was standing in the shallow end of the spectrum. Which oddly remained the deepest. These were the wounds left unburied. The wounds that penetrated my heart, mind, and present daily, bleeding through my every thought. As I was trying to work through these past hurts, I was equally trying to repair my relationship with Jared. He supported the idea of me fixing myself but not in an active way. He often deterred me from going to life group and church.

I felt like a tightrope walker scaling the canyon of myself, with one foot balanced on Jared, the other on God. I wanted them to merge into unison and both be part of my life. God had revealed that, through me, Jared would see who he was. So that became my mission. I wanted them both.

34

That summer our families took separate vacations, but Jared and I declared that we were back together, although I continued to question his faithfulness. We spent the Fourth of July at one of my family get-togethers followed by a lake weekend at his friend's lake house.

In one of my sessions with Natalie, she told me she was met with opposition.

"Michelle, you are holding on to something that is preventing God from moving forward in you. We can't continue until you are ready to surrender God's way."

I assumed she was meaning my drinking. Jared and I went out from time to time and partied and drank together. We had some wild fun, but we were together. After all, I had prayed God would return Jared to me, and he had revealed that I would show Jared the power of God.

I carried doubt and uneasiness in my heart and gut but figured that would numb in time. Even with those uneasy feelings, Jared quenched so many of my desires. I felt wanted again but wondered if he wanted me completely and only. I had a partner again, someone to dream with and go places with.

We stayed on the go most nights and took many weekend trips. His time was valuable to me. Everett never spared any, so I appreciated Jared's more. There were a couple of times that summer Jared accused me of being unfaithful. The worst accusation was of me being with Rex. The difficult part of that was that Rex and I had been a thing once, but that was over and a memory before Jared and

I ever met. Rex convinced me to lie about it back then, which rolled over to lies now.

I couldn't let it continue. I had to fess up. And when I did, Jared exploded! I had never seen him more angry. He said he was being told that Rex and I were sleeping together now. Rex was involved in an on-again, off-again marriage and, at Jared's approval, was told he could stay at our house whenever he needed. There were several nights Rex would come in, but always either Jared or his son would be there. We were never alone, and nothing happened between us.

You would have thought someone had sent Jared a videotape of Rex and me together. His anger and jealousy soared with intensity. He told me he just didn't know if he could believe me or ever trust me. Once again, I fell to his mercy. I pleaded for forgiveness and sought his favor again, to find worthiness in his eyes. I didn't understand why he was so strongly accusing me of this. He knew of my faithful nature.

I shared with my life group my constant struggle to believe Jared in the Ellie situation. Without much detail, I told how I had hurt him too, but he always believed the best in me. I asked for prayers to reveal clarity and direction. I felt like such a failure, not having the ability to move past assuming the worst and be able to trust him. I will never fully understand the workings of the mind and body. My gut continually felt like it was juggling a set of knives, but my heart fell deeper in love with him every time the sun rose.

35

Every Labor Day weekend my family has a reunion. I was so proud to be able to show up with Jared at my side. I wasn't a total failure! This marriage is going to work. We are together and happy. That's exactly what my beaming smile told my family. Just don't look at the torment rumbling inside.

A few days after our blissful family reunion, a Thursday to be exact, life trudged on as usual. It was lunchtime, and I had finished seeing patients at one facility and was leaving to go to another. I climbed into my car, ready to fire it up, when out of the absolute silence a clear statement resounded in my head.

"Jared is at the camper sleeping with someone."

I froze. It wasn't a thought. It was a clear, concise statement. Bold. Solid. A statement so intense you could sink your heels in and stand on it.

My heart raced, but I couldn't get my body to move. My brain was tripping over everything I could find to reason with.

"Jared is at the camper sleeping with someone," it boomed again.

My body was overtaken with trembling. A deep knowing was released inside me, and the tears streaked down my cheeks.

"Move, Michelle, move."

I picked up my phone to call Jared and nonchalantly verify his busy day. It went straight to voicemail. Jared's phone has never gone straight to voicemail. I started my car and, with quivering hands, started driving. I got on the interstate and began praying.

"God, if he is sleeping with someone, please let me find out."

I decided if he didn't answer before my exit, I was heading straight for Post. I uttered another prayer for him to pick up. Each time I dialed, his phone responded with voice mail.

As I came upon my exit, my head turned to the right, wishing I was going a different direction. The distance between the two points had never been so far apart. I filled those miles with prayer.

"Dear God, if he is cheating on me, please let me find out."

I hated saying those words but longed desperately for the answer to them.

I approached the guard shack and presented my ID as normal as a ghost-white face and twitching hands could do. I wanted to hurry and get to the camper, but it was also the last place I wanted to go. I turned into the campground as my eyes searched ahead of me to find his empty parking spot, but it wasn't so. I pulled in and parked behind his truck. My lungs scraped the air for breath. On the back side of the camper was a car. Answers were beating at my brain, begging to be grasped.

I stumbled out of my car and walked straight to the extra car to inspect it closer. There were leis hanging, all girlie-like, around the rearview mirror. My heart sank a few notches closer to the truth. My eyes were too broken to produce tears; they took on a state of shock, as did all of me.

Operating in a mode outside of myself, I went to the door. Locked. I skipped knocking and went straight to banging, which only resulted in my hands hurting. I called Jared again to which his voice mail answered. I sent him a text, "Open the door!" I banged again with my fist and teeth clenched. *Who?* was racing through my head. I went for the key that Jared had showed me he kept hidden. I unlocked the door, dreading the scene on the other side. The door failed to open. The second lock, the one that can only be locked on the inside was firmly in place. I banged and yelled, "Open the door!" I could hear shuffling inside and continued to yell louder as the tears ripped from my eyes.

My heart was pounding somewhere down by my toes as it had completely sank trying to escape the pain. My calls met with his voice mail again.

"Open the door or I'm going to tear it down!" I fiercely screeched. I searched for something to aid in my demise of the door. I pulled a pair of jumper cables out of my trunk and used the handles in prying the door open. Neither worked, and they were both left bent.

I text again, "I'm not leaving!"

Nothing.

I sat. I watched as the pieces crumbled. The last three months I've spent rebuilding my dreams with him. I tried cautiously holding my heart as it continued to plunder deeper in love with him. I sat. I had pushed myself to trust and believe in him. I've been trying to white out his pleas to Ellie, only to deepen them constantly in my head.

This is me, Jared. The one who anchors her existence in you. I'm slipping further into disbelief. Hold me. Stop me. Save me. I'm drowning. I can't breathe. Can't you hear me?

I fell to the ground as my entire body released foreign moans and whimpers from each and every pore. This can't be happening. I see his truck. I see a girl's car. The camper is locked. Do I really hear someone in there?

Jared, please! At any moment, come and rescue me from this nightmare! Tell me you love only me. Put my heart back in place and tell me I'm worth it. Whisk me away to the time when you held me on a pedestal and no other woman existed. I want to feel that again, to live with the you I had before doubts.

I jump up and beat on the door, yelling and crying. My fists are red and swollen, but the pain has no caparison to my bleeding heart. My call still goes straight to voicemail. I sent another text.

"Let me in the camper. I'm not leaving."

Finally, after an hour of banging on the door, I get a text.

"What are you talking about?"

"I'm at the camper, and I hear you in there."

"Where are you? You are starting to freak me out. Are you okay?"

"You know I'm not okay, and I'm not leaving!"

"Where are you? You are worrying me."

"Open the camper door, Jared."

"I'm in class over at PEC."

"No, you're not. Your truck is here, and so is some girl's car."

"Rodney picked me up, and we went to lunch. He dropped me back off at class. Meet me over here at PEC."

"Oh, heck no! I'm not stupid, and I'm not leaving. I'm about to break the camper door down. It's locked on the inside. I know you're in there."

"Kent must have locked it when he left for school."

"You can't lock it on the inside unless you are in there. I'm about to bust in."

My blood is boiling, and my body is convulsing as I grab the jumper cables. I hear the lock slide out of its holding place. Jared opens the door.

He stands there with full confidence and an innocent look on his face. Sitting at the table is a young girl I recognize, Valerie. She had dated Rex. She isn't wearing such an innocent face.

With a low, deep, rumbling voice, I fire at her, "Are you sleeping with my husband?"

She shakes her guilty look back and forth in a no answer.

I clench my red, swollen fists, gearing up to punch her with my anger. Instead, gritting my teeth, I turn to inspect the bedroom. The bed being made can't cover up the happenings I've encountered. Jared steps in and lifts up the bed and pulls out a set of keys.

"Valerie needs to leave," he says.

I ask the obvious. "Why are her keys in the compartment under the bed?"

"I had her hide in there so you wouldn't see her."

My every muscle has begun to ache from being constricted with anger. So many words are waiting to be launched from my tongue. All I can mutter in broken voice is "Why?"

"Let me explain," he begins. "I know what it looks like, but it's not what you think."

"Really, Jared? The old standby?" Now the words spew vehemently as I pound his chest, hurting my battered fists. "Why? How could you? I thought you only wanted me. We were in the middle of putting us back together. I can't believe this!"

"Michelle, Valerie was here to give me information about Rex. There's some issues going on military wise, and I'm trying to clear them up."

"Why would you have her come to your camper, blinds closed and door locked?"

"I locked the door when I heard you pull up because I knew you wouldn't believe me. I asked her to hide under the bed. I knew if you saw her, you would assume the worst. She's mainly here to clear up what's going on with you and Rex."

"Oh my goodness! You are really going to throw this back on me? You should have met her in a public place if this was all innocent."

"She called, and I happened to be here for lunch, so it made sense for her to stop by."

"No, Jared. None of it makes sense."

The hurt inside boils up over my anger, and I start sobbing, unable to maintain any composure. He reaches to hold me, and for a few seconds, he is my protector, and I melt into him again. My mind snaps back to the situation, and I push him away and run out the door. I cannot take being here any longer.

I drive off with him standing in my rearview mirror. The events of the last several hours rehash in collision. Everything has come to an end. The sun is shining, and people are on the roads driving. Why? Do they not know? Life is over. Nothing exists in the same light as it did this morning.

Confusion cuddles me like a warm blanket. The way he has been holding me, making love to me, so intense. The words affirming his love to me, promising I'm the love of his life, there is no one else. No man has ever poured such love and attention on me. That's all I've ever wanted—to be loved and cherished. Please tell me there is an explanation for all this. I don't want this to be taken from me too.

36

Jade is shocked when I spill the events of the day to her.

"It just doesn't sound like him, Michelle. He is so crazy about you and has tried so hard to help you."

"I know. I don't get it. I want to believe that Valerie was only there to talk about me and Rex, but he left me banging on the door for an hour!"

Several hours later, Jade calls me back.

"I was so upset, I had to call Jared. He swears nothing was going on. He is really freaked out about losing you. He says he panicked and locked the doors."

"Yeah, but Jared doesn't panic. I know him. No matter what is going on inside him, he is able to maintain a calm, cool composure."

I find myself alone and tormented again. The emptiness of the house magnifies loneliness. I could lay here bleeding to death, and no one would know. My life has become insignificant to everyone around me. A life with Jared has been the only thing I have had to cling to. If he isn't here to protect me, then who will? This day I had seen a side of Jared that I didn't see a way to justify. Finding the texts between him and Ellie hurt, and for the first time, I felt intruded to being his muse. I carried the blame for that. I pushed him away.

The depth of his lies as I stood there banging on the camper door pounded in my mind. A sheet of aluminum stood between us. I could hear him, he could hear me, yet he attempted to deceive me that he wasn't even there. Lie after lie as I stood there broken and crumbling. I had never met anyone capable of that level of deception, standing in the middle of truth but bending facts to manipulate belief.

The sound of his truck interrupted my thoughts. I needed my husband to hold and love me. Jared had offered answers and repairs to all things broken in me. I wanted him to have answers to this too. Although this day opened new questions about who Jared really is, he was holding every piece of my existence. I had given him access to all of me. My every thought and every move was dictated by him. I didn't keep enough of myself to be able to maneuver through this.

Help me, Jared. Make sense of this for me so I can continue to love you.

He speaks with such eloquence I question the deceit my eyes offered in the scene of the day.

"Michelle, you know how hurt I've been over finding out about you and Rex. Since Valerie had dated Rex, she was telling me stuff, trying to help me figure out what has really been going on between you two. I should not have locked the door, but I panicked. I know you have been struggling to believe me about Ellie. I knew if you saw Valerie here, it would be hard for you to believe me. I was trying to protect you from that." He looks so deeply into my eyes he gazes at my soul. "You are the only woman I want for the rest of my life. I swear nothing was going on. I'm so in love with you and fall deeper every day. You are more than I ever dreamed."

His silver tongue slathered me with the answers my heart wanted to hear. My head could not justify anything he was giving me and whipped me left and right with reasoning. I was taunted by his words versus the images replaying the day. It was too overwhelming. My anger for having to experience any of this reached its boiling point.

"Just go," I fumed with tears.

As he drove away, I was angered even more that he would leave. How could he not insist on holding me? He knows I need to be held. He knows I'm incapable of existing without him.

"Come back," my brokenness whispered.

Within a few minutes, he texted me, "I really didn't want to leave. I want to hold you."

"Then do," I replied.

SHED

Our bodies met with each other as though they had been starved of human touch for decades. My mind escaped the plague of images it held and let my desires take over. We dove headfirst into that insane, dangerously beautiful dance that always bound us together.

37

The sun rose again the next morning, but I remained in the middle of my nightmare. There was no escaping the events of the day before. Jared woke up and loved on me as usual, acting as though nothing had taken place. After he left for work, I met with the woman in the images of my mind, crying, unfolding on the ground outside of the camper. I wanted to tap her on the shoulder and tell her she is worthy of so much more. I wished I could hold her and soak up the tears she released uncontrollably. As I bent to whisper to her, the makings of her unfolded and blew away in the wind of my breath. She was so broken.

Fortunately, this was the weekend of our women's conference at church. I would be surrounded with my ladies. Ashlynn was getting to come with me, so I had to hold it together. She had seen enough of my downfall.

Music has always been an emotional experience for me. As hundreds of women gathered in one building to call upon the Lord, the song "Oceans" began to drift through the air. There was no chance of holding it together. I'm not sure if Rhonda sensed it or the Holy Spirit nudged her, but she leaned in to hold me up and allowed me to come undone. Several of my life-group ladies encircled me as I explained the last twenty-four hours. They held me with compassion and prayer. I could see in their eyes the pain they carried for me. I was so thankful not to be alone as I faced this.

Rash decisions lineup with many of my character defaults. In an attempt to gain knowledge and control of the situation, I sent Jared's first ex-wife a message.

"Have you ever had any reason to suspect Jared was cheating?"

"Call me," she replied.

As soon as we went to break in the conference, I stepped outside to call Kelly.

She told me how Jared had always been very flirtatious and she had suspicions but was never able to prove anything until the end of their marriage. She discovered he had been sleeping with a girl on their volleyball team. She said when he was married to Ellie, that Ellie had contacted her, asking the same question.

I told her what had happened.

She said Jared had sent a photo of a girl, bragging to Kent that he was seeing a younger woman. "Vanessa?" she asked me.

"No. Close enough. Valerie," I muttered.

"Michelle, there is no reason for him to have a girl in his camper, middle of the day, blinds shut and door locked."

Two images traipsed through my mind battling for my belief. The Jared that had many times rescued me in my drunkenness, encapsulated me with love and attention, the one that opened his arms to me as I tiptoed barefoot in the sand to give myself to completely, and the Jared becoming clearer and closer through the fog, telling another woman he was still in love with her and wished he was holding her. The one capable of looking at me disintegrate before him as he remained enclosed in his camper with another woman. I sought after truth with my eyes closed and head turned, not wanting to go the direction it was taking me.

I felt trapped in the middle of a tug-of-war game: my head versus my heart. Jared and I had long talks about the Valerie situation. He held my hands; locked eyes with mine; spoke in the calmest, truest sincere voice his reality of the day. He was so hurt and looking for answers about me and Rex. Valerie was the closest source to the matter. There was absolutely nothing between them. He needed answers to determine if he could or should trust in me. He was trying to find a way to salvage our love.

He was hurt that I didn't have more confidence in him. He polished all that off with how intense his love was for me and that I was the best thing to ever walk into his life. He said how difficult it was to push past the image of Rex and me together, but that his love was strong enough to try and pleaded for me to do the same. By the end of the conversation, I felt inadequate at my attempts to trust him and keep us together.

38

Near the end of September, we were invited to a pool party for some of the guys returning from Iraq. I had been behaving with my drinking since starting to church, only drinking occasionally. This evening I had a few beers. Jared and I were sitting on the patio talking.

"Hey, you wanna get in and swim?" I asked him.

"Sure!" he replied.

"My suit is in the truck. Do you care to grab it?"

"Why don't you just go skinny dipping?" he suggested.

I gave him a very puzzled look. "What?"

"Just strip and go."

"You wouldn't care for all your friends to see me naked?" I asked in surprise.

"No. As long as no one touches you."

My jaw dropped, and a very uneasy feeling crept up into my stomach.

"So if you think it's okay for other men to see me naked, how do you feel about seeing other women naked?"

"I don't see anything wrong with it. I think women's bodies are a work of art," he commented.

"Jared, I'm the only one you should ever want to see naked. That's intimate."

"I'm not out looking for it, but if it happens, it happens."

"And you wouldn't turn away?"

"Why would I?"

"Because you are married to me, and that is something only you and I share. It's part of our intimacy."

It wasn't until this conversation that I realized how different our beliefs really were. This added another layer of questioning the man I was with and his values.

39

Dressing up is so much fun, so you can imagine my excitement for Halloween. My costume had to be sexy and extreme. I chose a Cleopatra outfit—shiny, gold, and form fitting. I decked Jared out as my gladiator. I wanted Jared's eyes only on me. We looked pretty amazing. We had two Halloween parties to go to. One of my life-group ladies and one of Jared's military friends.

We went to mine first. I knew most everyone there, except a few couples. I mingled and introduced myself. One of the ladies was very pretty and had on a low-cut top. Most of what she had was hanging out, but so was mine. I was visiting with her when Jared stepped up. I didn't think much of it. I excused myself to the bathroom, told Jared I'd be right back. A few minutes later, when I come back, Jared was gone. I looked in every room but didn't find him. Someone told me he had stepped out on the back porch. As I walked out, I spotted him sitting next to the nearly topless woman, lost in a ga-ga gaze. He may as well had been salivating.

Feelings of inadequacy and intrusion crept in. My husband was looking at her the way he should only be looking at me. I had dressed sexy to captivate his attention. I was not willing to share. I sucked up my feelings and sat on his lap to love on him and gain his attention. I had been grilling him about Ellie and Valerie to which his responses always left me feeling incompetent to love and trust him as well as he did me. I knew saying something would be a losing battle.

If he would just move back in, it would clear all my worries about his activities and confirm his commitment to me. The thoughts of his possible infidelity never left my mind. The reality of his lies and deceit of that day were undeniable. He stood behind his reason of searching for truth about me. So maybe this was my big challenge. Nothing can grow or be strengthened unless it is challenged and tested.

One of my biggest deficits was trust. I faithfully continued my pursuit of God. Was he leading me to press beyond myself and enter into a realm of trust like I had sworn I'd never do? I wasn't able to with Johnny. With Everett, it was over long before it ended. My love for Jared was able to bypass all the pain and even grown deeper. I was so foolishly in love with him.

40

My kids stayed busy with activities, so many weekends, I'd stay at my parents. One Sunday, when I had them mid-November, on my way back home, Jared texted me.

"Have a surprise for you." Then he wouldn't answer my calls and texts. He loved to taunt me with excitement.

Nearly my whole drive home, I vented to Jade. Not only was she my best friend, she has a degree in social work. Her advice was extra meaningful. She had been present through this entire struggle. I tried explaining my tug-of-war. How is it possible my heart is loving someone deeper every day when it is that someone that has caused me to question everything they are and is pushing my trust beyond its capabilities? Him not living under the same roof magnified all my worries. She understood my doubts. She also pointed out that I was coming from an already wounded viewpoint.

As I turned on our road, my eye caught a glimpse of the camper. Thinking it was only a wishful mirage, I didn't go full-blown ecstatic until I pulled in the driveway. There they were, Jared and Kent, unloading and settling back into our home. I gushed a sigh of relief. He's back. Everything he has told me and promised is true.

My heart celebrated his return with gratitude. He was giving us another chance. It had been a year since we lived under the same roof. I carried the affliction daily of being the one that ruined our marriage so quickly after it began. I got lost in a swamp of emotions and alcohol, pushing him away. His actions had been questionable but without concrete proof or admission. I felt responsible for removing the first brick of our foundation. He was allowing me to redeem myself.

My heart succumbed full throttle to him. He owned every crevice and crinkle without challenge. Like it had been propelled forward with the snap of a rubber band. I wanted to exceed my original, broken attempt at loving him properly. He stepped away from me, yes, but he didn't completely leave like Everett did.

I doted on him, which is typically my nature. My drinking had subdued that characteristic. Alcohol breeds selfishness.

41

As if he could hear my thoughts, Jared took me to dinner one night, not thinking I noticed he was wearing his wedding ring. When I returned from the bathroom, he had mine on his pinky. (I had noticed it missing when getting ready for dinner.) He slipped it on my finger and gave me that same smile and wink as the day he said his vows to me.

Unsolicited memories plagued my ever-growing utopia. Jared was a member of a secret pilot's club called QB. They met monthly. One evening when he mentioned the upcoming meeting, a memory flashed to mind. It was while we were dating. Jared had sent me a picture of one of the pilots sitting in a plane with a topless young woman on his lap. I remembered it so clearly when the memory crept in. I was disturbed by it at the time as the man was married. Jared thought it was hilarious, saying they had got her drunk. When I mentioned it, Jared explained that only on special occasions, they would have topless waitresses. I told him I was in no way okay with that. He promised he would avoid those meetings for my sake.

I remembered many times Jared mentioning how everyone said he was like his uncle. That they both loved women. Several times he had said how much he liked being sneaky. Each time he did, there was a look of excitement in his eyes paired with a sly grin. I had overlooked those the times he had said it, thinking I was being a shrewd for letting it bother me, but here it was dangling before me with an unexpected irritation.

Many instances started getting my attention. One of the most unsettling involved his dad. It was a few weeks before Christmas, and

Jared's parents were visiting us for a few nights. His dad's back had been hurting. Jared suggested I give him some exercises. I had tried explaining several he could do. He looked puzzled, so I got in the floor to demonstrate. The look that washed over his face left me with an enormous feeling of disgust. I immediately left the room, trying to escape the odd discomfort.

Hoping my embarrassment was displaced, I casually brought it up in conversation. Me, Jared, my son, and one of Jared's sons were playing spades. I told Jared I gave his dad some exercises for his back.

He said, "Did you show them to him?"

I said, "Yes, I demonstrated them so he'd understand."

"I bet he liked that!"

"Huh?" I questioned.

"He may be old, but he's still my dad!"

Whoa! So Jared is okay, almost encouraging his dad's inappropriate thoughts of me? I would never be okay with that.

Maybe I was coming out of the alcohol-induced haze I had been in from the time I had met Jared. How could I have missed so much? He and his boys were constantly talking about sex and pointing out other people's physical appearances, whether good or bad. They were sharp with cutdowns to someone they found unattractive and very quick to point out desirable features of what they liked. Not in a general "she's pretty" comment but singled out and descriptive. It became frustrating and even hurtful. I found myself somewhat joining in on the game. I was quick to scan my surroundings and compare myself. Everywhere we went, I could feel Jared's eyes searching for something pleasurable to take in.

Traversing the canyon with one foot on Jared, one foot on God was fiercely exhausting, but I continued forward. The Holy Spirit had spoken three purposes over me so loudly I kept them held closely. When church announced the upcoming mission trip for Haiti, I knew I was to go. I had carried the desire to reach others abroad since I was a little girl. I attended the informational meeting and was choked with tears and conviction to be a part of the team. Jared didn't meet my revelation with the same level of excitement, but I told him I was doing it. He casually said, "Maybe I'll go too, to make sure you are safe." Another meeting was scheduled after the holidays.

Christmas has never been without excitement in my family. My sister Leah; her husband, Rick; and my nephew Landon drove in from DC to spend the holiday with us. My sister Crystal and her boys were there, my parents, and all of my kids. It was like everything was coming together. Jared and I took all our kids to the mountain to have Christmas with his family. We surprised the kids with a trip to see the *Nutcracker* in Memphis, the zoo, and ice skating. All the kids seemed happy to be back together.

Even Jared's favorite holiday, NYE, went over quite well. We went to his best friend's for their annual party. I participated in the games without getting too wasted. Our agreement was that I would not drink without him. Everything appeared to be mending.

Unknown to Jared, I was driving myself insane. I searched the camper top to bottom, left to right, every nook and cranny, searching for evidence. My gut carried a sick, twisted ball of doubt and worry.

My stomach was where my heart met with my head. They were continually rumbling for truth. My heart would present one fact, only to be argued with a reality my head carried. It was a never-ending battle.

I felt there was a section of activity Jared was keeping hidden from me. I had circumstantial evidence but no hardcore undeniable proof. It was unbelievable the way he had continued in our daily lives as though none of the craziness of last year happened. He acted as though it was wiped from his history until I would bring it up, which was often. I questioned his every move. When his phone lit up, I was looking over his shoulder paralyzed with fear of what I might find. It felt as though it was waiting for me around the corner. Truth was playing hide-and-seek, cackling inside with anticipation to jump out and suck my dreams away again.

Several times a week I looked through every drawer and cabinet on his side of the bathroom. I ran my fingers through the pockets of his clothing. He was going back and forth from the car to his truck driving to work. I searched both. He always kept a shaving kit with him. He had a container of pills so he would never be without his medication. One pill looked odd to me. It was blue and had a unique shape. One was cut in half. I found more in his bathroom drawer in packaging. When researched, I found it to be generic Viagra.

I didn't understand why Jared would not tell me he felt like he needed those. Unless it wasn't for use with me. I counted all the pills just in case. My self-imposed inquisition was consuming all my being. I was afraid to make any plans without Jared. I feared what he might do if I wasn't around. I became the type of person I despised. I was suspicious of everything he said and did.

It got even worse when Jared was moved back into aviation. For several years, he was chief at Range Control. I knew all the guys there and didn't feel threatened. Aviation meant a completely new group of people, moreover, flying. As in overnight trips. To top it off, he would be flying with the pilot that Jared had sent me a picture of with the topless chick in his lap.

My life group had been a lifeline of sanity and reason for me. I shared with Christy my maniacal behavior and how I carried torment every second of my life. When I was with him, I scrutinized his every breath. When I was not with him, I obsessed over what he was possibly doing. She told me to continue to pray and seek God's will. She reminded me that God gives confirmation through peace.

Something had to give. I asked Jared if he would be willing to start marriage counseling.

"Yes!" he replied. "You are driving me crazy!" he joked as he flashed me that smile and tossed me a wink. He knew how to cover his jabs with cuteness. Those winks must have been dipped in poison. My heart fluttered every time.

You would think the universe would pause or at least slow down when you find yourself high centered in crisis. Seems like that is when it chooses to spin faster, really piling it on as it sits back and taunts with laughter. Jared and I decided we didn't need such a huge house. Kent was the only one living with us full time, and he would be graduating soon. The company I was working for lost the nursing-home contract, so my hours were dropped to very part-time, six to ten hours a week. We decided to sell our house, buy a bigger camper to live in while we flipped houses. I would go to real-estate school to handle all our buying and selling. Jared was up for retirement soon. Luckily, being placed back in aviation would get his training current so he could fly with the airlines.

43

Jared had decided to go with me on the Haiti trip, which called for training and preparation. In the midst of all of that, we started marriage counseling. Jared chose the counselor himself. I was just relieved to have intervention. Spinning my wheels of insanity was depleting my energy. I persisted my interrogation of Jared nearly with each breath I took. I needed continual assurance from him that he had not cheated on me with Ellie or Valerie. It became common for him to stop, clasp my hand, peer into the depths of me, and, with a strong, immobilizing voice, affirm his faithfulness to me. It was like a verbal trance, but there remained a portion of heart immune to his words.

Unloading a brief history of events in one hour is challenging. Unloading mine and Jared's brief history, loaded with extreme events, deserves a medal of some sort. In our short time together, we had scaled mountains most people may climb once in their lifetime. I wonder how difficult it was for our psychologist to subdue a look of shock and keep from running out of the office? I am sure he had to pull at least a dozen books off his shelves for reference after we left.

I liked him right away. He made several biblical references and acknowledged his faith. He had done extensive work with many forms of addiction. He had also coauthored several books and made many trips to CA for speaking engagements. He listened with a look of really listening. I could tell he would be impartial. I was comfortable and confident with him.

It quickly became evident Jared was frustrated with my inability to let everything go and move on. Our counselor pointed out to him that there should not be a timeline for me to deal with my hurt and anger. Trust takes time to rebuild. Jared tried putting my drinking on the same level of breaking trust. And while I fully understand my level of deceit, alcohol is not capable of returning intimacy or emotion. The world of passion that I gave my husband had been tainted, and I felt robbed. His adamant denial did not wash away my feeling of invasion. I was not sure that anything would.

Jared had voiced from the beginning that he thought one-on-one counseling with me would be beneficial. About a month in, our counselor agreed. So marriage counseling became Michelle counseling with the intent of joint sessions from time to time. Using his voice of confidence and influence, Jared had the counselor convinced of his faithfulness to me and that I had extreme trust issues. Although my mind was clouded with doubt, my love for Jared was undeniable, and my desire to save my marriage remained.

44

After only a month on the market, we had an offer on our house and prepared to move. This coincided with our yard sale for fundraising our Haiti trip. We still had two of almost everything since most of our married life thus far had been spent separately. My furniture, dishes, and appliances ended up being the chosen set to go. I shopped for a suitable camper since I was not working much and it narrowed down our choices. We did not have time to find a house to flip, so Jared decided we would move onto Post.

Truth was, I would move anywhere to be with him. He had so much power over me. Maybe he was aware of that. Maybe not. I could spend every moment with him, and it still not be enough. He read me so well. He knew when my hand needed to be touched. Without saying a word, he could tell when my lips were asking to be kissed. He laid sweet words to my ears when my doubts were creeping in. His wink was never too late to knock me off my feet. Time after time, we made our breathless journey into ecstasy, slipping through the hands of time as if we owned the world. I liked living in the escape of reality. I dreaded the moment my heart and mind would battle to the final victor. The heart can only trick and subdue reality for so long.

All my hope was in Jared. "Michelle counseling" had my full effort. If there was a way to fully trust in Jared, I wanted to find it. My heart failed to heed my warnings to walk softly, so the rest of me searched to secure its position. I wanted so badly for Jared to see and feel the power of God. I wanted to build us back together with God

SHED

as the foundation. I knew if he was at the center, my heart would be safe.

Knowing it was coming didn't prepare me for it happening.

45

Jared had been flying almost daily, but he received an assignment to fly to CA for a mission that lasted several days. We had discussed it in depth several times, and Jared assured me of his loyalty. The fact that he was always paired with the same pilot, the married one that found it acceptable to have a naked young woman in his lap, magnified my anxiety. I presented Jared with different scenarios and asked how he would respond. After the camper incident, I wasn't sure if he knew acceptable boundaries. There was obviously an issue if he thought discussing any matter in a locked camper with a young woman was anywhere close to okay.

Fear. Fear is ugly and debilitating. It's like superhero strength gone bad. The adrenaline rush of a destruction junky. You gain X-ray vision into events that may or may not take place in a futuristic world you create and plant yourself in the middle of. It all takes place in a flash, leaving you the whiplash of insanity.

I could see the scene unfold before me: Jared having drinks at the hotel bar after dinner, eyeing a young lady a few seats over and sending her another of what she is sipping. He slips her his sly grin and tosses in a wink. He lives for the thrill of the challenge. The wedding ring is already in his pocket, pressed against his thigh, reminding him of how sneaky he is, adding to his excitement. The rush flares all the way up into his eyes, giving him an attractive glow of confidence. His tongue is so slick and practiced the compliments gently glide to her ears. He has watched and read her, easily knowing how to reel her in.

The biggest thrill was seeing if he could do it. Since she's already in his room, it only makes sense to deliver what he has built up to. While she's in the bathroom freshening up, he sends the sweetest message to his wife.

"This bed is so cold, and my arms so empty without you. Good night, pretty girl. Love you with all my heart."

"I'm missing you like crazy. Love you bunches," she replies.

His ability to deceive her gets him all the more enthralled into his seduction.

Little does he know the hell brought down on her through the vision she is trapped in the middle of. The sting of his chase, the wink that belonged to her, his promise so easily tucked away in his pocket. She tried to be brave and strong. She tried to tell herself it was only a flash of insanity. But the flash stung her heart so deeply it laced poison through her veins. The pain so excruciating that her tears ran as red as blood. Her prayers too weak to reach heaven; she only had the strength to reach for the bottle.

The next morning brings uncertainty. The scene was so clear, the pain so sharp it still stings. But the empty bottle staring me down reminds me I'm only a fool. Alcohol may numb the pain, but it also clouds reason. What felt like a glimpse of reality was a drunken, distrusting wife letting her past catch her again.

I started the morning with strong coffee and large doses of hating myself. It wasn't enough to erase my guilt. I envied Jared being able to put my mistakes behind him and trust in me. Everything I asked him to do, he did. Why couldn't I do the same for him?

My failure to believe him lined up with the texts between him and Ellie, the look of Valerie shaking her guilty face back and forth, and the lies Jared fed me that day. The compression of them sunk my scarlet *R* deeper into the core of me. Its branding sizzled as it pressed further into my soul, claiming me as its own. I hated myself more with each passing minute.

Jared sends me the sweetest good-morning messages, telling me he had to dream about me because one night without me was too much to bear. My heart smiled and skipped a beat, while my mind met with the image of another in his arms, empty wine glasses on the bedside table, his wedding ring having rolled to a stop under the bed as his pants were flung across the floor. The torture incessant, refusing to loosen its grip.

Unable to withstand the sting any longer, incapable to push aside the vision of stolen intimacy, I pour vodka into the burning wounds. I succumb to its strength quickly and easily. He turns into a distant haze, blurring his connection with anyone else. He lays in bed alone. His words of adornment ring louder in my ears as they gain credibility to belief. The insanity softens into a bearable state, giving me the hope of surviving until his return. His wedding ring gleams as it encircles his finger. *My love, my love. My one and only love.*

Just like that I wake up to Sunday. I hate that I found my way to the bottom of another bottle. That is not the person I want to be. The visions of him with another woman are so clear it is like I'm a hologram spectator. He continues his seduction as though I'm invisible. Does he not carry me in his heart? Does he not see my face or feel my touch? I know no other way to escape the torturous thoughts. I hope Jared doesn't find out about my drinking. He stands so strong in his commitment to me, but I have failed again.

It is so hard to go to church knowing how big of a disappointment you are. So I don't. I join the online service from the comforts of the camper, where I can hold myself in misery without having to put on a smile. My prayers must not be good enough to reach heaven. I can't count how many times I have asked God to take away my desire to drown myself in alcohol. And peace. Where is the peace that I hear everyone talking about? I have asked God into my heart. Does even he find me unworthy? Unwanted by God. That's pretty tough to swallow.

I guess I'm guilty of placing myself in a whirlwind of heartache, but I don't understand how to get out. I'm dizzy and am not even sure which direction is anything but upside down. I desire to seek God. I can't undo the feeling of him coming down and touching my heart that one Sunday just over a year ago. I have no doubt his presence has unveiled truths to me that only he was able to know. I have cried. I have prayed. I have thrown myself in the floor while doing both and asked God to unchain me. But here I remain, empty bottle on the counter and visions of my husband with a woman that is not me.

The two worlds collide and trap me in the middle. When I'm in Jared's arms, I'm certain he wants me. His love meets so many dry, broken, forgotten places and fills them, quenches the dehydration of years of being starved. At the same time, it feels robbed. Our intimacy is invaded. I feel it. I'm falling into a hole of the blackest darkness so thick it squeezes me as I fall. Both my hands reach up. They can't stretch out any further, seeking saving. Two hands reach back. I struggle to clasp one, either one. I just need rescuing. I graze fingertips that radiate security and comfort, but it's so dark I'm unable to see whose hand it is.

46

Doctor White and I had been focusing on dissecting my thoughts instead of me going haywire with them. I must say this weekend was a fail of epic proportions. He had given me a book to read about thoughts and breaking them down to see if there was any evidence or reason to support the thought. To look at it logically, not emotionally. There was even a graph and step-by-step instructions. Problem was, where was option 2? The option of not having captured the thought but letting it go haywire? And option 3: The thought went haywire and you reacted and did the last thing you wanted to do and the main thing you promised not to do.

I really did try. When the vision pulled me in, I struggled to turn my head. To find my Jared promising himself to me, looking into his eyes, and only seeing my reflection in them. But the thoughts were so much bigger than me. They were thoughts twisted with feelings, and they were rooted into a deeper knowing than I could explain. They were so strong. I wasn't sure I would ever be able to control their powerful force.

Checking my phone, I noticed that Jared had called last night. We had talked for a good amount of time, but I had no memory of it. Chances were he was aware of my drinking. I hoped he didn't know of my failure, but luck did not tip my way often. It's a terrible feeling waiting for someone, knowing you have disappointed them but not knowing if they know.

I missed Jared with a sickness like I had never missed anyone with before. Being trapped in the vision of last night made me miss him even deeper. Maybe because I wished I was there to defend my territory. Or maybe it was the guilt for allowing such a vision to come alive, suck me in, and unleash my forbidden poison. It was that thin line between passion and hatred that I tiptoed so frequently, daring myself to grab its danger. Desiring more of it while praying for protection from its sting.

Whether Jared knew about my drinking or not, I could not tell him about my vision. It was so real and excruciatingly painful, but it was of my creation. He had called, text, and given me affirmation of his love and faithfulness, just like I needed. I could read the disappointment in his first glance at me. That look hurt worse than any words could. The need to love him more in order to outweigh my failure kicked in. My body cried out the apologies of my heart in a way my words were unable to do.

47

At my next session with Dr. White, I told him everything. He was the only person I shared my vision with. I didn't care how crazy I sounded. I wanted help. I told him Jared gave me wavering answers on what he thought was acceptable boundaries in a marriage. The instability of his answers increased my insecurities. Each and every single day the knots in my stomach twisted tighter, and I slipped closer into the realm of insanity. I was watching myself lose it while everyone around me was telling me I was the problem and I had to fix it or I was going to take our marriage under.

Dr. White referred me to the psychiatrist in the same building to put me on medicine to help with the anxiety and, probably in his notes, the "insanity." He told me I needed to look at Jared's commitment to all the things I had asked him to do and that he was doing them. He said I had to change my focus and only I could control that.

I decided to start fresh. I wanted to make one more sweep through all of Jared's things to give myself a foundation of trust to move forward on. I paid extra attention to his flight bag and uniform. I gained confidence as I turned up empty to any phone numbers. Then came the overnight bag, the blue-pill holder, so little but so unsettling. One of the generic Viagra pills was missing. In a rage, I threw them in the toilet and flushed them. I sat and sobbed uncontrollably as flashes of my vision returned. Instead of becoming numb and familiar with the scene and his words of seduction, larger pieces of my heart were dissected and thrashed into shards scattered as far as I could see.

SHED

I had to stop the insanity. The pill could have been used with me. That is what I was choosing to believe. Although my kids did not know what I was wrestling with, I knew they were aware of my stress and uneasiness. This spiritual, emotional, and mental torture was unraveling the person I wanted to be. I knew I was near the end of being able to endure it.

48

Our mission trip to Haiti was a month and a half away. I set that as a deadline. I knew God would draw near as we were leaving everything behind to enter into a foreign land. I prayed that he would speak to Jared and reveal himself to him on this trip. I prayed for his heart to soften to desire to live in the guidelines God had designed. I prayed for the peace to be released from the torturous suspicion I lived in second to second. I wanted to be freed from the heavy despair on my soul caught between the two worlds I wished would collide and bring life instead of torment.

The decrease in my workload allowed me the time to search for houses for us to flip. That was more time-consuming than I had expected. My poor Ashlynn had dealt with scoliosis for years, which only worsened, even with therapy. It was determined that she would need a rod put in her back to maintain alignment and prevent further curving. What was only supposed to be a one-night hospital stay turned into a week.

Ashlynn's system was unable to "wake up" from the anesthesia. She vomited continually and was in so much pain. Seventeen years old but I saw my baby lying in that hospital bed, exhausted. It broke my heart not being able to help her. At the same time, Jared's dad was put in ICU for complications with his kidney transplant from a few years earlier. His hospital was down the road from Ashlynn's. Jared was back and forth and still had to work. I only left Ashlynn twice that week to run home and shower.

Everett and Lilith had come to the hospital the day of the surgery. I had my mom and dad with me, and Jared was in and out due to work. A few days into Ashlynn's hospital stay, Everett came on his own to visit Ashlynn. It was the first time in the three years since our divorce I had to be around him more than two minutes.

I discovered the definition of PTSD that day. There was no controlling it. All the old feelings of disgust and hatred boiled up like they had been simmering the entire time, just waiting to spew. I sat holding it in as long as could. When I was unable to do so any longer, I ran to the bathroom to vomit. The sound of his voice made my skin crawl, and everything internal shook. I couldn't look at him. My stomach twisted and held hurts that did not know where to go. They were all clawing me on the inside. My breath was shallow and quick, eruption peeking out wanting to release. It poured all through me as I somehow gained the strength to barricade it internally.

That night, in the few hours Ashlynn was able to stop throwing up and rest, I curled into a ball beside her bed and held myself as the eruption drained from within.

I needed Jared. He was overloaded too, trying to be with me and his dad both. When he came to the hospital the next day, I sunk into his arms and melted. He held me as my protector, and in those moments, I felt secure. We had lain awake many nights as he journeyed back in time with me to walk through my nightmare. No one else had been there with me. He squeezed me as my body trembled. Through tears and broken sentences, I tried explaining the eruption taking place inside. I was so afraid. It was completely unexpected, and I just wanted to be there for my daughter.

49

Ashlynn was put through all kinds of tests and had to have a tube run down nose, into her stomach. She was barely able to rest and couldn't keep pain meds down. It was terrible. Her roommate was a girl of the same age with spina bifida. She had never known the feeling of walking. Her mom said she had been put through hundreds of surgeries. The majority of their lives had been spent in this very building. I knew my daughter would get better; we had the end in sight. She would get to walk out of this hospital. This seventeen-year-old beside us would never have that opportunity. I ached for them both.

Everett and Lilith came to visit Ashlynn one day, and I entered back into my undesired world. Seeing them love on each other and happy made me so angry. All the ways he hurt me and pushed me aside, and here he is happy? He doesn't deserve to be loved or to be happy. The unfairness burned inside, along with all the other kindling of emotions roaring with flames.

Thankfully, Ashlynn took a quick turn for the better and was released to go home. She was looking forward to sleeping in her own bed. Everett met us at the hospital and took her home to rest. Missing sleep, a shower, and my husband, I headed for the camper.

I needed him on so many levels, mostly to help me escape. One thing I knew for certain, Jared had never failed to scale the line of passion and hatred with me. Our whirlwind of intimacy had burned my memories of Everett so many times before. I needed that fire to burn the flames of eruption that had been ignited before they flared out of control. He had saved me so many times before, but I pressed forward to scale the line on my own. He was there with me, but his grasp only grazed me as I passed by. I was falling into a torment I had buried. Now tainted, his touch no longer saved me from myself.

Wandering through the old familiar territory on my own again, alone in the nightmare, it became darker than ever before. The dim light Jared had offered for a time, now extinguished, left a gaping black hole. Darkness became even darker. Darkness. It's the only thing I can see. Nothing.

50

Eyes wide open all night. Sunlight creeping in but not piercing me. Light does not reach a bottomless pit, but pain does. Pain and memories. Words and broken dreams. Failures. The pit is where they gather. The darkness feeds their strength and takes yours. In my weakness, I had placed my hand in Jared's, trusting his promises to rescue me. His embrace had felt warm and secure but now left me holding a facade, falling aimlessly.

With Jared unable to supply my escape, I turned back to my drunkenness. The look of Everett's face blurred, and his touch was unable to prick my numbness. The Jared I had come to picture layered with Valerie and Ellie faded into one figure again. The heaviness of my mind relaxed. The picture before me became tolerable to navigate. Maybe cloudy prayers can't reach heaven. In my hazy awareness, I uttered words for rescue, but I don't think they left the universe.

Jared's dad was still in ICU. The doctors and nurses were up and down with their assessment of his future. Unaware of my condition, Jared asked me to meet him at the hospital. Sure, I could pull it off. I drove to meet him there. I had been unable to fool him for some time now. He knew right away. He was too overwhelmed to be very mad at me. Again, I hated to have hurt and disappoint him.

In the middle of the night, Jared got a call from his mom to hurry in. A few hours later, he returned and silently climbed into bed. I rolled over and put my arms around him.

"Jared?"

"He is gone," he softly said.

SHED

I think the shock prevented him from crying. I held him and let the tears flow for us both.

*****

The next morning I found him sitting on the edge of the bed, sunken down like a young lost boy. My heart broke for his pain. I walked over to him and grabbed his head and pressed it into my stomach as I rubbed his back.

"I am so sorry, Jared."

"I expected him to get better. He's my dad," he sobbed.

"I know," I whispered.

"And I'm pretty upset with you too."

We were two broken people unable to hold each other up.

I was weaker now as I trudged through the memories of Everett. My heart was broken deeper with the hurts accumulated from loving Jared. The load of brokenness heavier and heavier. He wavered on his belief system of boundaries, what was acceptable and not. Jared needed to grieve his dad, and I needed to suck it up and love him through it. We spent the week off and on at the mountain. His mom is a strong woman. She faced the loss with bold acceptance and determination to handle running their cabin and property with barely a pause in her step.

You could feel the absence of his dad. He was a man people respected and admired. His intelligence could be seen in the many contraptions he developed on the place. The family gathered for a picnic one Saturday as a memorial service. Several shared memories, laughs, and stories. His fondness of other women was something the family laughed about. It was something that made me pause and question.

The escape the mountain brought was difficult not to get wrapped up in. You could stand outside in the daylight and see no other visible structure. At night, the millions of stars transported you to a universe beyond pain and heartache. Memories melted away, time slowed, and the beating of the heart intensified with grandeur. I loved Jared with an intense fever. The kind that scorches all the good in its fire. It had slowly burned who I was until what I had left was barely recognizable.

We had one counseling session before our mission trip, my deadline to receive peace. I had to have clarification of Jared's beliefs and boundaries. I tried to get him to accept mine. I could not feel secure with his. I would never find it acceptable for him to soak in the pleasure of another woman's body. The counselor agreed that it was an interference of our intimacy. Jared danced around the subject until the counselor pointed it out to him. After that session, Jared decided he did not like our counselor and suggested going somewhere else.

The mission trip brought excitement to me as it had been a desire from such a young age. It was also filling one of the purposes revealed to me just over a year ago. Unfortunately, my heart was also heavy with the deadline I had given myself. If I was not able to find peace in my relationship with Jared by the end of this trip, this marriage was not God's will for me. The agony was literally killing me. I was torn between serving two masters, finding my heart and devotion ripped with each foot going a different direction. I longed to feel loved, security, and peace.

My life group was praying with me over this trip. Not only that we would give the people of Haiti a glimpse of God's love but that Jared would also see it. I knew if his heart was going to be penetrated by God, it would be in Haiti. Jared made sure to let our mission group know that he was only on this trip to ensure my safety. He told everyone several times that he did not go to church and it wasn't something that interested him.

*****

Our first day in Haiti we visited the village we would be working in. We got to meet and play with the kids. They were so loving and joyful. The dirtiest, smelliest kids with the sweetest, most genuine affection. They were easy to adore.

Jared and I met outside our cabins before bed to talk and share a snack. Our very first night here and he says, "There's a lot of pretty girls here."

"What? Everything we saw today and that is what stood out to you?"

"Well, most church groups you think of unattractive, mousey girls, but there's pretty girls all over. Not just with our group. Even the cabin next to mine is full of pretty girls, you can see in the windows but can't see much."

The feeling of not being his everything stung deeply.

"If they were changing and you could see, you would turn you head, right?"

Hoping mine and Dr. White's point had given him some realizations.

"You don't still think it's okay to see other women naked?"

He stood firm in his belief. "I think women's bodies are a work of art. They are beautiful. I don't think that's wrong."

I began to cry. The reality I had been wrestling with was becoming undeniable.

In some of our downtime, we joined in a volleyball game. One of the ladies playing was an attractive, fit woman. Jared was somewhat flirtatious with her. What bothered me more were the thoughts I could hear him having. I had never experienced this before and felt I was reading too much into the situation and maybe somewhat insane from the heartache. Whatever it was, it made my heart hurt.

Our group loved Jared. He was very helpful and captivated the guys with his Black Hawk stories. He loved impressing people like that. I found myself searching for him every time I stepped out of my cabin, afraid he would be flirting with one of the many pretty young girls here. I despised that feeling.

Several days into our trip, on one of our village visiting days, we met a beautiful Haitian lady. A group of us were on a man's front porch praying and sharing about Jesus. She came up to us and handed over her newborn. She was stunning. I could hear the thoughts Jared was having as if they were mine. It was scary because I wasn't sure what was happening, but I knew they were his thoughts.

It was so painful to find myself trapped in the middle of his invasion of our intimacy again.

Please just stop! Why are his thoughts in my head? This is so insane. I can't even confront him about this. How do you ask someone to keep their thoughts to themselves when they don't know they haven't been? It was bad enough he was having them and not even attempting to stop but go deeper with them. If he could see how much this was breaking my heart, I wonder if he would even stop. I was beginning to feel that his sexual desires overpowered anything and everything in his life.

51

The cabins we stayed in had no air-conditioning. We each had tiny battery-powered fans we attached to our bunks to give some relief. It was hot and sticky, uncomfortable, but that was not what kept me up that night. It was here, in Haiti, on this mission trip, I had begged God to show himself to Jared; but he was speaking to me. He was showing me Jared's thoughts and had been. I just didn't realize it until now. I was coming to know him better than he knew himself. Meeting his thoughts, his reality. The way he was constructed his whole life: sex and performance centered. I began to mourn the person I thought he was.

One day in the village, during our playtime with the kids, I sat for a moment on the rock wall to rest. A young girl sat a small space over. She looked maybe fourteen. All our focus had been on playing and loving on the young kids. I wondered if she felt left out or tired of "the Americans" trying to come in and help. I had learned a few common phrases and attempted to communicate with her. Our translator over heard my sad attempts at French Creole and stepped into help. Her name was LoveMyca. She opened up about her life and how she enjoyed seeing us come to help. The next day on our work day painting houses, she came looking for me, and we visited more.

Something happened that day that was hilarious and disgusting. Some of us girls really had to go to the bathroom, and being in a remote village, there are no bathrooms. The mission group we were with had just completed a quad of houses and a latrine in the center. So we took turns using the latrine with the other girls standing side by side to act as a door. I decided to squat over the latrine, but as I did, my phone slipped out of my back pocket and bull's-eye to the bottom! It took me a moment to realize what had just happened.

"Was that your phone?" one of the girls asked.

With my mouth still open in shock, I shook my head yes. We erupted in all kinds of commotion trying to figure out what to do. Some young Haitian men standing close by came to see what was going on. Our entire group stopped painting to take a look at my phone sitting about fifteen feet at the bottom of the concrete latrine.

A moment of despair struck me as I realized all my memories from our trip were in the photos on my phone. The Haitian men didn't waste any time. They gathered buckets, wire, tape, a pile of supplies to attempt to rescue my phone. With the help of our translator, the guys all worked together to retrieve my phone. Thankfully, twenty minutes later and a little dusty, my phone was recovered. After a good cleaning, it was as good as before it hit bottom.

The next day, during our playtime with the kids, LoveMyca brought me a gift. She had knitted a cell phone purse for me in red, white, and blue. She asked me if I would come to her home and meet her mom. I asked our translator if that would be okay. He said we weren't supposed to, but he didn't think the leaders we were with would mind. He said in Haitian culture being invited to someone's home was a big honor. They lived in one of the homes our mission group had built. They had dirt floors, only one twin bed, but the family had smiles and open arms. They were so happy we took the time to visit. LoveMyca shared with us her hopes of becoming a nurse in the future. We learned a lot about their culture and struggles that day. Our translator helped us exchange information so we would be able to stay connected.

Until meeting LoveMyca, I was so wrapped up in my dilemma. I came to Haiti wanting to let the people know that they weren't forgotten and for Jared to see God. I didn't want anything back. God is such a giving Father. He knew I was seeking truth. He was opening my eyes to painful things I needed to know and showing me through the people of Haiti that he sees my heart, that my heart is loving and caring and can make a difference.

Saying goodbye was more painful than I expected. After our last playtime in the village, I hugged LoveMyca and her brothers, then loaded up on the bus. I looked out my window and waved goodbye. She walked beside the bus until we were going too fast for her to keep up. The tears rolled as if I was leaving behind a part of myself.

When we left for the airport a day later, the bus was quite full, so Jared and I had to sit in separate seats. He ended up with one of the young girls from our group. She must have said how all the painting had caused a crick in her neck for Jared to have started massaging her. Normally, it wouldn't have been a big deal, but his thoughts would not quit cycling through my head. With the only words between us being his thoughts in my head, my anger toward him soared.

Our flight was delayed, and we ended up with a longer than expected layover. We were all tired, some sick, missing a hot shower, and decent food. As if my irritation was not enough, Jared started massaging another one of the young girls. At this point, I was completely ticked and stormed off through the airport. Jared isn't the type to own up to doing anything wrong nor to apologize. I can't stand disagreement. I went to speak to him about how inappropriate he was being. He told me he was just being nice and I was overreacting. I told him it bothered me and that should be enough for him not to do that.

We did not speak again until we had landed, picked up our luggage, and were in the truck. I told him how much it hurt to see him massaging the girls and not once offering to massage me. I expressed how difficult it was trying to believe him about Ellie and Valerie and seeing this made it all the more difficult. He tossed the blame back to me, saying how nothing had happened between them and I needed to let it go. I was preventing us from moving forward.

I had missed being wrapped up in his arms for the last week and needed to feel him against me. Once we got to the camper, I apologized to him. I told him how exhausting it was but that I was working hard to let things go.

The deadline I had set for myself had approached and come to an end. The peace I desired continued to elude my reach. In its place was more disillusionment with my husband. Who I was and who I wanted to be stepped further back, being sucked into torment, swirling into darkness. My soul was desperate to be quenched with relief.

Again, I opened up to Dr. White. Throwing out my concern for how crazy I sounded, I told him how I could hear Jared's thoughts. It was outrageous and terrifying to experience, but I knew God was revealing truth to me. Thankfully, he was a man of strong faith. He could see the struggle in my eyes and, somewhere in the midst, my sanity. He could see the rope I clung to getting shorter, loosening my ability to hold it together.

He urged me to choose my direction. The conflict was worse than trudging water. It was causing me to drown. He requested the next session to be with the both of us. I told him I had to have direct clarity on Jared's beliefs and boundaries. I could see it, but I wanted to hear it from Jared instead of working from my assumptions.

We moved forward with our plan to flip houses, and I spent most days searching for a suitable one. We had nearly all of the money from my savings that we had put as a down payment on our house. My goal was to be able to buy and flip out of those funds instead of needing to borrow. One evening in the kitchen of our camper, I came across a withdrawal slip. Jared had taken over $30,000 from our savings. I fumed with anger and tears. He said he took that money to pay off our credit-card debt. Problem was, all the credit cards were in his name, and I had no idea what was on them. Jared made very good money and should not have any need for credit cards.

A family beach trip had already been planned for the end of July. I went forward with the trip, praying for my last hope of peace and for God to show himself to Jared as he had revealed to me that he would.

God showed up in a big way but, again, not in the way I requested, desired, or hoped. Jared's thoughts invaded my head space louder and more vivid than before. We fought the entire trip. He kept wanting to play volleyball with a group of young twenty somethings. Several times I asked him to go to the beach with the kids and me, but he declined, wanting to stay in the room and rest. Then I would find him mixed in with the young, attractive group playing volleyball.

52

I cried most of the way out of Florida. Somewhere in his heart, Jared had sympathy for me. He wanted to stop in Biloxi and have an evening out, just me and him. We took all the kids to dinner, then back to the room. Jared and I went to the casino for drinks and games, just like old times.

Only it was not old times for me. I saw Jared from a completely different perspective. I saw a man I loved so deeply but was unable to validate any trust or belief in him. My heart broke to hear the thoughts that ran wild in his head about other women. I despised having to realize that I could not declare his faithfulness to me. I had to look at him knowing that in the middle of making love to me that he had given himself to others. I was not able to be his muse or hold his heart in my grasp alone. The battle between my head and heart was coming down to its final victor.

My stubbornness argued with my insecurities. I had no solid, concrete proof of Jared's infidelity. What if I am wrong? What if all the destruction I had caused and endured was telling me I was not worthy of love, so I was sabotaging myself? One thing had become undeniably clear: I could spiral no further down this black hole.

In our marriage counseling session, I told Dr. White about Jared's participation with the volleyball games at the beach. With my insecurities, he agreed it was out of line. I demanded Jared to fully disclose what he thought was proper boundaries in a marriage. He said he would not go looking for it, but if a naked woman crossed his path, he would not turn from it. I left that session with more conviction that Jared was not the person I needed to be with.

I spent that week in deep prayer. I pleaded with God to release me somehow from this torment. Everything inside me was begging to get out of this marriage. The thought of living with a man I continually questioned was a death sentence. Chasing God with one foot and Jared with the other was literally tearing me apart.

"God, one way or another, give me absolute proof, either of Jared's faithfulness or of his infidelity."

We had made an appointment with a realtor to look at a house we were interested in flipping. Not knowing how to proceed with Jared, I went along with viewing the house. It was impossible not to get excited and swept into the possibilities. We shared ideas for changes and improvements. Jared was looking at deploying within the next nine months and wanted to make sure he had me set up with a place to live before he left.

A few days later we took the kids with us to see the house. They were all bubbling with excitement and wanted to help with the project. Jared wanted to make an offer.

I met his enthusiasm with hesitation. The man standing before me no longer resembled the man I had given myself to. Each attempt I made to move toward trusting him left me with more questions. I shared with him my fear of never being able to trust him and that I did not want to live like that. At first, he got mad.

"Our love should mean as much to you as it does me. If you love me enough, you will stop all this worrying and accusations and let us be happy."

"I've tried so hard, Jared. You have seen me struggle. You know I love you. Something inside my gut is preventing me from trusting you."

He turned on that smooth, soothing voice that he had used to mesmerize me countless times before. His arms wrapped me snugly, close to his chest so I could feel his heartbeat. The smell of his cologne made my head float back to a time when he knocked me off my feet and left me breathless, unable to get enough.

"Michelle, you are the only woman that has my heart. I have not been with anyone else, and I only want to be with you forever. Trust me and let us move forward with our dreams."

Instead of comfort, angst topped off above capacity level. It was a Saturday. Despite my concerns, he called our realtor to tell her we wanted to put in an offer. Luckily, her voicemail answered. With Jared working outside and the kids riding bikes and playing tennis, I went in to a still, quiet camper. I felt time was running out.

I lay in the floor and folded myself into a fetal position. I had come to the end of myself. With Jared incapable of saving me, I reached up in search of the touch that offered comfort and security. I made a final plea.

"God, help me. I can't do this any longer. Reveal to me once and for all proof that Jared has been faithful or proof that he has not."

I had been doing research on my phone for colleges for Ashlynn. My data was nearly used up, so I asked Jared if I could use his since he had unlimited. Feeling like the remnants of myself were nearing suffocation and no longer able to tolerate the anguish imposed by loving Jared, I searched his phone for answers to quench my misery. Numerous times before I had scanned his phone, flipping through texts, apps, and email. This day something compelled me to go to his Sent email.

As many words are in the English language, sometimes it is still impossible to connect them together to make sense. Unable to tell myself exactly what I found, I knew it was the piece I needed to link me to answers. Jared had sent himself an email from his personal account to his military account. It was from something called Pic Lock 3 Ultimate. It listed a master passcode and a decoy passcode. I snapped a picture of it so I could look it up. The knowing deep within me released a roar of disdain for what this would uncover.

When I think of myself, I have always thought of little, weak, insignificant. *Strength* has never been a choice word in describing myself. Weak, unable to bear heartache, choosing to soak it in alcohol instead. Too insignificant to stand up for my feelings and desires so I took the stripes of others. Little thought of myself so giving more to others. But maybe in the midst of all that did lie strength. The strength to subdue the desires of my flesh for the purpose of others. Not in a healthy way obviously. But the inner strength I had all along was emerging in a new way.

Once again I had to lay aside my desires. I wanted to rip my clothes, scream so loudly the earth shook, and run as far and fast as I could until land ran out beneath my feet. The hand that I had reached for several times, grazing but not grasping, was now firmly in my grip. The comfort and security fully radiating in me to make what I needed to do possible.

Setting aside the knowing flowing inside me and the curiosity roused by the email, I had kids to tend to. I attempted to adopt Jared's skills of weaving a facade. I went into mom mode. I cooked a dinner enjoyably for everyone, followed up with game night. Being an intensely emotional person, reigning the emotions in can be difficult. My heart was breaking down aware of betrayal on the other side of the steps I knew I had to take. The kids perceived my behavior was not typical, so I told them I had an upset stomach. Which was completely true, yet only a pinhead to the disgust rumbling through me.

When everyone was in bed and Jared sound asleep beside me, my focus went back to the email. The tears made it difficult to read the details of this app. I knew I had never seen it on his phone. As I read on, I discovered that even the app is hidden. The home screen is camouflaged as a black icon and not easy to find. I wrote down the details knowing I was too shaken to remember them.

53

For the last year and a half, Sundays had once again meant church for the kids and me. With the growing ache inside me, I told them I did not feel up to it today. They loved the church we had been going to. I am sure part of that was the change they had seen in me, but they understood me not feeling well.

Jared, Lucy, and I cooked breakfast for everyone, with Jared completely unaware that I had begun to pull the threads, unraveling truth. After getting all the kids fed and occupied in activity, I asked Jared for his phone again to continue my research. He looked at me in complete innocence not knowing I had pierced through his lies, seeing a glimpse of evidence with more beckoning me, silently waiting. He gently placed a kiss on my lips. For the first time ever, that is where it stayed. I didn't drink it in and relish its sweet tenderness. It didn't exist anymore.

I sat inside with the kids as I did my college research. When I was satisfied that they were focused on their activity, I slipped into the bunk room to shift my research. This was the moment my head and heart had been battling for, the final victor. I hoped with all parts of my flesh that the photos would be full of me, only me. All of Jared's proclamations of faithfulness confirmed, and I could finally lay to rest the clawing inside my gut.

I followed the instructions I had written down. Coordinating trembling hands and eyes that feared the truth was a daunting task. I gripped so tightly that hand that now offered my strength. The black icon was in the exact place they said it would be. As black as the hole I had been falling aimlessly into, the darkness that encapsulated me and prevented light from breaking in. This dark blackness that haunted me held the answers to my freedom. I keyed in the passcode.

There, right in front of me, before my mind could process what my eyes had captured, my stomach had already fallen to my toes. My dreams were slipping out the back door, and my heart was knocking punches into the panic button. It couldn't be stopped. Truth was seeping into my doubts. Reality was putting out the fire of my dreams. I was completely unaware of to what depths I would meet the answers I'd been searching for. This was one of those moments I didn't want to be right. I'd take being wrong to have my dreams back. Undo the skid marks on my barely beating heart, please!

There was a file of me, but there were also five others. Of all the times I had been overtaken with trembling, combined they were only a speck to the tremors that ran rampant through my system now. My emotions melted into tears, running wild with the tremors. The pieces of my heart so scattered they were unrecognizable to their former frame. A strength came from outside of myself and ordered my mind to operate in sensibility.

I grabbed my phone to take pictures of what I had found. Two of the files were his ex-wife's. Over sixty nude professional photos of Kelly, his first wife. The file of Ellie was a compilation of old and new photos, no nudes. As expected but not prepared to encounter was the file of Valerie. Photos so explicit vomit launched from my stomach into my throat. My mind barricaded my heart, not allowing it to soak in the magnitude of the discovery.

The other two files were names unfamiliar to me. Upon opening one of them, I recognized the young Black lady. I had met her at a cookout when Jared was chief over Range Control. He had taken photos of her in demeaning displays. He even had screenshots saved of his nasty, racially derogatory conversation to her. I guess he was proud of his dirty talk with her.

My heart was pumping triple time, and my lungs were screeching in search of oxygen. The trembling made it difficult for my limbs to move properly. I feared my entire system would disintegrate, unable to function due to the overload it was being given. Ashlynn must have heard my sobs or felt my shaking through the camper. She found me in fragments on the floor.

"Mom, what's going on?"

There was no way to pretend I was fine. "I just found out some information I wasn't expecting," I replied.

"Mom, you need to breathe."

I composed myself as best I could and told my kids we were leaving. We were to meet Everett later for them to go home.

Jared had been working outside on the tool trailer we had purchased to start flipping houses. He was surprised to see the kids and I leaving earlier than expected.

"We are going to stop for dinner," I explained.

Shock has effects on the physical body that are impossible to hide. My pale skin and glassy-eyed look caused him to ask if I was okay.

"Fine," was my only answer. No kiss or "I love you," which had been my standard farewell.

He stood puzzled as I drove away.

The kids and I stopped to eat dinner. The vomit lodged in my throat made it impossible for me to squeeze down a bite. Feeling the tears rising up, I ran to the bathroom to avoid my kids having to see me breakdown. I sent my sister and Jade a text message telling them what happened and asking for advice. I knew approaching Jared face-to-face would not be a good thing. Jade told me to stop by after dropping the kids.

I needed my best friend. I was incapable of making rational decisions. Jade and I sat on her front steps. I was still trying to process what I had found. Lies, deception, pain, shock, intense heartbreak, disbelief, confusion, anger—I was full of intense emotions cycling through me all at once. Jade asked me how much I had left of my savings. I said, "Forty-five thousand dollars." She told me I needed to go home to Jared, act like nothing happened, load up my things in the morning, and go straight to the bank to withdraw the money. My sister said I could stay with her. Jade told me not to confront him, knowing he would manipulate me.

So we had a plan for my physical being. I did not know how to manage what was detonating through every cell of my heart and mind. All the images were churning with Jared's words and expressions of love. How? So many nights he held me while I cried with frustrations at not believing him. He swore to me he had not been with anyone else. Worse than that, he blamed me thousands of times because I would not let it go.

Countless times he looked me in the eyes swearing to me I was the love of his life. He coated me with his warm, soothing words, words I had never heard from any man before. He wrapped me in his spell, declaring he would protect my heart and heal all the wounds that had left their marks. I never stumbled. I fell right in holding his gaze as my comfort. Falling never felt so exciting and effortless. He gave me such security. I gave him all my secrets, hurts, doubts. He twisted them into a beautiful picture where, although so broken, he made me his priceless masterpiece.

Having given him all of me, I had nothing left to hold me up.

"Jade. Focus on what Jade told you, Michelle. It is time for you to do the pretending."

I set my mind on the task at hand, but my heart was a wild card. It had not been able to cauterize the flood of tears pouring forth. What if Jared saw the bleeding from my chest? I stopped at the liquor store on base, the only place that sold on Sundays. If I numb myself, maybe I can play the part of a girl with an unbroken heart.

I chugged as much as I could, as fast as I could. It had been five hours since discovering the photos, the excruciating pain clawing me, relentless to give way. I parked, sitting, waiting for the alcohol to infuse through my every facet, begging it to hurry and release its stillness. Once I began to feel its release, I continued on to the camper.

Jared met me outside with a big smile, saying, "I have been so worried about you. You left earlier without much of a goodbye."

I smiled back, hugged him, then entered back into my black hole.

My things could not be packed quickly enough. Being in this camper felt like being in an alien world to me. It looked different. It felt different. In the photos of us, I now saw deception and sickness in his eyes. I saw myself standing beside him so fooled. I looked at her with sympathy, now seeing the man behind the facade. I wish I could yell to myself, "Run, you idiot! You are walking blindfolded into a trap!" She probably wouldn't hear me anyway. She was nursing her wounds with his adoration.

As much as possible was crammed into my Pathfinder. I went straight to the bank, nervous that Jared had found out my plan and beat me to it—that is usually what he did. Thankfully, the money was there. I drove to another bank and opened an account in my name, then went to work.

About lunchtime, I got a text from Jared asking where all my things were. I sent a message back, telling him to ask Valerie or Joriah. When he gave an idiot, not-knowing reply, I sent him a few of the pictures I had found to help his memory.

He replies, "Who are these girls, and why are you sending me these?"

I have no energy for this.

When I finish work, I have to swing by the camper to pick up Buttercup. My things are loaded, so I hope to be quick. Jared is at work, and I don't want to see him. It's not a house, it's a camper, but we had made it a home. Again, it felt so different now. I didn't mind giving up my 3,200 square-foot house and moving into this camper. Just as long as I could be wrapped in his love, anywhere would be home. As I stood there with memories flashing around me, the feeling of a fool swept over me. More than anything, hurt hung my heart low.

I sat at the table to write him a letter. My heart was bleeding, and I wanted him to know, although no words would be sufficient to the extremes of it. A few sentences in, and the door opens. No words even come to my mind. I simply look at him as I'm sitting there, coming undone. His eyes carry a look I have never seen and will never forget. A look of sorrow and shame, but it does nothing for explaining. Oddly, for a moment, I feel sorry for him. It's as if his eyes are saying, "I couldn't control it."

"I never wanted to hurt you." He bends down in front of me.

I scoot back. "No! Why?"

"Michelle, I love you more than I have ever loved anybody."
"Why?" I repeat.
Nothing.
"You even have pictures of Kelly. I'm assuming when you went to visit Kent you screwed her."
"No, she just wanted me to have them."
I can't even deal with his thinking. I get up and leave.

On the way to my sister's, I stop at the liquor store. I can't be me anymore. My chest hurts. My stomach hurts. I can't stop the breaking of me. I want out. I want to die. The pain keeps getting worse. The horrible photos won't stop appearing. I can't go anywhere to get away from it all. I douse myself heavily with vodka, the only way I know to ease the insanity.

54

The next day I barely found the strength to shower. Jared keeps sending me messages telling me my drinking is to blame for our breakup. It stuns me that he continues to deny the reason for my leaving. I text my life-group girls—Christy, Rhonda, Jackie, and Barbara—to tell them what has happened and ask for prayers.

The rest of the week I work my few hours a day, barely able to function. I can see people around me, and I see my body move, but my mind is lost in a swirling world of madness. Pieces of my 2.5 years of knowing Jared tumble a lifetime torment. I am unable to hold any food down. "How could he look at me while he was stabbing my heart?" I force the alcohol down in objection to the plaguing thoughts.

That Friday evening Rhonda calls me. I had been in bed most of the day. She had just seen the movie *War Room* and pleads with me to forgive Jared. Whoa! I'm really taken back on that one.

"Rhonda, he has done nothing but deceive, manipulate, and cheat. I'm broken. I can't forgive that."

"Michelle, unforgiveness will hold you back. God can't release his goodness in you if you hold that in your heart."

I love and admire Rhonda so much. I know she has my best interest at heart.

"Pour it all out to Jesus," she implores.

All week I had floated through every minute like a zombie. I had not prayed once. Not really wanting to but understanding the need, I slipped out of bed and glided to the floor. Without effort and with no words, my heart sank into God's hands. The tears ran with no holding back, and he caught every one. He read each beat of my heart and gently guided me to his presence. In an intensely intimate yet delicate manner, he held me close. A feeling so raw and real it will never leave my heart.

The Holy Spirit spoke words to my being as I lay crumpled in the floor.

"This is not who I created you to be. I have an amazing purpose for you to fulfill."

This isn't who I want to be either. That very moment in the floor of the bedroom, I became his. Only his. There was not a single speck of myself that I did not want to give him.

All to Jesus, I surrender. All.

My prayer turned into thankfulness.

"Dear Father God, thank you for ending my misery. Thank you for reaching down and guiding me to truth. God, it hurts in a way I'm afraid will haunt me forever. Please ease this pain. Rock my heart in the arms of your love. Help me to forgive. I'm so angry. So, so angry. I don't know how to forgive this. I need you to show me. My heart loves Jared. Help me to unlove him. I know when I cry you're there. It must hurt seeing me so hurt. I know it had to be hard for you to reveal these truths to me, but it was the only way. And, dear God, I'm so thankful. Thank you for releasing yourself within me. I'm all yours."

I had experienced the truth about Jared on a deeper level than anyone ever desires to go. His thoughts cycled through my head, shattering my own. The vision remained a fresh imprint that I wished would stop visiting me. The photos were date-and-time stamped and infiltrated memories of us with their explicit deceit. I knew for certain God had shown me who Jared really was. I was uncertain how to breathe while mourning the loss of my future with him and the intimacy I thought was so rich and pure.

I believe now more than ever before that God works in reverse. He has gone ahead and taken each step we will ever take. Knowing our steps, he walks back through and places people, situations, and gifts in the exact places he knows we will be needing them. It's our choice to see and accept them.

Going to church that Sunday was a struggle. I walked in and straight to the back where I knew I would find Rhonda. She grabbed me, and I collapsed into her. She held me as the brokenness flowed out. I was so weak she sat me down and left to get Christy and several other women to pray over me. These were not light prayers but deep, heavy-hearted prayers as these women had been with me through the struggle. God had gifted me with some amazing godly women that would help direct me in his way and give me hope.

I placed myself in prayer. I didn't know how to forgive, but I wanted to. Not only did I need to forgive Jared but also Everett. When you have been wronged and your fate has taken a sharp curve you didn't see coming and didn't want to take, anger fiercely moves in. I had been hovering there with Everett and did not want to sink further with Jared. This was my chance to unblemish my life and set things right. Having the photos stuck in my memory made this an enormous task. I was also now faced with the decision of turning him in. I was terrified to do anything out of vengeance. My intent was to undo myself, not tack on more bad choices.

The two young girls in the files I found were Jared's subordinates, two were ex-wives, the other I did not know. In the military, infidelity and fraternization are heavily punishable. Knowing Jared misused his power and authority shocked me. More than anything, when my eyes scanned the photos, I saw him turning his back on our intimacy and tainting it with a sick sexual obsession. I felt him pushing blame on me while he held me as I cried tears of shame and hatred for myself in not being able to move past things I thought had happened but to trust him that they hadn't. He held me down while standing up on my misery, arrogantly proclaiming his self-righteousness.

My heart was so burdened with deep agony it was impossible for me to carry. The more I handed it over to God, reaching outside of myself, the more he leaned closer. I told him I was too overwhelmed with heartache to face Jared with clarity.

"I love him, God, and I want to help him. But I am too broken to even carry myself. I surrender Jared to you. Please move in his heart to give him healing and the desire to do the right thing. I unchain myself from him and ask your will in all areas of my life."

In the midst of my undoing, God spoke life to me again. He revealed that this struggle will be a testimony. He gave me a vision of writing a book and speaking. Neither of which fall into my capabilities. I was in no form to argue or doubt God. He had shown me in enormous ways his power and ability.

"I don't understand how any of this is possible, but I do know you make all things possible."

*****

Dr. White could tell in a quick glance that something had happened since our last visit. I explained to him my finding the explicit files hidden on Jared phone. I told him I believed God was revealing to me a sick sexual addiction of Jared's.

"I'm so, so sorry, Michelle. The last few sessions I saw red flags but didn't expect this. He had me convinced he was telling the truth. I can't diagnose him. But I can say, with what I have seen, I think you are on the right track. I have done this over fifty years, and Jared is one of the best manipulators I have ever seen."

He warned me Jared would stop at nothing to continue to control and manipulate me.

"Block his number, any access to your social media, change all your passwords. He will infiltrate every connection to you that he has."

It was difficult for me to see the man I loved in this light, but not one single thing about him surprised me anymore.

Every waking moment I was not obligated, I spent in prayer and reading the Bible or spiritual motivational books. God had freed me, was calling, and I wanted to answer. My heart was so tangled in Jared's lies, manipulation, and deceit the knots were grueling to unravel. He sent one text after another asking me to see him and saying how much he missed me. I replied that I was so hurt I couldn't see him, that he had no idea how the photos were plaguing my mind. When he replied with, "What are you talking about?" I fumed with anger. Forty-five minutes later, he says, "I love you, miss you, wish you were here. Sorry you're upset." His games were exhausting.

A week and a half after finding the photos and leaving, Jared sends me a message implying he has filed for divorce.

"I'm sorry, I hope you can find the happiness I couldn't give you. I cried all the way back from the courthouse. I told all my friends how much I love you, but the drinking just wouldn't stop. I will love you forever."

My heart lurched in pain as my head swam in disbelief.

Thankfully, that was life-group night. I looked forward to the love and sanity it offered in my world of craziness. We were in the middle of our series "Free Indeed," another blessing God had deposited on his journey through my steps. It is a series about breaking free from bondages and exposing the enemy. Christy had us close our eyes and ask God what he wanted to reveal about us. He gave me the word *empowering*. He revealed that he is creating and molding me to empower others through my struggle.

After life group, Barbara, Jackie, Rhonda, and Christy gathered around me, laid their loving hands on me, and prayed. I could feel the power. Jackie asked us to pray for her daughter and unborn grandson's health due to some complications. She anointed each of us and herself with oil and prayed a prayer of healing. She prayed with strong conviction and faith. I had never been a part of something so powerful. Jackie has a gift of faith and uses it fully. It amazes me. I left feeling empowered and strong.

The next day after work, I decided to get more of my things from the camper. It was early afternoon, so I didn't have to worry about Jared being there.

As I am gathering my things, he comes in.

"Hey! What are you doing?" he says like nothing is wrong. "Give me a hug!"

"No, Jared, I want to know why."

"I just want a hug, then I will tell you why."

"I'm not hugging you. I just want to know why."

"Michelle, you're never satisfied with my explanations," he says.

"Let me hear what ya got. Why?"

Then the lies roll.

"Those aren't my pictures."

"Jared, they were taken in your camper."

"It wasn't me. I let a buddy use my camper. He would bring girls here."

"Oh really, Jared? Then why are the photos on your phone?"

"He sent them to me to hold for him to give back to him later. I forgot they were even there."

"Jared, that is the biggest lie I've ever heard. One of the photos shows part of you in it."

He continues to argue with me that it's not him and to look closer. I'm so furious at his level of denial that I just storm out, leaving my things.

Jared had said he was going to his mom's, so the next day I make another attempt to get my things. He comes in again! I'm shaking with frustration. I'm in the bedroom gathering my things. He asks me to sit on the bed and talk to him. Thinking I may finally get some answers, I sit.

"Michelle, I filed for divorce because your drinking wouldn't stop. I love you, and I want to be with you, but I can't handle the drinking."

I look at him in absolute shock.

"Jared, I left because I found files of you having sex with other women. This has nothing to do with me drinking!"

He looks me in the eyes—that deep, soul-penetrating look—and turns on his trance-inducing voice.

"Michelle, you're the woman of my dreams. I would never do anything to hurt you. A buddy of mine asked to use my camper. I didn't see a reason not to let him."

The trance swirls my head with confusion. I try to rationalize all my findings over the last week and a half. I try to make sense of it all so I can continue loving him. The deep knowing inside presses in on me. I'm so in love with him, but I can no longer love him.

I snap back to reality and plead with him. "Jared, this is me. I opened my world to you. Please give me the truth. Can you not see how much your denial is killing me more and more?"

I am stunned at the continued lies. I had thought somewhere deep inside that he really did love me. I was wrong about so many things. I was wrong to hope he'd release me from his continual torment.

With crying eyes and a bleeding heart, I go to leave. He follows me out.

"I can't imagine my life without you. If you would just stop drinking, we could be together."

I can't even process. My mouth is unable to find any words sufficient for the moment. My eyes look at him with a crushed desperate look of betrayal. As I go to climb into my vehicle, he grabs me and hugs me. As we pull apart, somehow we end up kissing. The intense fever started burning me again, but all the good had been scorched, only leaving ashes of pain.

*****

It was Labor Day weekend, time for our annual family reunion. It was this time last year I had found Jared with Valerie at the camper. I was so stupid to ignore all the signs and stay with him. Had I chosen to be with Jared but not seek God, he would have remained there, waiting. But because I sought him with desperation, he continued to speak to me and reveal truth. I continued to seek him in desperation for healing, strength, and wisdom to put one foot in front of the other as I walked away from Jared.

Jared was clearly not going to make that easy for me.

"I keep thinking about our accidental kiss. I need more of your touch."

I should've blocked his number like Dr. White advised. My wounded heart soaked up his words. At least, I meant something to him, and that felt good.

My heart throbbed in pain with each automatic beat. Good thing the body is designed to be self-sufficient with certain abilities. If it weren't, my breath would have ended long ago. My heart too cluttered of pain to remember to breathe. Family is comfort for me. Although I didn't feel like visiting, I wanted to go to the reunion. The familiar laughs and voices were like a warm blanket. Several times my mind drifted to the previous reunions Jared attended with me, and that deep pain would overcome me. Then the love of my family would surround me and ease my thoughts.

My cousins have always been a close group. I tell them how I feel God is leading me to turn him in, but I'm so afraid. One of them says it is my responsibility; another says there is always more under the surface. They are all in agreement.

One cousin asks me, "Could you live with yourself if you don't? No matter what you decide, we are all here for you."

"Can I live with myself if I don't?" Honestly, I am just trying to figure out how to live. I have a job, a few hours a week, which is nowhere near enough. I have no place to live. I want to be closer to my kids. Do I leave my support network? How do I protect myself from Jared? He knows my weaknesses. He knows how I function. I'm struggling to simply open my eyes in the morning because that means I'm still alive. And that means with every breath I draw, there is strength enough for the memories and pain to circulate. They flow on automatic with the beating of my heart. My biggest need is to separate myself from the debilitating pain in order to function.

55

Ashlynn had asked me to go to her church on Sunday. It's a small country church, and I'm ashamed to say I had low expectations. God must have sent the preacher a memo because I felt like he was preaching to me. His sermon was about how God has gone before you and has prepared the path you will take. He will give you strength and supply your needs. You have to have complete faith. You must surrender all; God wants to carry you through. He has a purpose he wants you to fulfill.

I had been ignoring Jared's text. This particular night he text, "Since you refuse to talk to me, I need your sister's address." I knew it was so he could have me served with divorce papers. Twenty minutes later, he texts, "Miss you!"

So many things plague my mind. I'm actually playing out a "trial" in my head of Jared being court-martialed. I'm struggling about how everything will go down. I stop myself. God has gone before me. I'm so tired of being stepped on, not standing up for myself. This time, although I'm scared, I have faith.

"God, this is in your hands. I surrender to your way. You are lifting me up. Your ways are higher and stronger than any weapon Jared can form against me."

*****

Labor Day, the girls and I go to a get-together at my cousin's. We spend the day talking, eating, and swimming. Memories follow me everywhere. I have a slight break down as I think about Jared and me being here on the Fourth of July. That is also followed up with images of him and Valerie date stamped on the same day.

That evening we go see the movie *War Room*. It is so nice to see God's power and promises rolled out in a two-hour time frame. This family is in the middle of a spiritual battle. They stay in faith and choose the weapon of prayer. As outsiders, we get to see their story in different phases and perspectives. If we could look at the end of our lives, like watching a movie backward, it would be so much easier to push through the bumps. That is where faith is so important, to know that God has been all the way through, even to the credits.

Jared called me four times that day. Seeing his name displayed on my phone makes my heart jump. Then all sensibility steps in and reminds me that my heart is no longer safe with him. I cycle through the roller coaster that leaves my heart dismantled in the end. I force myself to focus on the goodness of God that promises safety and healing. Healing. That sounds so unreachable right now. My night ends with messages from Jared begging me back.

In preparations for the divorce papers I know Jared has coming, I have an appointment with a lawyer about filing a counterclaim and my next steps. The retainer fee alone will be $2,500! I also have a counseling appointment. Dr. White warns me that Jared would never be in agreement with a counterclaim because he has to maintain control. He thinks it will be a long, drawn-out court battle. He also advises me to be tested for diseases. My mind hadn't even gone there! He warned me that Jared would step up his game in trying to get me back.

About 6:00 p.m. that evening, an officer served me with papers. I knew it was coming, but to go through the process completely ticked me off. The officer said Jared had been hounding him and was a total jerk. I'm sure it was because he couldn't wait to beat me to it and relish in his control. Reading the papers took my anger to new levels. He wrote the papers himself and as if we were in agreement with the terms. He cited as reason for divorce to be that wife made life intolerable for husband. That bit into me like a ton sack of tacks.

I blazed with anger! What kind of man files for divorce against his wife after she finds photos of him having sex with other women?

An egotistical, arrogant one! I wanted to pull up my big-girl panties, march right on to Post, and unload the photos to his superior officer. I'm thrown into anger and fear. Jared always has the upper hand. The army would never believe me.

Deep moaning ripped from my chest as, again, I stood over the dry, empty canyon of myself. I had been traversing the space for so long, but the other side had not inched any closer. The fog started to lift and dissipate from among the horizon. My screeches of pain echoed back to me, but they were not carrying loneliness with them anymore. The crevices that displayed bareness began to trickle small signs of life. The shadow I had been standing in began to dim as the light softened its darkness. The rumbling earthquake quieted as I clasped the hand that had grazed me so many times, waiting for me to reach back.

I had displaced my control into the wrong hands, giving the task of my comfort, peace, and happiness to a source incapable of offering the supply my soul craved. The canyon remained deep and wide, but my feet were no longer split, walking separate directions. They had chosen the path, placing one foot in front of the other. The horizon became clearer and closer as I changed my focus. My hunger for God's word was insatiable as his peace began to fill me. That hand that now holds me gives me calmness and the sensibility not to make rushed decision that are typical for me.

When all this hit, I wanted to run off to Italy to pull close to my grandma. I miss her so much. I would love to be able to talk to her about all this and hear her thick Italian advice. I decided on a mini-trip instead to my sister's in DC. Oddly, my cousin from Italy will be there too, like a small piece of Grandma.

My niece is five and a half months now, and I haven't met her yet. This trip will be a much-needed lift for my heart. I'm focusing on learning all I can about forgiveness. I read the entire flight looking for how to achieve what seems so impossible. Flying through the clouds, I toss out the window prayers to heaven.

"God, please help me to forgive Jared and give me guidance in proceeding with the divorce. Please take away this pain. Sometimes it's so heavy my chest feels crushed."

Sleepless nights followed me to DC. It has been three weeks now, and everything remains freshly pressed in my mind. I wake up countless times with the images taunting me, reminding me how much of a fool I had been. The prick of his deception stings more as I continually search for reasoning. Not understanding makes the pain pierce deeper. His adamant denial twists the knife lodged in my heart. The nightmares chase me into my canyon. It had once been a dry, treacherous, gaping hole but has now become my safe place, my area of seclusion where God now holds my hand as I journey to the other side with more clarity.

In the early morning hours, I read as I wait for everyone to get up. Forgiveness is such a mystery to me. It must be achievable, or God would not have ordered it. My biggest hold is the idea that forgiveness means acceptance of the behavior. I feel if I hold on to my anger, my disapproval of the behavior will be clear. If I let it go, it's like what happened was not wrong and wounding. It's even more difficult to forgive when that person is continuing to be hurtful. My desire to unblemish my life presses forward in my learning.

My niece and nephew do my heart so much good. We enjoy a day at the park, and I always love time with my sister. Time together means so much to me. Nico, my cousin, and I have plans to meet my friend Alexis for dinner. She moved here almost a year ago with her fiancé.

I haven't seen Nico in many years. When I was about nine, my family took a trip with Grandma to Italy. That was the happiest I had ever seen her. Nico has visited the US several times since. We Metro into the city to meet Alexis and Zac. Nico and I get into a deep conversation about love and loss. We are both in the process of trying to get our hearts to move on. Hearing his Italian accent gives me comfort that a piece of my grandma will always be in my heart.

It's so exciting to see Alexis happy. She asks me where Jared is, so I fill her in.

"Wow!" she says with surprise. "I really thought he was a good guy and so crazy about you. Michelle, you need to realize he did you some good. This isn't the same Michelle I saw two years ago."

I ponder on that one. No one is aware of the insane roller coaster. Inadvertently, he may have done me some good. He caused me to come to the end of myself.

Dinner was good with great conversation. I hug my friend and wish her well, not knowing when I'll see her again. Nico and I walk down the street to a little bar. We sit and talk while he sips on a drink. He invites me to come stay with him in Italy. Oh, how I'd love the escape, to run away from the chaos! But I know the pain would find me there too. The only way to escape it is to face it.

Nico and I Metro back and meet my sister and her friends at a wine bar. They are all tipsy and talkative, sharing about their families and husbands. They all have husbands that are present and involved with their children. I think that will be an ache that will never leave my heart.

I was able to sleep in some the next morning, and it felt so nice. How is it my heart can hurt as soon as I wake up? I'm so thankful to be surrounded with family. Leah and I enjoy some alone time out to lunch. A little while after we get back, I breakdown. I go to Leah's room, cry, kneel, and pray. So much is weighing on me. I need discernment. I have decisions to make, but I'm so afraid of making the wrong ones.

That night Nico and I sit outside and talk. He is very insightful and doing some soul searching himself. He says he can see the pain in my eyes and prays I receive relief.

My last day in DC, Leah, Nico, and I go into downtown for lunch and take a walk down to the White House. The air is nice and refreshing. I always love downtown DC, no matter how many times I go. The history and beauty fascinate me.

The questions cycling through my mind have been nonstop but thankfully distracted. Now on the plane home, I'm alone with them again.

"Did he ever really love me? How could he hurt me like that knowing how fragile I was? How could he promise I was the only one as he was being unfaithful?"

Instead of ordering a drink, I pray, "Dear God, please make it stop hurting. Help me to control my thoughts."

I find myself wanting a message from him, to know he misses me too.

The nightmares haunt me all the way to my heart and prick me awake. I lie in bed alone and curled into a ball as I realize I can't wake up from my reality. The visions chase me into daylight. I force myself to remember the discoveries about my husband. The dreams of a life with him disintegrate as I wash myself with truth. The mourning begins fresh as the revelations sink in. The love I tried to give him returns to me in a tattered package. It bears the stamp of rejection. It covers the warning label marked "Fragile" as though it were invisible. The wounds so heavy my attempt to get out of bed knocks me to the floor. The debilitating pain pours out at Jesus's feet, flowing like a river.

"I don't understand. How could he be so heartless, to have done all these things? Take me, God. Unbreak my heart."

My prayer continues as I try to put my mascara on, followed by dabbing it off my cheek as it is streaked from tears. My sister asks if I am okay. I explain to her that it is just one of those days. It's impossible to adequately describe the deep, throbbing pain. I feel God is there with me. I know he sees and understands the hurt and knowing that gives me comfort.

Work was short with multiple periods of breakdown. Jared is in Fort Rucker for training, so I go to Post for my workout. I go by the camper because I miss being there. I miss being on Post. I miss the life I lived with him here. I want to see if there are any signs of him missing me. Beside the bed, he has one of our wedding photos and a small bottle of Crown. Good. Maybe he is a little tormented too.

Last week it was laid on my heart to tell Rhonda and Jackie the full truth including my struggle with alcohol. Christy and Barbara already knew, and it was not my intention to mislead or hide anything from any of them, especially when I had been asking for prayer and guidance. I asked Rhonda if I could meet with her and hoped to be able to talk with Jackie soon. Rhonda said yes and asked if Jackie could meet with us too since she was in town. It was a God-given opportunity.

Part of me was nervous to reveal the complete truth about myself. I could run no longer. I had come to the end and met with my undoing. The shame that had held me back was loosening its grip. With the glare of truth, I knew these two were godly women, valuable in my spiritual battle.

They met my honesty with love and support. I felt another layer of rejection peel away from my overburdened load. I shared about my deliverance, God reaching down and telling me who he created me to be. Jackie mentioned Celebrate Recovery, which was one of my first spirit-led revelations. We clasped hands, and they prayed over me. The loneliness I had felt began to vanish, being wrapped in encouragement.

Seeing the *War Room* inspired me to get serious with my prayer life. I bought the book *Battle Plan for Prayer*. Top of my list is Jared—to have the proper way to deal with the divorce, to be able to forgive him, and for the healing of my heart. The book is very specific; and I follow it exactly, keeping a notebook, very detailed.

My prayer life has an exact plan. As far as a job and living situation, there is none. I'm afraid to make the wrong decision about anything. I excel in that area. I found a PRN position at a home-health agency I applied for to supplement until I figure things out. In the middle of taking an exam required to apply, Jared sends me a message.

He says something about picking up my jet skis.

I simply reply, "Okay."

Then he asks if we can get together and talk, he doesn't like what we are doing.

"I don't either," I reply. "But I know beyond a shadow of a doubt what you were doing. Please explain how and why so maybe I can find some healing."

He doesn't stray from his lies. He accuses me of being obsessive and dramatic. If he could see the torture in my eyes, would it stir his heart even a pinch? I'm too weak to see him but strong enough to hold to the truth. He ends the conversation, luring my weakness.

"I just want to hold you, feel you, smell you…forever."

The blur of my tears prevent a reply.

When my tears ease up, I read some verses on forgiveness. I pray, asking for something to prick his heart. It's so painfully clear that Jared is not who I need him to be and I must walk away. I ask God to prick his heart to reveal truth to me. The level of torture his continued denial is causing is pain on another level. Having photos of his infidelity is excruciating. His continued lies make me feel like I never meant anything to him. If he ever felt a twinge of love for me, he would release me from the sadistic manipulation binding me to chaotic insanity and allow me to come to terms and find healing.

Luckily, I don't have work today, so I'm able to make it to Brock's tennis match and Josie's volleyball game. It's a huge dose of goodness for my heart. Ashlynn and Josie come with me to Mom and Dad's to stay the night. I sit down with the girls and tell them what is going on with Jared and me, not details, but that I left him. I tell them how much of a relief it is to be out from under that burden and how much God is speaking life into me.

The sea of insanity billows my mind into an early morning. Waves of love, hate, lies, and dreams crash together leaving me a castaway secluded to a heart so full of pain rescue is a fleeting thought. A distant hope to be discovered, then disappearing, as reality appears on the horizon. My body automatically folds into the floor. I pour my heart out to Jesus, asking him to take me from this world and end my misery. But then he reminds me that he needs me here and that I'm not alone.

I fix the girls breakfast and send them off to school. I have work, then life group tonight. Jared doesn't leave my mind for a second. I had not replied to his text last night, not wanting to start the back and forth again. I am working hard on forgiveness, so to be encouraging, I send him a message telling him so, that it will come layer by layer, but I'm releasing the process to God. He replies that I'm condemning him to a life without me.

My afternoon is spent reading about forgiveness and praying. I don't know if I'll ever get to the other side of this, but my heart has developed an intense gratitude for the saving grace I've received. Nothing has marked its intensity, so I press forward, wanting more.

The hunger growing inside gives glimpses of hope to my parched soul.

Christy's and my life-group girls are another drink of water to my heart. We continue the "Free Indeed" series. It's about how the devil searches the earth looking for weak ones, scouts them out like a wolf. He preys on them; watches their habits, weaknesses; and, when they're at their weakest, attacks harder and doesn't let up. He keeps going until they are devoured.

After life group, I sit in my room at my sister's reflecting on how deceitful Satan is. A message from Jared interrupts my thoughts. He says how much he loves me and misses everything about me. He doesn't like having to file for divorce, but he did because of my drinking. He really doesn't want a life without me.

"Are you crazy?" I reply. "I left because I found photos of you having sex with other women!"

He completely ignores the issue and sends me Bible verses about love and marriage. My brain enters into a real of disbelief. I have never in my life seen such insanity! I'm fuming with anger, and somehow my heart takes on more pain. I am so wound up and exhausted. I put my phone out of reach, lay down in bed, and read scripture to calm myself into sleep.

*****

The next morning my phone has a flood of texts from Jared claiming it's not him in the photos, that I need to look closer. The one photo of him with clothes on is clearly him in his favorite underwear. I know, I bought them. When I mention that, there is no reply. Defeat swarms my mind. I have no job, no retirement plan, no home. My chest is hurting, feeling like the many times I have had pneumonia. What is going to happen to me? I feel like a cloud of doom hovers over me. I pray for God to reveal his plan to me. The pain weighs so heavily on my heart, not lifting. *God, I trust you.*

I call Natalie from church, telling her I want to do Freedom Prayer. This time I'm ready. She sends me paperwork and tells me it will take several months. I know it's a step I need to take. In the meantime, I'm holding on to God's promises. I've seen his promises in the Bible and in my friend's lives. I picture myself walking in darkness, scared, but I'm holding his right hand, and I smile with comfort.

Kent calls, but I don't answer. Anything connected to Jared hurts. He leaves me a voicemail asking if we can have dinner. I feel so bad just up and leaving him. I also remember Dr. White's warnings that Jared would use any resource available to get to me, and I feel cautioned.

Jared never replied to my message about the photo of him in his underwear. I should declare victory at his inability to argue back, but I don't. I plunder deeper into insignificance. I don't matter enough for a response. I matter even less against the truth. My heart is begging for scraps to disprove my findings, not wanting to release the intimacy it looked so long to encounter. Sleep eludes me as much as the truth. I dip into each of them in small doses, but pain brings me back. The saying is that the truth shall set you free, and it surely does. It never says it's easy or painless.

At 3:45 a.m., the cycling chaos pulls me out of bed. My bleeding heart is not worth a reply? I wonder who he is holding. How did he candy coat the explanation that he lives alone in a camper? I'm sure it was a well-executed sob story how he tried his best to save me, but it wasn't enough. He just wishes a woman would hold his love as significant as he holds hers. I have scenarios scattered throughout my mind. They each start and end with his lies and deception.

"My heart is broken, and you don't even care?" I message at a decent hour.

"I'm hurting too," he replies. "I feel like I'm wasting my time explaining. I disprove one thing, and you move on to the next."

"I'm ready to sit down and talk. I need answers."

He says he thinks that would be good. "Just be productive and not angry." Then he sends a bunch of sweet messages. His words are a combination of everything I ever wanted layered under my biggest fear of infidelity.

Dr. White has told me many times that Jared would not admit the truth to me. I feel that if I can get him to look me deep in the eyes and see the lost girl he found once upon a time that he would save her again. Save her with truth. I had to make an attempt. I knew beyond a shadow of all knowing the truth. I desperately needed his release from the agony of his lies.

I declare the intent of my final attempt. Jared may or may not allow me the truth. Whichever way it goes, I have to pick myself up and move forward. If he admits it, it will be a weight of insanity lifted from my shoulders as I feel I've been banging my head against a brick wall.

I hope to find understanding and move into forgiveness easier. If he doesn't admit it, it will be another twist to the knife already wedged in my heart. It will reveal the level of his cold half-heartedness and deepen the realization that I'm not enough. No matter what, the truth stands in God's revelations to me.

The kids and I spend the weekend at my parents' house. It's so nice to have supportive, loving parents. We grill out, watch movies, and have a nonstop laugh session. Saturday, Josie and I are working on a puzzle, and Ashlynn is watching *Grease*. The song "Hopelessly Devoted to You" hits me unexpectedly, and I walk to the bathroom to hide my tears. They erupt from deep inside with no end to the brokenness. Ashlynn knocks on the door to check on me. She finds me crying and wraps me in a hug. She tells me she's proud of me for leaning into God and doing things the right way. Josie comes in and hugs me too. I hate for them to see me like this, but some things are impossible to hide.

Sunday, Jared texts me about us getting together to talk.

"Are you wanting to talk to work things out, or are your intentions to badger me so you can get closure?"

Does he really think I would come back to him? I carefully answer him, not wanting to push aside the possibility of getting the truth, but also not wanting to lie.

"I need you to be completely honest with me in order to move forward. There are things you can't deny that need to be answered."

Then he asks if I will be able to move forward, put all this behind me, and work on us. My reply is that it all depends on him. If I start getting lie after lie, I'll walk out the door. I didn't add that my intentions are to be able to move forward without him. I didn't add that I was begging God to reverse time, remove his infidelity, enter Jared's heart, and let me return to the dream that had been demolished. We decide to meet Tuesday night. He asked me to come to the camper for privacy.

Monday was fairly uneventful. I decided I would attempt to record mine and Jared's conservation. My hope was to get his confession, and if I did, I wanted to be able to replay it to myself. I wanted to be able to confirm that I haven't been insane this whole time and knowing Jared the way I know Jared, he would later deny his confession. For fear of his future manipulation, I needed to be able to access the truth at the pressing of Play, to hear his own words and to not be given into his games.

Tuesday wakes me with my nervousness. This is the day I plead for truth and an ending to a portion of my pain, to be able to slip out of insanity's grip. I drop to the floor to enter into a gut-wrenching prayer to God. First, I thank him for revealing the photos to me so I could have concrete evidence. I thank him for the desire to turn to him this time. I ask for a hedge of protection; for God to soften Jared's heart and mind to give me the truth; for God to rise up his army behind me; for the Holy Spirit to give me the words, strength and composure.

I have an afternoon appointment with Dr. White. I am so jittery and completely sick to my stomach with the upcoming evening blazing through my every thought. I tell Dr. White about my struggle to understand and forgive Jared. He explains that I may never understand and forgiveness will take time. Then I tell him about the plans for us to meet this evening. The movement of his eyebrows and wide opening of his eyes speak his thoughts before his words do.

"Oh, Michelle, I strongly advise against this. I'm afraid you may not be strong enough yet. I would hate to see Jared manipulate you back into his arms. I'm afraid you will not get the truth you are hoping for. Why do you feel the need to talk to him? Is he going to be any less convicted? People have been charged with murder by evidence, still denying it was them."

I explained that I needed to do this for me. I want and need to know how he could and why. His final warning gave me great pause.

"Be very, very careful. Jared is a master, one of the best manipulators I have ever seen, and I have done this over fifty years."

Back at my sister's, I attempt to prepare myself. The recorder does not come with a manual on how to tape a private conversation. When I go to test the recorder, a bright, red light comes on. Ugh! I look for a black Sharpie to cover it with but am not able to find one. An ink pen does nothing. I find a pink piece of construction paper, fold it up, and tape it over the bright red light. Perfect! You can't see the light at all. I decide to wear a black bandeau so it can hold the recorder and prevent it from slipping down.

In the middle of my preparations to secretly record our conversation, Jared text and asks when I will be there. I told him it would be about an hour. Then he asks if I would want to eat dinner with him. So maybe he is living in an alternate universe where this isn't one of the most difficult moments of life waiting in front of him. Truth is, he apparently does live in an alternate universe to think all the things he has done are okay. Bad thing is I have been stuck hovering between normal and this insane world.

I've not been able to eat all day. My head has been spinning since my eyes opened, and when I did make it from lying down to actually standing up, my body would not hold still from complete dizziness. I tell him I don't want to have dinner. I'm coming to have a serious conversation and that is all.

Besides a black bandeau, what does one wear as appropriate attire to hopefully extract and tape a confession from one's husband? I pause for a moment to question myself. "Am I crazy?" The clear, concise answer is "Yes." I grab a loose T-shirt and some jean shorts to appear as normal as my abnormal self can right now. The most important thing to put on is my armor of God. I can't attempt this evening without it.

I also pray, "Dear Father God, please give me the strength to overcome the temptation of my physical desires. Give me strength to guard my emotions and keep my focus on the task before me. Please, please, please give me the confession I am looking for so I can unchain myself from the insanity. Circle me with an army of angels to protect me. Fill me with the Holy Spirit to give me the proper words, wisdom, and discernment. In Jesus's name, Amen."

I'm as prepared as I possibly can be. My body is awkward in functioning because of my trembling. I have only shaken this badly one other time. Oddly, it was a year ago this very month, a week shy from the very day, I made the same drive I'm about to make this very moment to Post. My intent was to find truth then. My intent is the exact same tonight. God boldly revealed truth to me when I pulled up to find Valerie locked in Jared's camper. I have felt a fool the entire year having believed Jared over God's revelation. In my continual seeking of God, he gently pulled me closer to the truth yet again, revealing the photos to me, giving me truth that had kept my stomach in knots with my knowing but not having evidence. Evidence in hand was not enough to shatter Jared's lies.

Here I stand at his mercy, asking for him to look upon me with grace. I confess that I put Jared above him and am so ashamed. I desire to return fully to him. Placing nobody and nothing above him.

I make the seemingly long drive to Post as the trip a year ago circulates through the pain of photos, lies, memories, and fears. I can't allow Jared to overcome my knowing. I hold so tightly to the rescue God gave me. The feelings of being wanted and cherished by God are so profound Jared stands dimly in its shadows. "I can do this." I feel strength being released inside me, and I know where its release is coming from. It's not of me, thank goodness.

I hold his hand stronger than ever before. My humanness continues to release its trembling in my body, but nothing can shake my foundation. This time when I pull up to the camper, his truck is the only vehicle there. I sit for a moment, tuck the recorder in my bandeau, then go to the door. I pause as I realize I no longer live here and knocking would be appropriate.

"Come in," I hear from inside.

As I step in, I'm unexpectedly overcome with the feeling of missing home. That's what this place had become to me. A place of safety and comfort. But then I see Jared, and the feeling of safety and comfort is quickly replaced with pain and fear. My eyes dampen. I don't want to do this, but I must in order to move forward.

He steps toward me and gives me a hug.

"We can sit on the bed and talk," he suggests.

"No," I say firmly. "The table is fine."

"That seems a little formal," he remarks.

"Yes, it's appropriate," I state.

He has the speakers set to one of our favorite stations. I tell him I need to go to the bathroom before we start. I fiddle with the recorder not knowing if any of this will actually work. I control my finger as steady as possible and press Record. I place the recorder in the center of my chest so the speaker is facing outward and will hopefully pick up our conversation. I make my bandeau as secure as possible, put my shirt back in place, remind myself to breathe and focus boldly on seeking the full truth.

As I begin to step down into the kitchen area, Jared zips over and catches me on the step. He stops me face-to-face. "I like you on that step," he says.

No, no, no. Please don't. I already can't catch my breath. Please don't try to give me the touch my body has ached for the past month.

I've cried myself to sleep with the sharp pains of desire clawing at me. My trembling system is clouding every function that typically comes natural. I'm having to concentrate on how to breathe and how to put one foot in front of the other. My words shake from out of my voice box.

"Please let me sit down." My eyes cling to the tears, not wanting him to see my emotions, only a millisecond from complete meltdown.

He has had extensive military training in hiding true emotion and focusing on the mission at hand. I have had none. My emotions rule my every heartbeat. My eyes, my breath, my touch bear my caring despite my desire to not be revealed. Clasping God's hand is my only source of strength to accomplish his will in this situation. I tuck myself inside of him, the safest place I've ever known.

We sit at the table—Jared on one side, me on the other. I have no script or plan for this conversation. Only the prayer that God leads and controls. My greatest desire is the confession so I can validate with my ears what my heart and mind already know. No one can fully understand the power of manipulation unless you're in the middle of its grip. Everything of reason defines that you are being manipulated, but it has some mystical twist to your intelligence.

My trembling is a combination of nerves and anger at being insulted of my intelligence. I want to get right to the truth. I want his mouth to say the words defined in the photos and repeatedly denied with his lies. He has thought this ahead a little more than I had. He wants to sugarcoat the happenings defined in the photos by explaining how in love with me he was and how hurt he was by my continued drinking, like that gives validation to him having sex with other women. I want to spew. I want to punch and kick and hurt him. I told him not to marry me. I told him I was an absolute, unworthy mess. He softly undid my untrusting heart so devastatingly so that he owned it for a time. He deserved none of my patience, but my heart is so true to its character that I gave it to him anyway, biting my tongue to let him have his moment.

His seemingly well-prepared speech described how hopelessly in love with me he was. I was the woman he had countless dreams about but never expected to find. He became aware of my drinking issue, but he saw beyond that. He saw my heart. Although it bore scars and deep veins of misuse, it beat with a true rhythm of love and compassion that is more rare than the purest of diamonds. It sparkled beyond his ability to resist. He loved to acquire anything that offered to be a challenge. Not that he cared to have it but to prove his ability to conquer no matter what it took.

His speech was nipping my patience bit by bit. I didn't care to hear about his love story, although I'm a hopeless romantic. It was all a fake story of deception anyway. Surprisingly, my eyes did not get stuck as many times as I had rolled them. I could feel the moment of truth edging closer. My blood stopped flowing, my breath already scarce, halted entirely. Time froze. Air stopped moving. Birds seized in their tracks. Every movement of time and space stopped beating, giving him his long-awaited moment.

After defining how deeply I had hurt him with my drinking, he finally said it.

"That's when I fooled around."

My lungs should have gasped for air, but they remained incompetent. That, that was his voice. His words sat on my ears. Although it took him seconds to speak, the words were barely able to enter into my knowing. I mean, I knew, but now I *knew*. His voice was saying the truth. His voice melts the truth. I hadn't been sure he was capable of such, although no less than condemned by proof.

I was unsure how to process. I was blank. He told me to breathe. I gasped for oxygen as if my lungs had never had any. I was too heartbroken to cry. I had hoped to enter some other universe where his faithfulness to me would be not just the words out of his mouth but actual, real-to-life gut knowing, and I could love him again. Love him in a way that would not leave me shattered and destroyed. I had known all along that was impossible, but I've always lived on the edge of fantasy. I could no longer reside there.

The truth had entered the universe, and it couldn't be reversed. He continued to mumble reasons for his unfaithfulness. They were words blurred in the farthest reaches of my mind. I was in my own space. He was there, but he was not. Slowly, I felt my pulse starting to vibrate. My lungs each sucked in a deep breath to help restore their starving. For the first time ever, I felt actual brain waves stirring to life. Tears finally escaped the impenetrable dam as for the first time in two years I was deemed not insane.

Two years he forced me to believe I always assumed the worst instead of believing in him. Two years he made me suffer, believing I was such a failure. Many nights I lay awake trying to figure out what was so wrong with me that I had such wounded trust abilities. I cried to my counselor wanting to be "normal." I did intense therapy, dissecting my thought patterns and trying to retrain myself to trust. I had known clearly by the photos of his infidelity. What broke my heart more intensely than it had ever endured before was the two-year deception that I was so abnormal and incompetent to be worthy of trusting someone that loved me so intensely.

As if all that was not enough, his next statement brought more numbness to my already altered state.

"Do you see why I had to lie to you? If I had told you the truth back then, we never would've gotten back together."

"Jared, look where I am now. You watched me suffer day and night with not being able to believe in you because of this feeling in my gut. You saw me trying to work so hard with Dr. White on trying to believe you. You even lied to him and said I just wouldn't let it go. He put me on medication because of my anxiety due to my failure. You left me outside banging on the camper door while you were locked in here with Valerie for over an hour. I have had to live with torment believing everything was my fault. How many times did you tell me I just needed to believe you and get over it?"

"Thousands! I didn't want to lose you."

"But you were okay with watching me suffer? Not just suffer but live in torment? Complete and absolute torment!"

"I just kept thinking you would get over it."

An explosion of the deepest, fiercest pain collided with an anger I must have laid claim to through my Italian ancestors. The culmination of all his deceits, lies, manipulations, and selfishness manifested into my reality. My words were barely understandable as I questioned how he could look in my eyes daily, seeing my pain of struggling to move forward. So many times as I made love to him I told him to promise me I was the only one.

"Jared, when you found me, I was already so broken by Everett. You knew my fragile state. I repeatedly asked you to leave me alone. Why? Why, knowing my past, did you pursue me? I told you I was a mess. My best friend, Jade, and even my mom warned you." In the most broken, tear-filled language, I asked again, "How could you?" I knew it was my voice, but I had never heard something so heartbroken, that it even made me gasp for air.

Deserving of so much more, the only answer I got was, "I don't know. I just wanted you to be mine."

I had expected that if he loved me as intensely as I loved him. "I don't know" was just not acceptable. I had to have more.

"How did things with Valerie start?"

"I saw her on camp from time to time, then we started texting. She said she was attracted to me and liked me better than Rex."

"So you just flat out asked her to come to the camper so you could have sex with her?"

"It just started happening."

"You know, Jared, I don't have one of the best memories, but some things are ingrained in my mind. These photos you uploaded are date-and-time stamped. The dates you were entering explicit, pornographic photos of you having sex with Valerie were also some of the same dates you spent with me. For example, Fourth of July, 7:30 a.m. you are uploading sex with Valerie. Then, noon, you come to a family gathering at my cousin's. You were there as my husband, separated, but obviously trying to put us back together. Many of the dates you were having sex with Valerie, you would come and stay the night with me. That is extremely sick." My anger was skyrocketing! "Now toward the end of July, you start entering files of a young Black girl. Now who is she?"

"Just a girl," he says.

"Oh! Just a girl? How did you meet this girl?"

I already knew who she was, but I was curious to see if he had caught on yet that I was much more intelligent that he had given me credit.

"I met her playing volleyball."

"Oh, volleyball? That is interesting. If my memory serves me correctly, and I know it does, I remember meeting this girl before when you were chief over at Range Control. She was under your command and attended a cookout we had. Sometimes I'm very surprised at the details I remember. I also remember her having a very large muscled-up boyfriend."

"Your memory surprises me too."

"So how in the world did you weasel her into coming to your camper to have sex with you?"

"I don't know, and I don't see how any of these details are productive for us."

A blood-wrenching response from the deepest depths hurled forward without any pause.

"You don't know how this has destroyed me! I fought to keep myself from giving you all of me, but I failed enormously! I trusted you with more of myself than I trusted me with, so you have all of me. I've relied on you as my source for every movement, even every breath. I've put you as my source above everything, even God. How dare you suggest that I understand that it would be reasonable for you to do this!"

My blood was pulsing so profusely that I couldn't sit still. I jumped up, paced, stomped my feet as hard as I could. So much anger was lurching from every atom in every space of my body. Then something that surprised even my own ears came from my very mouth.

"I could understand you trying to get over me and turning to someone else. I did that too, but after a few months of talking to these other men, I realized how wrong it was, and I stopped. Then we decided to get back together. But you continued your sick activities and then got involved with the young Black lady even after we got back together. And Ellie again!"

"When you and I decided to get back together, I stopped. The date-and-time stamps are all wrong. When we said it was us again, I hadn't done anything."

"Oh, for the love of everything under the sun! How stupid do you really think I am? I'm totally sick of you consistently insulting my intelligence."

"Michelle, I mean it. When we decided it was us again, I stopped everything. The day you caught Valerie here at the camper, she was here because I had told her you and I were back together."

"Jared, I caught her here in September. We got back together in June. And why would you have her come to your camper instead of meeting in a public place? Nothing you say makes sense."

"She was having a hard time letting things go. She called, and I was at the camper on my lunch break, so it made sense for her to come over."

"So it also made sense to keep me locked out over an hour while you are lying to me that you are not even there?"

"I knew you wouldn't believe me."

"I don't think I have ever told you the story of that day. I may have, but it's worth repeating because it was so incredible. I had been struggling for a year with believing that you and Ellie were not involved sexually. She showed me the texts you sent her telling her you still loved her and wanted her back. That was so painful, but I felt I pushed you back to her. I bore the responsibility of that with great defeat. I felt in my gut that you had a sexual relationship with her. You knew this because I questioned it nearly daily. You were so good to look me in the eyes, hold me, and swear you never had sex with her.

"While we had been separated, I started attending church and life group. Jesus became a person to me, not a religion. It was something more powerful than I had ever experienced in my entire existence. Shamefully, I put you above him, but I still sought him. I sought after him in ways I never had before. I had felt him touch my spirit, and I knew I wanted more, but there was also you, and I didn't know how to merge the two. It was agony looking for a way to have you both.

"Anyway, the disturbance of your untruthfulness grew in my gut. It became so painful. I prayed, actually begged, for a way out. This is going to sound completely insane to you, but I really don't care. Lunchtime, I was getting in my car to go to another facility when this booming thought sounded in my mind, *Jared is at the camper sleeping with someone.* It caused me to freeze because it was such a foreign thought. It did not belong to me. I was so puzzled, I couldn't move. Then, as if it was not still echoing in my head, it said it again, *Jared is at the camper sleeping with someone.* I knew. I just knew it was God."

"My attempted phone call to you went straight to voicemail. The drive to camp was a nightmare. I knew I would find you here with someone. I knew it was God telling me so I could be relieved of a marriage that was wrong for me. God was answering my prayer. He saw my pain and constant misery. He wanted to give me relief. I can imagine him looking down from heaven all those nights I cried. I bet he came down, laid beside me, and gently brushed my tears to the side. Nights when my kids were heartbroken, I did the same without them knowing. I cried because I knew they were hurting. I used to stroke their hair gently, just soft enough to touch them but not wake them. I knew God was there doing the same. So knowing the pain he was about to have me witness, I bet it was heartbreaking for him. Having to reveal the truth to me in a blatant manor, his daughter, knowing she was about to crumble, but knowing her future and that it was best."

The heaviness of emotions was more than I could survive. I felt myself coming all the way undone. Those feelings coursed through my veins with a prickling force I was no match against. I had screamed at the top of my lungs for relief that never approached me. Words weighed down with heart break lodged in my throat as this moment I had been waiting for was finally before me. Choking down the words and shoving back the tears, I had to press forward in the strength gifted by God.

"Did you know I cried my entire drive to camp that day?" my broken, trembling words continued. "I knew I would find you here with someone. I hoped to be wrong, but I knew I wouldn't be. When I turned the corner and saw your truck in front of the camper and a car behind the camper, the person I tried to believe you were changed in a half second.

"It's astounding how quickly the brain can process. The you I wanted that hid the truth stepped aside, actually disappeared. I saw clearly the real you. No facade. Before the pounding on the door and all chaos broke loose, I sat for only a moment. A moment was all it took for every dream I had envisioned for us to disappear with the vapor of you. God had been preparing me for that. Unfortunately, the big, loving heart he gifted me with was going to be an entirely different project."

I had to rehash the events of him leaving me locked out and banging on the door for over an hour.

"The magnitude of the lies that day, Jared, that is not normal. Do you not understand how extreme your lying was that day? I was standing there with you inside, hearing you talk, but you were telling me you were somewhere else. That is extreme deception. People don't do that. Why did you take such sick pictures of these women, Jared?"

"I was trying to do everything I could to get over you, Michelle."

"No, you weren't! You spent more nights of the week at the house with me than at your camper. I felt like your rotating door, Jared. It was always whenever you wanted me."

"Michelle, I messed up a lot. I'm sorry, I wish I could turn back time and stand by you like I promised I would. Truth is, you're the most amazing woman I've ever met, and maybe it took all of that for me to realize it. I don't want to lose you. We can still have all those dreams we talked about. I can't lose you. I don't want to lose you."

"Jared, I don't either, but I have to. I don't trust one single word that comes out of your mouth. Not one. I love you so much, like in love with you, but you are incapable of being truthful or faithful. God has shown me who you are, and I have to walk away."

He got in the floor on his hands and knees where I was sitting at the table. He laid his head in my lap and sobbed.

"Please don't give up on me. I gave you chance after chance with your drinking."

"Seriously, Jared? You knew I had drinking issues before you married me! I had no clue you had screwing-other-women issues!"

"Michelle, I'll do anything you want. We can go to counseling again. I'll go to church."

"Jared, I tried my hardest to get you involved in church. You always made fun of it or had some critical remark about the people or sermon. You made me cry over it several times because it spoke to my heart with such meaning then you would ruin it. Counseling? You couldn't pay me to go to counseling with you. You lied the entire time we went and made marriage counseling turn into 'Michelle' counseling.

"As far as chances, I gave you more than I said I would ever give any man. My birthday, only five and a half months after our wedding, I discovered your inappropriate relationship with Ellie, but I listened to you—stupidly! I gave you another chance. Then about nine months later, I catch you at the camper with Valerie. Doors locked, blinds closed, phone off, banging on the door over an hour, extreme lies trying to get me to believe you're not there. Now a month ago, I find sick photos of you with five women, two of them your ex-wives, on a hidden app on your phone. You have spent the entire month lying to me that they are not even your photos. Someone asked you to keep them for them. Oh, how nice of you! Like why would anyone have collections of photos of your ex-wives? Ugh! The whole thing makes me want to scream! It's completely impossible for me to trust anything about you!"

"Michelle, I will really do anything. You can put one of those trackers on my phone so you'll always know where I'm at."

"Jared, I don't want to live that way. It wouldn't work anyways. You would be at work screwing some girl on your desk. You will find a way around anything. That is one thing I believe about you 100 percent. You love to be sneaky, and the biggest thrill is getting what you want in the sneakiest, almost-getting-caught manner. I think you have a sick sexual addiction and need help."

"Michelle, I think you're right. But my addiction is you. I can't live without you. Please don't leave me. When I'm with you, I'm the man I want to be."

At this point, I was bawling. I had to leave him. There was no way around it. There was no fix. My heart was head over heels in love with him. I was more in love with him than any other man I have ever loved. God had clearly revealed to me that I could not have him. He had shown me who he truly was. I had to walk away.

"I need to go," I quickly said. I needed to go before my sensibility left me.

"Please don't!" he begged.

I jumped up and hurried to the door. I grabbed the handle turned my head to the left and looked into the bedroom. I'm not sure how long I paused. I contemplated lying on the bed, Jared coming to hold me and make love to me like many, many times before. My heart, my neglected body—they desired him with fires that were redder than red. They were that orange hot of fires that have been long burning. I was in the danger zone. I flung open the door and ran. All the while he is yelling, "Please don't leave me!"

I had been trembling all day, and by the time I made it to my vehicle, it was even worse. I survived. I heard some of the most painful things I didn't want to hear but needed to.

"Thank you, God!" I started the car and began to drive off. I stopped at the end of the road, removed the recorder from my chest. The red light was on. I assumed that meant it recorded everything. How well? I was too shaky to test it out. I pressed Stop and laid the little recorder in the cup holder.

An immense pressure eased itself from my overloaded brain and emotions. He confessed. I wasn't crazy. He added more lies to the pile and insulted my intelligence even more. On my drive back to my sister's, he texted me, "Please come back to me."

He really is insane. People make mistakes, I get that. I'm the queen of mess ups; but when people realize their mistakes and change, really work and try, that is commendable and should be encouraged. He did none of that. It was lie added to lie and covered up with more lies, coated with deception. He was a master of epic manipulation and the Lord of all things to his personal pleasure. After being a victim to his continual blame, his enforced shame at my inability to forgive and move on, his front- row seat to my misery as he egged it on once again left me in shock. Was he really warped enough to believe that I could possibly accept his behavior and move forward? Nothing shocked me where he was concerned. Absolutely nothing.

My nerves finally began to calm some, and my head started to clear. The rest of my drive I thanked God profusely.

"Thank you, Lord, for the strength to not give into my flesh, the strength to stand firm, the confession, and the ability to pull off recording it."

When I got to my sister's, I checked the recording. All ninety minutes of it was there. I had become a woman of caution, so I decided to make a copy of the recording. I downloaded an app on my phone and played the recording to copy to the app. I closed the bedroom door to allow it to copy.

I sat in the living room to read some of my devotional books. I was blown away with God's provision yet again. After about thirty minutes of reading, the doorbell rang. I had no doubt who it was. Jared stood there with a long face and a lost look.

"Can I have just a few minutes of your time, please? I have a request."

I couldn't imagine what now. I told him he could come in for a few minutes and I would listen. We sat on the couch. Several times he reached for me, then apologized and said it was just so automatic.

"What is so important that you had to drive here after we just spent a few hours taking?"

"I have an idea," he started. "I want to withdraw my complaint for divorce. I want you to really consider staying married to me. I know I did so many things wrong. I want a chance to do things right this time."

Is this guy for real? If he could see the thoughts tripping over themselves in my mind, he would run. He has not listened to one word I said the entire two hours we just spent speaking. It's totally, completely impossible for me to ever trust him!

I've been trying to figure out how to respond to his divorce complaint. Number one, it completely ticked me off that I discovered his infidelity but he ran to file against me. Number two, he lists him as the plaintiff, me as the defendant. Number three, he listed that my indignities made his life miserable therefore giving him a reason for divorce. I had spoken to three lawyers for advice on filing a counterclaim. I didn't like the terms he wrote up in the settlement. Him withdrawing the divorce would give me time to figure out how to properly go forward with the divorce. I wouldn't, however, lie to him.

"Jared, as I have repeatedly told you, it's impossible for me to trust you. I tried this entire last year and wasn't able to do it. I can't. You have cheated and lied our entire marriage. I deserve so much better than that. I will not stay married to you."

"I could have and should have tried harder. I lied and put everything on you, but now the truth is all out, so we can actually be honest and open and work on us."

"Jared, just last week you were trying to get to believe that the photos were a buddy of yours and you let him use the camper to screw women."

"But I told you the truth tonight. Now we can start fresh. I love you so much. Please don't leave me!"

I could faintly hear the recorded conservation playing in the bedroom. I was hoping he wasn't paying attention. Maybe he thought it was the TV or radio.

"Jared, I caught you in several lies tonight, and the only reason you confessed to them is because I had you backed into a corner with proof. I truly believe that you are incapable of telling the truth. I don't trust you at all. Even with you in my eyesight, I don't trust you. I don't trust or believe anything about you. You filed for divorce. Do what you want with it. I'm telling you right now, I will not stay married to you."

"Just a chance. All I'm asking for is a chance."

"This is my sister's house, and I'm sure she wouldn't approve of you being here. It's time for you to leave."

About five minutes after he left, he texts me to ask if he could bring me something to eat. Oh my goodness! The guy really doesn't get it! I simply replied, "No, thanks. Good night."

I really expected his confession and me declaring I wouldn't stay married to him would put an end to his madness. *I did end his denial*, I thought. Another kind of crazy opened. He declared his deep love for me and said he was going to fight for us. The realm of insanity opened wide, sucking me in again against my will.

Jared sent me messages.

"Remember the power of patience and forgiveness," followed by five Bible verses.

I didn't reply.

The next morning he sends me loads of pictures of us, declarations of love and more Bible verses. He also asks if he could see me. The man has gone from one extreme: lies, deception, and denial to the opposite extreme of Bible verses and not giving up on us. He is the oddest person on planet Earth. Sadly, he is dragging me in with him.

About lunchtime, I finish working in Nashville and figure I'll go by the camper, catch him screwing some chick, and he can finally stop all his "devoted to us being back together" crap. I drove onto camp, and his truck is parked at the camper. There is no other vehicle there. I assume he picked her up on his way. I park several roads over where I won't be seen, but I'll definitely not miss him leaving or who he is leaving with. I sit and wait for twenty-five minutes. His lunches are typically thirty minutes, so he has to be leaving soon. Out of the corner of my eye, I see a car pull right up beside me.

Unbelievable! It is Jared and Kent. I'm so irritated. Instead of me catching him, he has caught me.

"What are you doing?" he asks.

"Just thinking."

Okay, so I left out the details of me attempting to play detective.

"Kent just had a root canal. He would really love it if his Mommachelle would come tuck him in."

I am such a sucker. I already felt terrible for leaving Kent. Several days before, we made dinner plans for that night. He had asked many times, and I had finally given in. I had no idea he had a root canal scheduled and asked if he needed to reschedule dinner. He said he would rest the afternoon and would be ready to eat come dinner time. I tucked him in, hugged him, and said I would see him this evening.

Jared follows me out of the camper. He starts in again with the lies about the files being dated wrong, blah, blah, blah. I'm really so sick of hearing his crap. I shut my eyes and expel all the air from my lungs in frustration. Unexpectedly, he grabs me, holds me tight, and kisses me deeply. It's been an entire month that I've been physically starved from him. My brain is dead set on what needs to be done and is finished, complete, and past done with him. My heart, my lips, my body—they have not received the full memo from my brain. My head swirls with that euphoric feeling it's been craving.

I lean in, press even harder into him, and kiss him with passion that is uncontrollable. When my brain is finally able to snap me out of the trance and deliver the message to get the heck out of there, I pull back.

"I've got to leave!" I tell him.

He gives me that look, the look with the sly grin. He knows I still want him, he knows the part of me that does anyway. Danger is written all over his face, especially deeply into his eyes. I know it's best for me to completely avoid him. He saw a piece of my heart when he looked into my eyes. He knows he still owns a part of me.

After what happened with Jared earlier, I'm nervous about keeping my dinner date with Kent. I'm afraid Jared will show up. I know he saw the weakness in my eyes earlier. I know it's his character to take advantage of weakness. Luckily, Kent is there waiting for me—alone. All of me relaxes. The threat of Jared has been dismantled. Kent is so talkative. He says how much he misses me. He says nothing has been the same since I left. He says all Dad does is lie in bed.

"Michelle, can you please come back?"

"Kent, did your dad tell you why I left?"

"Yeah, he said you found some pictures of other women on his phone and thinks he was cheating."

"It's quite a bit more than that. He confessed that he was. That is all you need to know. That's why I can't come back."

He said he has a football game on Friday and asked if I would come watch him. I told him that I would love to watch him play, but it's best that I not come. Seeing his dad is not a good idea for me.

A text message from Jared pops up.

"Hey, why don't you order a margarita and then Kent can drive you here, and you can have drinks with me?" (Devil-face emoji.)

I told him he knew that was not a good idea and that after dinner, I'm going home. Then he tells me that he dropped Kent off and Kent needs a ride to the camper. I was totally pissed!

"Why did you drop Kent off? He has a car. I thought he drove here?"

"I needed to do some work on his car, so I dropped him off."

I was furious!

"Jared, you know me coming to the camper is not a good idea. I'll meet you at the gate with Kent, but I'm not coming onto camp!"

While I'm sitting at the gate waiting for Jared to come get Kent, he calls me.

"I need you to bring Kent to the camper. I've been drinking, and if I get caught driving on camp, I'll be in big trouble."

He really does think I'm a complete idiot! He has had this planned out the entire time! Having no choice, I drive Kent to the camper. Jared is standing outside waiting for me. He comes over to my door. I rolled my window down, trying to avoid getting out.

"Will you please come sit with me at the campfire?"

That one little sentence, and I'm suckered. His kiss from earlier in the day was still smoldering on my lips. I wanted more, but I knew better. I made attempts to keep myself safe, but they failed miserably. His schemes were thought out more than mine. As soon as I set my foot on the gravel, he scooped me into his arms. I made no attempt to resist him.

The last look I gave him earlier in the day, he saw way too much. My eyes are literally the reflection of my heart and soul. He saw himself when he looked at me. He knew that even though he had broken my heart and crushed my spirit, that I was still his. He had broken my heart into more than a million pieces, it would be impossible to number them, but he knew with only a partial glance that his name was written on each and every piece. He owned me.

The thrill of knowing how deeply he deceived me and that he could still own me added to his game. It enticed him deeper. Could he ever own all of me again? My mind was aware of his sick, tawdry sexual addiction. My spirit had been reclaimed by God. He had never faced a greater challenge than what I had just become to him. As much as he had wanted me before was in no comparison for his desire for me now.

As he kissed me, he felt no resistance. I leaned in, pressed against him and radiated the fire of my desire directly into him. I was taking him into myself, drawing in the touch and passion I needed, until once again, my mind caught my emotions and simmered them down.

"I have to leave," I said with sudden desperation.

As I got settled into bed, Jared texted me.

"I don't want any more nights without you. Good night, my love. Holding you felt wonderful."

With the thrill of his new challenge, he could barely sleep.

56

Friday morning I awoke to several message, photos, and love proclamations from Jared. He said after I left last night that Kent thoroughly chewed him out.

"'She is the third mom to have left me. You better fix this and never hurt her again.' You are very loved and very missed. Please don't let me have ruined this. We can have a wonderful life. I will never hurt you again. Can I pick you up tonight, and you can go to Kent's game with me?"

"Jared, I love you. I think you have a strange sexual addiction and need help. I'm sorry, but this is something I just can't take."

"I will go see Dr. White. I'll do whatever he recommends. The only thing I feel addicted to is you."

"I just can't," is my short, direct reply.

I received a message from the company I had applied for PRN work. They said, because of my DWIs, they would not hire me, even though it had been two and a half years ago. That, combined with Kent's comment last night, "You're the third mom to leave me," I was feeling so emotionally defeated. I went to my sister's and climbed into bed. I tossed around the idea of going to Kent's game. It broke my heart for me to miss it, but I knew it was best for me to avoid Jared at all cost.

As painfully and deeply as he had broken me, holding him, kissing him, feeling his body next to mine last night was opening something inside me. It felt like a slow release of a poison that burned and soothed at the same time. It was burning my spirit and caution was firing up inside of me. The soothing of my desire was intense. It was a slow release of a soothing feeling, but it was driven with intense passion. Its attempt was subtle. Being a person of strong physical needs, I could feel the power hidden behind the subtlety. It was that danger that I was always drawn to. It was seeking me out again. I was completely unaware of the new challenge I had become to Jared. All I knew was something new was brewing inside of me again.

My heart was breaking, feeling like I was abandoning Kent. I knew the Holy Spirit and Dr. White's warnings about Jared. My sister had come home, so I took my balling self into her room and plopped down on her bed to talk. I told her how terrible I felt about Kent. She reminded me about Dr. White's warning.

"You're dealing with a master, Michelle. He will use any means to get to you, even his own son."

I knew she was right. I decided it was best to skip the game and just sit home, being a ball bag, not having any clear direction to my life.

At five thirty, the doorbell rang. Crystal hopped up from the bed to go answer it. She returned a few minutes later and said, "It's for you. It's Jared. He's insisting on seeing you."

I'm sure I'm looking completely wretched, but what does that matter? I open the door, and there Jared stands with his confident smile, roses, and the football-mom shirt I had ordered.

"Please go to Kent's game with me. You know how much it would mean to him." He knows exactly how to get to me.

"Jared, you know it's best for me to stay away from you. I would love to see Kent play, but I really can't go."

"You know I want you there with me badly, but I understand your hesitation. Please go for Kent. It would really mean so much to him." He holds the purple football shirt up to me. "Purple is definitely your color. Please?"

"For Kent," I told myself. The poison was rumbling through my veins, thirsty for another touch. Another kiss. To be held, anything to be quenched. The spirit was whispering its warnings.

"It's okay," I responded. "I know I don't need to get back with him, and I'm not going to. It's just a harmless football game."

On our way to the game, Jared says he's hungry and wants to stop for a bite. We stop at one of our favorite fast-food places. As we are walking in, he grabs my hand.

"This just feels right," he says.

It does feel good, I think. I've missed my hand being held.

Once we get to the game, Jared runs around to my door. As I'm stepping out of the truck, he grabs me, pulls me close, and kisses me deeply. It's as if he's sucking the poison up through me, and my head begins to swirl. I'm spinning, and all I want is more of him. He holds my hand as we walk.

"Did you see the picture I sent you? The one with half a heart on each other's hand, and when they are clasped together, it makes the heart complete? I want us to get those."

We find a seat at the top of the stands. Kent sees us, smiles big, and waves.

Jared rubs my back. "I'm so happy you're here." Sitting watching the game, he keeps rubbing my shoulders and back, squeezing me, kissing me, telling me how beautiful I am. "I miss you so much. I don't want to do anything without you." He gets teary-eyed. "I'm so happy you're sitting here beside me."

"I can't stop thinking, did you rub their backs too? Take them to dinner?" I ask.

"It wasn't like that. It was just sex. Just an act. It was nowhere near like what we have. Please stop thinking like that."

"You can't expect it not to be on my mind. It may have just been an act to you. But to me, it is consistent images, literal images that scroll through my mind on play at all times. There is no Pause or Delete button to them. The pain of violated intimacy is a pain that I see no end to."

I try to remind myself that I'm here for Kent. It frustrates me so deeply that Jared thinks he can rub my back and, like a genie, poof! all the memories and hurts disappear. I wish! At the end of the second quarter, Kent gets hurt. He's unable to play the rest of the game, so we decide to leave.

On the drive home, I bring up our money situation that Jared had drawn up when he filed for divorce. His proposal was to finish paying off all credit-card debt and I would get whatever was left. Possibly $5,000 to $10,000. I told him I was getting screwed. Before we married, I had $87,000 in savings, and he had between $30,000 to $40,000 in credit-card debt. I was in complete disagreement with his proposal. He said none of that matters anyways. He is going to withdraw his complaint for divorce. I told him I still stand firm on my decision to divorce him.

He turned, gave me his sly smile, and wink. He grabbed my hand. "We are meant to be together, and I'm not giving up. I'm not going to let you go."

I remained unaware that I had become a pawn in his game. A game that had become a deep- rooted obsession to him. The poison that the challenge released through him was different than the poison that burned and soothed in me. His poison was toxic. Not just to the ones he inflicted it upon, but also to himself. His poison was so toxic he would stop at nothing to feel its powerful burn. He craved the burn it released. The bigger the challenge, the sneakier the deception, and overpowering the most resistance released the level of toxicity that gave him the most intensified burn. Nothing manufactured could offer this level of high. No heroin. No cocaine. All he needed was himself and the skills he had spent his lifetime perfecting.

57

Saturday morning I have a load of messages from Jared.

"I slept well last night although I stayed awake thinking about you a lot."

My sister and I decide to go hiking. It's a gorgeous day, one to take advantage of. After several hours of hiking, when I get back to the car, Jared has a long message.

"I know you don't know what to do, but I know we both love each other and love spending time together. Go with me to Hot Springs. We can go to that German restaurant we both love, hangout at our favorite clubs, and stay at the Arlington. I'll have you back for church. I could even go with you. I really want to spend time with you. I love you with all my heart and feel lost when you're not with me."

He definitely knows how to tempt me. I love traveling, even short weekend getaways. My favorite German restaurant, we haven't been there in months. Going to our favorite club, well, that means drinking. Staying at the Arlington, obviously means being held, cuddled, making love, having my fleshly desires overfilled. And he tosses in church. I want to go so, so badly. I know it would be a huge mistake to spend time with him. My mind is set on divorcing him. It's far beyond impossible to stay with him. My fleshly desires are screaming at me! I could go just for the fun? Use him for a change? Tempting, but my conscience wins. I simply ignore his message.

A few hours later, another text from Jared:

"Couples massage at nine or ten thirty. Which do you prefer?"

Now he is appealing to my enjoyment of being pampered. The guy is really working me over. Again, I ignore it.

A few hours later, another message.

"Are you really not even going to answer me? Please go with me tonight."

"Jared, it won't change anything. I keep thinking about what all you did with those women. Not only that but you have lied and deceived me our entire marriage."

"Be with me tonight," he goes on.

I'm blown away that he's not getting it.

"*I can't!*"

"Okay, I understand."

Then he continues to send pics of us together, Bible verses, etc., as I'm stepping up my resistance, trying to get through to him, to get him to understand it's over. It's done. I can't and will not be with him. I'm unwittingly increasing his hunger and intensifying his challenge. His mouth is beginning to water, and the burn of his addictions begin to scorch him on the inside. His sly little smile brings forth a slight rumble from within. Almost like a laugh but it's laced with evil.

58

Sundays have become my favorite day of the week. I never thought that would come out of my mouth, but it's so true. I get lost in the worship music. It opens up my heart and spirit to God as if it's only him and me. As opposed to when I was a kid, I listen and soak in the sermon. I have made so many friends, and they truly feel more like family.

After church, one of my friends and I are going to a meeting about a women's wilderness weekend. We are planning a two-night, three-day backpacking trip. I've done a lot of hiking but have never done a backpacking trip. I'm thrilled to have the opportunity to take part in such a cool adventure!

On the way back from the meeting, Jared text and asks if I can talk. I told him I was in the car with friends but could call him in about thirty minutes. He says he needs to talk about some important decisions and a lot of them depend on me. He needs to talk in person. My sister text me and said Jared pulled up, realized my car was not there, and left. So apparently, he was planning to just show up and talk, not even ask.

When I get back to my car, I call him. He says he's down the road at one of our favorite restaurants and asks if I will come join him for dinner. I didn't want to have dinner with him, but I'm such a sap. I felt bad that he was already there and by himself. So I go.

"Why are you here?" I ask.

"I was driving myself crazy at the camper. I can't live without you. I have some ideas. I want you to give me a year. Let me prove to you that I can be faithful. I want you to take over our finances and even put a tracker on my phone. If you're not happy after a year, at least you'll be more financially stable. You have nothing to lose."

"Jared, you're not getting it. Those images are embedded into my brain. I gave you a year after I found Valerie at the camper. Your level of deceit and lies that day made it impossible for me to believe anything you tell me. You watched me live in agony that entire year. It's impossible! I'm not capable of trusting you. This is killing me. I'm so in love with you, but I can't trust you!"

"Michelle, I'll never be happy without you. You're everything I've ever wanted. Please!"

After dinner, we walk outside. The sunset is breathtaking.

"Let's drive toward the sunset," he suggests.

He knows how much I love them. We have our what used to be typical, casual conversation.

My gosh I miss him so, I think.

We drive back to the restaurant and sit to talk for a little bit. He leans over and kisses me. He still has that effect on me. Everything inside me tingles and melts. My heart goes back in time when I was his one and only.

"Come stay the night with me."

"I can't. My sister will be wondering where I am."

So many times my mouth does not consult my brain. This was one of those moments.

"She will be out of town on Tuesday. Maybe I can come sit by the campfire and visit?"

As soon as that came across my lips I wanted to slug myself. Brain! Where are you? Why are you so slow?

"That would be amazing," he says. "I'll cook us some dinner."

I'm so mad at myself. We've been studying in life group about leaving doors open. Doors that could lead to sin create opportunities. They need to be closed to guard yourself. How could I make myself so vulnerable when I know better? Why is this so hard?

Jared text me before bed. "Good night, beautiful. I miss you already."

*****

Monday I have my usual short day at work. I go to Post to get in my workout. I don't know how he does it, but Jared pops in. Maybe he has a tracker on me? Wouldn't surprise me at all.

"My gosh, you're beautiful! You're driving me crazy being hot and sweaty. I can't wait to see you tomorrow night."

I shrug. "I'm having second thoughts about it."

"I really think we need it," he says.

"Well, I really need to finish my workout. I have an appointment with Dr. White to get to."

Dr. White is completely shocked that Jared confessed to everything. He warned me again.

"Michelle, Jared is a master. He will now step up his game to get you back. You need to be extra cautious."

I didn't tell him that I had made dinner plans with him for tomorrow. What am I doing?

Before bed, Jared sends me a text. "I can't wait for tomorrow night."

59

Tuesday morning I wake up to a message from him.

"I am soooo in love with you! See you tonight."

I'm already feeling guilty. God has shown me so many times, in so many ways to stay away from Jared. I know I have to divorce him. I have very strong physical needs that haven't been met in a few months now. He's still my husband. I could just use him to meet my needs?

I make my mind up that that is what I'll do. It's so wrong, and I know it. God has clearly warned me to stay away from Jared.

"Dear God, I'm doing something tonight that I know is wrong. Please stop me. I'm so weak. I want to be held. I want to be touched. Please strengthen me to stop. God, this is not right. Why am I still going? I don't want to get back on the wrong path."

I don't stop myself. I shower and get ready. I pray the entire drive.

"Lord, strengthen me. Give me a way out."

I pull up, and he is outside.

Oh my, how I miss him. I miss this place. He helps me out of the car and hugs me. Oh my gosh, he feels so good. He smells intoxicating. I linger in his arms. I want to stay right here. I just want to be held and breathe him in.

"Let's go in. I need to tell you some things."

We sit on the couch to talk. He says he doesn't want us to linger on the past all night and be all serious. Then he tells me something I wasn't expecting at all.

"I had lunch with Allen (our Haiti leader) today. I told him everything. I asked him if he would be my mentor."

He said he wants a more spiritual life. He realizes he has been wrong about a lot of things. He says he has been praying every night. I told him I was proud of him, but this is something he needs to do for himself, not for me.

He had cooked us a nice dinner. He said he got us some alcohol to drink and relax. He mixed me a drink to go with my dinner. After we ate, one of our favorite songs came on. We slow danced. I was beginning to feel a nice buzz, was wrapped in his arms, relaxing. That was the last thing I remembered.

I wake up the next morning, in his bed and naked. I still feel half wasted. As nice as it felt to be held, there is no way I would have been able to have sex with him had I not been drinking. The other women would have been too heavy on my mind. Jared knew this as well. He knew he would have to supply me with alcohol in order to get me in bed. The man is skilled, intelligent, and he is probably still on his euphoric high from successfully sexually conquering me.

I feel so disgusting and defeated. My intention was to come last night and satisfy some of my physical needs. Now I feel violated, like I have let Jared start coming in again. I still stand firm on my decision to divorce him, but not only did I just crack the door open for him, I swung it wide open.

60

Ashlynn's senior pictures are this afternoon in Cave City. I have to pull myself together externally. Internally, I'm crumbling piece by piece. I had been feeling wanted by God. Now feelings of failure, mistake, and unchosen are beginning to dominate. I've given Jared the impression that we're possible again, and that is the last thing I meant to do.

Getting to be involved in Ashlynn's senior pictures was a huge blessing. I had been excluded in so much. Lilith actually invited me to be a part of this day. We took Ashlynn to get her hair and makeup done and then met up with the photographer. I had no idea where my baby girl had gone. Standing before me was a beautiful young lady. Luckily, I was able to disguise all the terrible yuck that was beginning to unleash itself inside me yet again. This day was all about Ashlynn, and she fully enjoyed it.

Jared had text me earlier in the day and asked if I could call him. He had something he needed to tell me. I said I was involved in something very important and would call on my way home. A little after leaving the kids at Everett's, I give Jared a call. He tells me that Valerie sent him a message, telling him I was harassing her on FB, calling her names and threatening her. I'm immediately pissed!

The day after I found the photos, I sent her a message telling her I hope she enjoyed screwing my husband and that I had the pleasure of finding the photos. That was about a month and a half ago. At the moment, I was completely infuriated. Having come to know Jared the way I do now, I'm sure Valerie told him a month and a half ago about the message I had sent her. One of the things that gives Jared his "high" is being the center of a love triangle.

He says, "I just wanted to tell you. I hope she drops everything, and we can just put it all behind us. Good night, sexy girl. I love you."

Putting himself at the center of a love triangle has just created in me the desire to fight for him and become the victor of his love. He moves the "Michelle pawn" one block closer in his sick love game. The high he receives is mild, but any high is worth any lie he dishes out.

He continues his game the next morning with loads of love messages. He is flying out on a mission but wanted me to know how much I mean to him before he flies off.

My day is a simple, typical work day until I realize Jared has deleted photos on my phone. I had saved the copies of messages Ellie had sent me shortly after Jared and I were married. The ones of him professing his love to her and asking her back. He also deleted the pornographic photos I had recently found. Now those I had on back up, thankfully. The ones from Ellie, I did not. He also deleted all her messages to me and her number from my phone.

Furious was an understatement. My drinking had been an issue throughout our marriage. He invites me over for dinner and supplies me with alcohol. His goal was twofold: wipe away the evidence I had of his infidelity and get me in bed. Here this man has been telling everyone he filed for divorce because of my drinking, but has been enticing and supplying the entire time.

I send him a message telling him how angry I am.

"You had no right to delete anything from my phone."

"Michelle, you are the world to me. I know every time you look at those photos or text messages, you hurt. I have forgotten it, and I pray you do too. I really want this behind us. I love you very much. I want us to move forward. We can't do that when you are constantly reminded of my mistakes."

Unknown to him, I have no intention of moving forward with him. I accepted his dinner invitation because my body was in desperation for touch. My lips missed being kissed even if it was with someone that had hurt me. My flesh was crying for attention.

"You still had no right to delete anything of mine. You also deleted several sweet messages that I had saved from you. Now I don't have those either," I grumbled through texts.

He responds, "I was a little foggy, only meant to delete the negative stuff. You are the world to me. I will repay any sweet messages with lots more if you'll let me. A day without you, and I'm craving your touch. Missing your beautiful smile."

I'm so irritated, but I'm also beginning to realize my feelings for him are changing. I still love him and miss him intensely, but I'm seeing through all he says and does. It's all about serving his needs and purposes.

It's my weekend to have the kids, so I drove to Mom and Dad's. The kids go to a football game Friday night. Saturday, we enjoy a walk together, and Josie and I start a Christmas puzzle. Sunday, my sister and nephews come for Mom's birthday lunch. We had an enjoyable weekend. I received text after text from Jared. How much he misses me. He feels like he won the lottery because he has the sexiest woman alive. Sunday morning he texted me and asked what time church services at NLC are. Later, he texted and said how much he enjoyed the service.

Questions start running through my head again. Is he really changing? Does God want me to stay with him and work within myself on forgiveness? I'm thinking about these things as I am driving back to my sister's.

I ask God, "Please don't be asking me to stay with Jared for the purpose of working on learning about forgiveness. Pushing myself to do something that, I don't see possible. Please, God, I don't see how I can. But if it's your will and desire for me, I know you will make it possible."

I'm crying because the last year with Jared I pushed, I struggled, and I was miserable. I don't feel in my spirit that God is leading me in that direction; but with Jared going to church, praying, and reading his Bible, it's making me wonder.

As all these things are running through my head. Jared calls. He asks me to come over. I told him no because I have something I need to do. Actually, I feel the Spirit cautioning me. He begs. He says he wants to take me shoe shopping. Are you kidding me right now? He knows I love shoes! He is working on me pretty hard. I keep telling him no. Then he says, "If you change your mind, I will be here drinking beer. I have other stuff for you too."

That does it. I give in. I'm going. I tell Crystal that I'm going to stay with a girlfriend of mine. She is having boyfriend trouble and needs a friend to lean on. I text Jared and tell him I'm on my way.

How can I be so weak? My heart always flutters when I see him. I'm so in love with him, but I know a life with him is impossible. So why am I going? God has shown me who he truly is and has attempted to keep me from him. He gently warned me when Ellie showed me the text messages. I didn't listen then. The warning against him got more painful when I found Valerie with him in his camper. Like a massive idiot, I didn't listen then either. I ignored God's warning and ran right back into the lion's den. I was miserable and yet again cried out to God for answers. If he was human, he would have laughed, turned his head, and said, "You stupid girl, you got just what you deserved." And that is what I deserved. But God had mercy and possibly pity for me. I'm sure I broke his heart by not listening to his warning. So when I yet again begged for a way out, as harsh and painful as it was, I found the photos. How stubborn and stupid can a girl be? Here I go again, and why? Why? Because I'm choosing to satisfy my flesh. I'm stupid, stubborn, and selfish.

Jared is waiting for me outside by the camper. In a matter of seconds, my flesh begins to drink in his poison. He grabs me, kisses me deeply, passionately. It begins to release the sting inside me. That sting is so powerful my desire burns for more. He fixes me a drink, and it does not take long for the release to flow through my veins. The lies and images disappear. I am back into the world where Jared has me on a pedestal and no other woman exists to him. With the past having disappeared, Jared and I can enter our uninterrupted intimacy.

MICHELLE MARTIN

This is the combination my flesh has been lusting. Jared, touch, intimacy, alcohol, sex, reversing time. At this moment, in the grips of alcohol, I'm able to satisfy my desires. The worry of tomorrow, when it all comes back, I don't care. It's all about satisfying me tonight.

61

I wake up wrapped in arms with no memory past the second drink. He makes love to me before getting out of bed and getting ready for work. I get up to get ready for work after he leaves. I'm so nauseous, dizzy, not sure how I'm going to survive my work day. I drive straight to the gas station and buy a pack of Angry Orchard beer. I drink three on my way to work to bring back a buzz and take away the hangover.

As soon as I'm finished with work, which is only a few hours, I start in on the rest of the beer. My plan to be with Jared last night was to satisfy my fleshly desires. Something I did not plan on or intend started happening. The feelings of being in love with him began to tug at me. Jared's old house, where it all began when we met, was on my way home. I decided to take the exit and visit the old house I had loved so much.

I stopped in the driveway of the old house. Memories pound though my head as the tears mourn all the loss. I loved being in this house with Jared. Our time here was before I knew the real him. He truly made me feel like a queen. I honestly thought he saw me as the only woman that existed on earth.

When we were in this house, his love was pure and untainted. More than anything I wished I could go back. I wanted our starry nights in the hot tub. Our swings on the porch swing as we overlooked the river below lit up with moonlight. I wanted that feeling back. The feeling that no other man had ever given me. The feeling that I was his everything, and if I was not by his side, the air was unworthy of breathing in.

I began to feel trapped again. The canyon I had been closing in on started widening. My footing started loosening. My foundation that had been firming my sturdiness began to waiver. My joy and peace were slipping into confusion and fear. The door I opened for Jared to satisfy my fleshly needs was allowing more of him in than I intended.

My drive back to camp continued with fear and confusion swarming through my head. The life I knew I wanted with God was now becoming foggy with the fleshly satisfaction Jared offered. I stopped at the liquor store and bought four BuzzBallz. I downed one, then drove onto camp. As I turned to go to the camper, I noticed Jared's truck there. I was not expecting him, so I crammed gum into my mouth to cover the smell of alcohol. We talk for a bit, have sex. He asks if I have been drinking and says he smells it on my breath. I told him it must have been from last night; I have been burping it all day.

I put on my workout clothes, planning to head to the gym. Since I have been drinking, I'm not feeling up to the gym. I decided to load up Buttercup, head to my sister's, and drink more to ease out of the hangover.

Plan fail. I wake up wearing orange and locked in a jail cell. I have flashes of hitting a car, my airbags deploying, the firefighter from church being on the scene. Where is Buttercup? Do they know I was drinking?

I bang on the door because I'm really clueless as to what happened and what they know. A short, stocky, unpleasant lady opens the door.

"Can I please leave?"

"We have to hold you for six hours. You have one hour left, and there's not an officer here to fingerprint you. You'll have to wait."

I start pacing. I wonder if there is any chance, maybe they didn't know I had been drinking.

There is some Kool-Aid beside my bed. I down it. I'm so thirsty! The faucet in the bathroom isn't working. I lay on the cot and try to remember what happened. I barely remember leaving Jared's. I know I had Buttercup with me. I remember exiting, and traffic was really backed up. I was afraid of slamming on my breaks and throwing Buttercup forward. I hit the car in front of me. My front and side airbags deployed. I was so terrified I had a difficult time breathing. I remember one of the firefighters from church being there. I was afraid to talk to anyone because they would know I had been drinking. I don't remember anything else.

I'm so thirsty but still can't get the faucet to work. I bang on the door. No one comes. I bang some more. Short, stocky and very angry girl finally comes to the door. I ask if I can go yet. She says it still hasn't been an hour and there still is not an officer to fingerprint me. I ask if I can please get some water.

"Use the faucet. Push hard."

After what feels like hours, they come to let me out. I asked if I could sign myself out, but of course, that's against policy. I felt I had one option: Jared. It's 12:10 a.m. He answers his phone. I asked if he could come to the Cobalt police station and pick me up.

"On my way," is all he says.

We had to call a bail bondsman, sign a bunch of papers. It took a while.

On the way to camp, he asks me what all happened.

"There's not much I can tell you. I felt hungover from us drinking the night before, so I picked up some beer to drink and make it through work. Then I still felt bad, so I got more to drink. I remember running into the back of a vehicle on my way to Crystal's. My airbags deployed, and I don't know where Buttercup is."

We climb into bed, and remorsefully, I make love to him.

As we are lying there and he is holding me, I ask him, "Why would you come get me?"

"Michelle, I love you."

We lay there holding each other. He drifts off to sleep. Now I really feel trapped. God warned me so many times about Jared. I still have not listened once. I'm sure he is fed up and doesn't want me anymore. I'm facing my third DWI. I may not have a license. I barely have any work hours. Jared still loves and wants me. He wants to take care of me. I love him, but I can't be with a man I can't trust. What if I have to be? Right now, he is my only choice.

62

The next morning Jared gets up and gets ready for work. He says he will come back later and we will figure it all out. I get up and have coffee with him. Jared says he wants to stop the divorce. He asked me if I would be able to get past everything so we can work on us. If so, he says he would help me. At that moment, I saw Jared as my only option and said yes.

After he leaves, I drink a beer that's in the fridge. I'm not sure what charges I'm facing. I already have no place to live. I'm completely terrified. I had gotten back on God's path and was doing so well. Now I feel my scarlet *R* blazing on my chest again.

I find a bottle of sake in the upper cabinet. I take a few swings of it. I'm trying to ease off this leftover hangover from days ago. I get to feeling fairly good, not trashed but not hungover.

Jared comes in at ten thirty, and we leave. He calls the police station and finds out there were three vehicles involved in the accident. I hit the lady in front of me, and she hit the vehicle in front of her. The third car had three people in it, and they went to the ER. One was a six-year-old girl. I have charges for another DWI, obstruction, and a refusal. He asks where we would be able to find my dog. They said to call animal control. He calls, and they have her.

We go to the police station and get the police report. Then we go to the wrecker service to look at the Pathfinder. All the damage is in the front. The front and side airbags deployed. I start picking up some of my things. There are two empty BuzzBallz in the floor, one unopened one in the cup holder, which I grab. Then we go pick up Buttercup.

On the way back to camp, Jared calls our insurance agency to get a rental car lined up. He tells me he has to pick his daughter up and take her to counseling but doesn't want me around her yet. He decides we will stop to get the rental and I'll drive it back to camp, then he'll go get Lucy. The rental place doesn't have a vehicle ready yet. Due to time constraints, Jared has no choice but to pick up Lucy with me there. We take her to her appointment, then drop her off at her mom's. Ellie is furious when she sees me in the truck.

As we are driving on camp, Ellie calls and is chewing Jared out for having Lucy around me. He had told her that he had kicked me out because of a drinking incident. He tells Ellie that he wants to stay married to me, and we are working it out.

When we get back to the camper, we start a campfire to sit around and talk. I'm totally irritated that he didn't tell Ellie the real reason I left. He has never been one for telling the truth and taking responsibility for his actions. Of course, he pinned it on me. I told him if he would tell her the real reason I left, she would be more open to us getting back together and not so against me being around Lucy. I told him it would be best for him if I wasn't in the picture at all.

"No. I'm in love with you. As much as you have hurt me, you have also given me more love and happiness than anyone ever in my life."

63

Each passing moment I gain feelings of being trapped. I'm not capable of loving Jared the way I did before. I'm terrified of what my future holds. God has tried so many times to save me from Jared. He has shown me in extremely bold manners to run from him. I have done the complete opposite and have ran back to him. I'm sure God has washed his hands of me and has his back facing me this very moment. How could he ever want me again? Each time he has rescued me, I've turned back to what brought me down.

My only option is Jared. I'm being forced to stay married to a man I am in love with but can no longer love. My future is resembling my torturous past.

Jackie text, checking to see how I'm doing. I tell her about me coming to see Jared and everything leading up to jail and another DWI.

"Michelle, Jared is not your source. God is. You are supposed to be running from Jared, not running to him. Now you have the spirits of guilt, shame, and unworthiness. Repent and bind up those spirits. Replace them with peace and comfort."

Her words sit very heavy on my heart and spirit because I know it is the truth. Every spirit she mentioned I brought in. I have felt them in heavy doses. They are what have taken away my hope and are making me believe Jared is my only choice, my only source.

The rental car place sends someone to pick me up so I can get the rental car. After getting there, they tell me they are unable to rent the car to me because I have no DL. Once again, Jared comes to the rescue. They allow him to rent the car. We go to lunch and switch vehicles. He leaves to go back to work. I stop at the liquor store to buy and replace his beer and sake I had drank. I also buy four shots for myself to have after I get back to my sister's.

I go the camper and replace Jared's alcohol, get Buttercup, and we go to my sister's. My poor Buttercup smells like residue from the airbags. I give her a bath. I can't imagine what she endured in this accident. I have so much guilt. I could have killed somebody! My heart becomes loaded with guilt in many areas. I down the four shots.

I don't understand the stupid things I do. Maybe it's the feeling of hopelessness? I don't know. It's Thursday, and I work in Nashville, then Casten. I stop at the gas station and pick up a twelve pack of beer. I have two on my way to work at Nashville. After working there and on my way to Casten, I have another two. Finishing there, driving to my sister's, I down the rest so I can trash the evidence before getting to her house.

Unexpectedly, my sister is home. She looks at me and immediately says, "You've been drinking."

Of course, I lie and say no.

"I need you to come blow in my car and prove it."

She has a breathalyzer from her DWI.

Crossing my fingers it won't register, but knowing better, I fail.

"You have to leave. I'm in recovery and can't have this in my home."

I don't blame her a bit.

I start loading my things in the rental car to leave.

"I have taken a picture of your license plate," she says. "If you drive off, I will call the cops. You need to call someone to come get you."

I call Jared. He says he'll be here as soon as he can. He hopes to bring someone with him to drive the car back. He's unable to, so we have to leave the car and plan to get it in the morning.

He is obviously irritated at me for drinking after everything that has happened.

"I can't believe you were drinking! You just got another DWI!"

I lied and told him I only drank after I got to Crystal's. Like that makes any of it better?

"I can't let you have the car for the weekend."

"I am supposed to pick Josie up tomorrow, have dinner with our family, and Race for the Cure on Saturday."

"I'll take you to work tomorrow and pick you up after. I would like for you to come to the mountain with me for the weekend."

64

The next morning Jared takes me to Cobalt to pick up the car from Crystal's. On the way, he says he will let me use the car to pick up Josie after he has made sure I've not been drinking. We can do our family stuff on Saturday, and then he wants me to come to the mountain afterward. I agree. We go back to camp so I can get ready for work. I asked him if he would please let me drive to work and back. I've kept him from his job enough. He agrees and leaves for work.

While I'm getting ready for work, I get a text from Jackie.

"Why didn't you go to life group on Wednesday?"

"Because I'm feeling hopeless, helpless, and I feel like giving up."

She replies, "You are listening to the lies of the devil. Run from temptation, not to it! Do you want this man more than God? You can't be powerful with God and pitiful with Jared."

"I don't know why the devil is attacking me so hard!" I complain.

"Yes, you do. Michelle, God has chosen you. You have a purpose, and you have great potential. Please don't let the devil steal that. You're in this mess because of your disobedience. You have been asking Jared to get you out instead of God. Repent. God specializes in turning messes into messages."

There is so much truth to her message that I tremble. What she said to me the other day, "Jared is not your source, God is," has been ringing nonstop through my mind. I don't want to stay with Jared because I know what kind of life it will be. It will be a repeat of the misery that God led me out of. I'm only with him now because I know he offers financial security. I may lose my driver's license. Without a driver's license, I would lose my job. Looking at Jared, I see security financially but misery. Looking at God, to me, is unknown. I must look at what I do know about him.

I asked him to save me from Jared, and he did. I asked him into my heart; he showed up. I've been tormented with the struggle between Jared and God, but every time I look to God, I feel a peace and joy that I have never known. Choosing God will give me that back. What about financial security? Where will I live? What about a job? Am I going to be able to drive? Looking at God, all of these are unknown. Before I stepped into disobedience and ran back to Jared, I had peace. At this moment, I'm back to torment. I don't know what, if any, provision God will give me. God has moved in my heart so many times, even though I mess up. He has never failed to take me back, and when I return, he still fills me with love and peace. I miss that peace and security.

I cannot keep turning my back to him after all he has done for me. Provision? I will just have to trust him. No amount of financial security is worth losing the feeling God has given me on the inside. I may have to live at my parents and walk to work at McDonald's or a gas station. The provision God will give me is unknown. The peace, joy, love, security—that is a promise. Choosing God is worth so much more than choosing Jared.

I know choosing God is the best choice. But saying goodbye to Jared, for good, is crushing. I have to let go of someone that I'm deeply in love with for someone that is even more deeply in love with me. I don't want to leave my church or move from Cobalt. Balston is in the middle of nowhere, but I feel God leading me there. What forty-year-old wants to have to move back in with her parents? But being there will offer safety from Jared. I know this will not go well with him.

The thought of all of it is depressing. I want to spend time with Josie and my family, but I'm such a mess right now. I don't want Josie to see me like this. I message her and tell her I'm sick and will not be able to do this weekend. Then I message Jared and tell him I will be spending the whole weekend with him on the mountain.

SHED

He doesn't know my decision to move in with my parents. I want to spend the weekend on the mountain as a goodbye. This will be the end to it all. I want the chance to grieve and close out all my dreams with him. My heart needs the time to come to terms with all things ending. I want to say goodbye to the mountain itself and its most stunning view of the stars I have ever seen. Goodbye to its nature and serenity. Goodbye to a piece of myself that will always be there.

65

When I finish my work for the day, I go to the camper to pack for the weekend. I work on Monday, but Jared has the week off and will be spending that time on the mountain fixing things at the cabin and barns. He asks if I can come back Monday after work since I don't work again until Thursday. I let him know that I'm planning to go to my parents so I can make Josie's volleyball game Thursday. There are two things I know for certain: I will be divorcing Jared, and I am moving to Balston to live with my parents. Everything else in my life is unknown, but I'm placing it all in God's hands.

During my packing, Jared calls to ask me to go to Range Control where Bryson works. He is one of the sweetest, most genuine guys I have ever met. We connected on a deep friendly level, and I have shared a lot with Bryson. We walk outside to talk, and I tell him about my DWI. He is disappointed but says he still loves me anyway. Bryson was the first person I confided in about finding the photos on Jared's phone. Bryson is very good at being impartial and loving both Jared and me despite our faults.

I tell him how deeply in love I am with Jared, but I don't feel we are capable of making it work. I told him that Jared confessed to everything, but I don't want to turn him in. Bryson tells me a little about his marriage and says, "Maybe the timing for you two isn't right."

I explain to him that I don't believe it ever will be. I'm not capable of ever trusting Jared, and it crushes my heart. He allows me to cry on his shoulder, and then I tell him goodbye.

On our way to the mountain, Jared and I stop for dinner. We have not been to dinner together in several months. I have always enjoyed going to dinner with him, sitting, talking, laughing, enjoying good food. I never had that with Everett. I'm crying. This, this has been one of my favorite things about us. We would sit for hours at a restaurant lost in conversation, lost in each other. How do you mourn something that you didn't have in a fifteen-year marriage and has meant so much to you the short time you have been able to experience it? Letting go of Jared is also letting go of moments he gave me, not understanding how much they meant to me. He has filled that void, but I know God is asking me to release him. So with that, I must also relinquish the gift of these moments because they have become tied to something that is now tainted and no longer life-giving.

As preparation for when I do tell Jared I can't stay married to him, I share about the conversation that Bryson and I had earlier. Sometimes the timing isn't right for people. He acts as though he doesn't hear me. He starts talking about different flight schools the military will be sending him to and how much he will have to be gone. As he talks about it, I live the moments. The sickness in my gut creeps up again, and I become a nervous wreck. I see the scene as he is talking: him going to dinner, sitting at the bar, and working his charm on a pretty young girl. He has no resistance; and knowing I'm sitting at home, waiting for him to return, drives the thrill for him to reach his desired level of "high."

That vision is another confirmation that this is the end. I will not live my life in that torture any longer. My heart sinks deeper into mourning. The more time I spend with him, the more clarity I receive that a life with him equals a life of stolen peace. We haven't even reached the mountain yet, and the grieving in my heart is already so unbearable. I know my love for all things about the mountain. Its simplicity yet intense magic is going to increase the magnitude of difficulty in saying goodbye; but it is a mountain I must climb in order to get to the other side.

We stop at Walmart to park my car and pick up a few things before driving up the mountain. He automatically grabs my hand. I love holding his hand. Luckily, it's dark, and the tears are able to roll down my cheek unnoticed. Inside, as I'm bent down in one of the aisles looking for something, Jared comes up, leans down beside me, and kisses me. I drink the moment in. I don't know how I will be able to function without affection and touch.

The drive up the mountain is full of curves and hills, dust spinning off the tires until we come through several gates and into the clearing. There sits the cabin, awaiting our arrival, with dim lights twinkling its hello. This will be the last time I will ever drive up with excitement and anticipation to the serendipity it openly offers. I have two days to soak it in, but I am already dreading my goodbye.

We grab our bags and go inside to a warm welcome from Jared's mom and Aunt Mary. The cabin is lacking in modern appeal. Even the bathroom doesn't have a door, simply a curtain you slide to close. The appeal of the cabin is the feeling of simplicity and comfort. Jared's mom has set up a mattress in the shop for Jared and me to sleep. It's attached to the cabin. An old junky shop and yet it is perfect. Part of me is experiencing Jared before my discovery of the photos. I didn't care where being with him took me. I just wanted any moment with him I could get. It's dark out as we climb into the bed. You can see a million stars twinkling in the windows. It's captivating.

This is my first time to make love to Jared, me being sober, since the confirmation of his infidelity. My heart cries as my mind is tossed back and forth between loving him and the haunting of the images. I force my mind to escape to give my body the chance to enjoy this moment. I'm unable to escape from my heart. My heart loves this man with the deepest, strongest, most intense passion I've ever twisted myself into with another person. I'm making love to this man with my soul as my heart is mourning the loss of him and the goodbye of us. He pauses, sensing my emotions. He looks into my eyes and sees my tears. They are tears of love and goodbye, but to him, they are only a symbol of my love as he is unaware of the goodbye pouring through them.

66

The smell of bacon cooking pulls us awake. I love waking up naked, wrapped in his arms. My body has never fit so perfectly into anyone else's. It's as if all my curves and bends were molded to fit his. I'm unable to resist kissing and rubbing him until we are making love, such is our usual morning routine. This is one of the many special moments I will miss. Again, my heart cries knowing this will leave me too.

After joining everyone for breakfast, Jared heads outside to get to work. I had received a text last night from Rhonda checking to see how I was doing. I fill her in on my arrest and DWI. I hate having to admit to the stupid things I did. I pick up one of my spiritual books and do some reading. Before I know it, it's lunchtime. Jared and I sneak upstairs to have sex before he heads back out to work.

I decide to take off for a walk. So much is churning through my mind. So I'm going to live with Mom and Dad. Okay. What about a job? I'm terrified. I might not be able to drive at all. I may have to do jail time. Even with all this looming over me, Jared wants to stand with me and help me. It would be so much easier. The bills would be taken care of. If I'm not able to drive, I would have him. But it's not right. Staying with him would pull me away from God. That has been part of my struggle since returning to church, the tug-of-war for my heart and devotion.

I put a post on our women's Bible study group, asking for prayer. I explained that I had stepped into disobedience and opened many doors that should have been bolted. I explained that now I have brought many unwanted spirits upon myself and am right back in the middle of a spiritual warfare God has been walking me out of.

Stuart, a friend of the family, had come in for the day to help work. They all come in for supper. We sit around the table enjoying food and conversation. I'm really going to miss Jared's mom. She is such a unique person. I've enjoyed every moment I have shared with her. I've often thought about asking her about their open marriage. The idea is so foreign to me. I can't understand being okay with sleeping with another man and knowing your husband is doing what should be shared only with you but is with other women. She would have opened up and shared with me, but the weekend is not about that. This is my goodbye weekend.

Stuart is sleeping in the shop tonight, so Jared and I go upstairs. He is exhausted. He has worked hard all day and has another long day tomorrow. Knowing I will have a more difficult time falling asleep, I pick out a movie to watch. We love on each other and cuddle. He drifts off to sleep as we are wrapped in each other. Our bodies so close, I love the feel of him next to me. My mind drifts off as usual.

All directions I try to go to make us work always lead back to lies and deception. My heart is having such a hard time accepting that this is over. I softly turn to be able to look at him. Tears stream down my cheeks.

"Farewell, my love," I gently tell him.

I don't know if he feels the flutter of my heart, some of my tears streaming onto him, or hears my soft goodbye; but he rubs on me.

"Baby, are you okay?"

"Allergies," I lie.

He gets up and steps out on the deck to pee.

"There are a million stars out here. You gotta come see!"

I step out and am in such awe my breath is taken from me. Middle of the night we both stand here, lost in the world above us. It's like every star the universe could produce has shown up to twinkle its goodbye to me. It's saddening and, at the same time, heartwarming. Like a salute to my appreciation of its unmatched beauty.

Shortly after we get back in bed, Jared is fast asleep. My heart, mind, soul, and spirit are processing and mourning so many things that sleep continues to elude me.

At 1:30 a.m. Sunday morning, Rhonda texts me as though the Holy Spirit was prompting her and she obeyed.

"You have to listen to the Lord. Stop listening to the devil. Jared is making you into someone that you're not." She says she has something for me.

At six fifty that morning, I get a really long message from her.

"You have been trying to negotiate with God. You are stuck between following God's plan without question and also trying to have your will and please God too…trust and obey!"

We make plans to meet Monday evening so she can give me whatever it is she's talking about.

Jared gets a call from one of the guys from Range Control. He informs us that Bryson's son was killed in a car accident last night. We both lay on the bed in shock and heart sick for him.

We go down to have breakfast with everyone. The guys go back out to work, saying they will return at lunchtime. Stuart is leaving after lunch. I send Bryson a message and pray for him and his family.

I continue in prayer about Jared and me. I pray for strength and to receive the closure my heart is needing. Jackie and Rhonda have been messaging all weekend. The continued theme is trust and obey. I have not been fully surrendering to God's will. I must obey and turn from Jared. I have to trust God for direction and provision. Although it means saying goodbye to so many things Jared gave me that were neglected in my fifteen-year marriage, it is also saying I am more worthy than the lies and deception.

I don't want to tell Jared my decision while we are at his mom's and after receiving the news about Bryson's son. Part of me is also being selfish. I want to be able to complete my goodbye and have my time to grieve without the interruption of Jared. I know he would work his manipulation and turn my goodbye into his pleading to keep me. My decision is solid in my head and spirit. It's my soul and heart that need the grasping of reality and last moments to breathe in the magic of the mountain and to experience Jared as untainted as I possibly can.

Stuart leaves after we all finish lunch. Jared says he needs either me or his mom to drive the little tractor to help him work. I quickly volunteer, throw on a ball cap, and head out with him. This is my final day to enjoy all I can.

I work for about an hour and a half. The weather is perfect, and the mountain glows with its beauty and fresh air. My lungs breathe in the oxygen and serenity. Although I am saying goodbye, a sense of peace washes over me. It is as if the mountain is blessing me and telling me how much it understands my need to leave.

Jared's mom drives down to bring us water. I drive my tractor over to Jared so we can enjoy our break together.

"It's so nice to finally have a wife willing to help."

Oh, that hurts in so many ways. Hurts me in knowing I won't return and he won't have that anymore. It also hurts because if I was so much of what he wanted, then why did he do what he knew would lose me?

After our water break, Jared says I can go back up to the cabin. I have completed all the work he needed me to do. I drive up the mountain slowly. It's a fairly bumpy ride, but as I'm going up, the mountain is releasing to me the beginning of my last sunset. I don't want to miss a moment. As I get to the cabin, I go in to get my Bible and come outside to read and witness my final sunset here.

Jared comes and sits beside me. "Nothing like the sunset on this mountain."

I shake my head in agreement because if I spoke, my emotion would have been heard. I lay my head on his shoulder, admiring the beauty of the colors, sad to know it was my last one.

"I'm sorry I've been so busy this weekend. We can drive over to the lodge at Mount Magdalene for dinner?"

That is the place where Jared proposed. I don't know how he would feel up to it after having worked so much. Unknown to him, this is my last night ever here on the mountain, in this cabin. I don't want to miss a moment of it.

"No, I would rather stay here and enjoy every minute with you," I say, knowing it will be my last.

After enjoying a nice, simple dinner with Jared, his mom, and Aunt Mary, we all go to the living room to relax. They put on a movie that I have no interest in, which is fine. I just enjoy being on the mountain, in this cabin, with all of them. While they watch the movie, I pick up one of my spiritual books to read. I'm content. I'm cuddled on the couch with Jared, and the mountain is graciously releasing its serenity.

Jared asks if I would like to watch a movie with him out in the shop, back into the bed where we spent our first night together here, the first time I consciously made love to him since the infidelity.

Knowing this is my last night forever with him, I excitedly agree, then ask, "How are we supposed to watch a movie out there? There's no TV."

"I'll run upstairs to get that one and get it all set up. How about you pick out a movie?"

They have so many movies I've never heard of.

"What is *Sirens*?" I ask Jared's mom.

"You guys might like it. It's pretty raunchy, lots of nudity. It was one of Jared's dad's favorites," she explains.

I don't get it. I just don't get any of it. How could she be okay with any of that? That is the foundation of Jared's upbringing: sex and nudity. It simply confirms more to me why I must step away from him. I pick a movie I am familiar with that has no nudity.

While Jared is getting everything set up, I step outside to capture a moment with the stars. It is truly mesmerizing. I can even see the Milky Way. I breathe the fresh, pure air deep into my lungs.

"Thank you," I tell the mountain and stars. "You have given me a goodbye I will never forget. A portion of me will always be here too."

I believe when you connect with nature, it intertwines with a portion of your soul. It stays inside you forever, and in return, it keeps a piece of you in gratitude of your admiration of its beauty and offers a piece of serenity you carry for eternity.

After everything is set up, Jared and I start the movie. He compliments me over and over, but each time he does, the images of the young girls pop into my head, and I find myself comparing my body to theirs. Those images will never go away when I'm with him. He starts making love to me, but something has changed. For me, it's only sex. My body is there enjoying the process, but my heart is gone. It has become simply an act. For the first time ever, I have sex with my husband. My heart made love to him for the last time nights ago. Unknowingly, my heart said goodbye to that portion of us. It is forever gone, forever done, and I am so deeply saddened.

Jared steps outside to pee.

"Michelle, the stars are even more breathtaking tonight. You have to come see."

The stars twinkle even brighter than a few hours ago. We stand there naked. Jared behind me, holding me. I cry. I cry because I will never make love to this man again. I may never see the stars in such a clear, more beautiful sky than this. And I cry because my goodbye weekend has come to an end.

67

Monday morning I get ready for work. Jared drives me down the mountain to my car. Looking in my side-view mirror are the final images of the cabin I will ever see. Knowing this is me leaving him, leaving it all, I can't stop the few tears that make their way down my cheek. Hiding them does no good as he can sense something is wrong with me.

"You need to consider what is best for everyone. That is what I'm trying to do. Ellie will leave you alone if I wasn't in the picture," I tell him.

"Yes, she would, and that would be the easiest, but that is not what I want to do. I want you."

This is my final goodbye to him. With my last kiss, I give him back the dreams we had been building together. I attempt to get back the pieces of my heart he has owned, but it's impossible. He will forever own a portion of me; and I, a portion of him. Even with all the lies and cheating, my heart is breaking knowing I am taking away his dream of having me. Unknown to him, our hearts are breaking together as I'm giving him up, choosing God. I remain wrapped in his arms, not wanting to let go.

I breathe in the fragrance of him that always intoxicates me. Will my body ever fit curve for curve into another man's? There are so many things I love about him and will desperately miss. Everything inside of me is collapsing. I can no longer deny God's voice and warnings. Each time I have stepped closer to Jared, the consequences have increased. As much as my flesh is desiring him, my spirit is desiring God more.

After getting into my car and driving off, heading to work, the complete undoing of myself takes place. There are tears in massive quantity. I scream at the pain of letting go, of all things ending that I thought would last forever. When the process has drained itself and there are no more tears, no more voice to scream, calmness fills me. I know I'm doing the right thing. I thank God for giving me my goodbye weekend. I thank him for taking me back although I had deliberately stepped into disobedience.

I ask that he guides me to his will. I know my disobedience will enter me into consequences of undesired actions. I ask for his protection as I walk forward facing the unknown.

"God, please give me provision as I rely on you as my source. I give you my faith, my trust. Lead me to making you my foundation. I know this path will be full of rocks to trip me up. I know I will not be perfect. Fill me with the Holy Spirit so when I do trip, I'm guided back to your path. I know you have chosen me, but with that choosing, I understand that Satan sees that too. I have become a target to him because of my choosing. Prepare me for the battle. Although you have chosen me, the path will not be smooth and simple. It will actually grow more difficult as Satan fights to win me back. I declare victory, Lord, because my heart now belongs to you."

Time to start cleaning up my mess! After work, I meet with a lawyer to defend me on my DWI. He is the one that represented me on my second, so he gives me a discount and only charges me $4,500. He faxes papers to Driver Control, asking for a hearing to see if I can receive a restricted license instead of losing my license for thirty months. A restricted license requires you to have a breathalyzer in your vehicle. My lawyer warns me that it doesn't look good. I caused an accident, and they have me for obstruction, saying I would not cooperate and also for a refusal to blow to be tested.

Well, when I mess things up, I go all out! My future is hinging on this hearing. This is an opportunity to lean in to God as my source. When you step into disobedience, there are consequences. God also promises never to leave us. I must do what I know is my part in this. Get into God's word, ask for forgiveness, repent, confess to others, and ask for them to join me in prayer and worship the majesty and greatness of God. What I feel is very significant is deep, honest, emotional prayer, a one-on-one with God. I am talking about throwing down in the floor, emotions wide open, Holy Spirit-filled praying. Intense, gut-wrenching, pure prayer.

I'm thinking all those things as I'm driving to Rhonda's. Just seeing her is a source of healing to my heart. I know she deeply cares and has been speaking truth and life into me. Her hug is a hug of family as that is what we have become. I'm quite surprised when she hands me what she said she was needing to give me. It is a Celebrate Recovery Bible. Celebrate Recovery was one of the purposes revealed to me when I started life group. So where this will lead? I'm not yet sure.

I continue on my drive to Mom and Dad's. It's an hour and fifteen minutes from Cobalt. I'm reflecting on all the events of the day. It has been a long one! In the midst of all that took place, I also had a counseling appointment.

Dr. White warned me again. "Michelle, you are not completely surrendering to God's will for you. You need to break communication with Jared. He will continue to step up his game, especially seeing that he was capable of getting to you. Remember, you are dealing with a master manipulator. God's path for you and your safety are riding on this."

They also increased my anxiety meds. Apparently, I appear to be an inner and outer mess! One of my concerns is how to break it to Jared that I'm moving to Mom and Dad's and I'm pursuing the divorce. I still love him, even through all the deception and heartbreak he has caused me. I don't want to do the same and harshly rip the Band-Aid. He is also dealing with Bryson losing his son and is asking me for advice on how to be there for him.

The final portion of my drive to Mom and Dad's, I pray over all the mess in my life. Choosing God and walking away from Jared is my chance to right all my wrongs. I understand Dr. White's warnings about ending communication with Jared. I'm not able to do that at this time because we have to communicate regarding me having the rental car and when I will be able to get the Pathfinder back.

68

The next morning I dive into the Celebrate Recovery Bible Rhonda had given me. This feels like the answer to my battle with alcohol. I'm so fired up and inspired. I send Rhonda a text, telling her how this is what I have been looking for.

"I want my life to be more than a testimony. I want my life to be a ministry."

I want God to use every part of me fully to do his work. Somewhere deep within, a new desire is beginning to burn. I have a new hunger for God; it takes me by surprise.

As I'm reading, God reveals to me three reasons he is leading me to live in Balston: (1) To be closer to my children and begin restoration of my relationships with them. To lead me closer to returning to being their mom again. (2) To lead me away from Jared. Creating distance, making the temptation to run to him more difficult and giving me the safety of being guarded by being in my parents' home. (3) God is leading me to a wilderness, pulling me away from all distractions so he can be one on one with me. He wants to be my one and only, to pour life into me, to pull me close to hear his heartbeat. Empty me of all pain. Tear me down so I can be filled with him and him alone.

When I felt God leading me to Balston, I was going, but I was going like a three-year-old—whining, kicking, screaming, pouting, fussing, even my bottom lip was turned out. And I was complaining. I was leaving the church and life group that had done so much to build me up. I was afraid. I wanted more than anything to be closer to my kids, but I was afraid that being pulled closer to where I lost myself the first time would lead me to losing myself again. God revealing to me why he was bringing me here was a blessing. Sometimes he lets us know why; sometimes, not. The important thing is even when you don't know, obey. Trust and obey.

I became excited and honored that God was choosing to lead me into the wilderness. He also revealed that I would have a year of healing, then a year of writing this book that I still thought was crazy, no, insane! I argued and told him he had the wrong girl! I followed my arguing up with, "But, hey, you are the big guy. You have never led me down the wrong path. You chose to save me, and I choose to follow you. Wherever that leads."

That evening I get to enjoy going to Josie's volleyball game. Brock had tennis practice, and when he is done, we go to dinner. Ashlynn and Josie even come back to Mom and Dad's with me to spend the night. I haven't even fully transitioned in the move, and God is already showing me blessings.

I have to work in Nashville and Casten Thursday and Friday. Having been kicked out of my sister's house, I decided to ask Jade if I can stay with her. I also want to tell her face-to-face about my DWI. I called to ask, but she had seen my arrest online. She thoroughly chewed me out, told me I could stay the night but that we needed to have a long talk.

I had been doing job searches online for some type of PTA work in Balston, any type of facility. I was coming up with nothing. Mom had been doing in-home care for the elderly for years. The man she was currently taking care of happened to be receiving therapy. Mom asked who the therapist worked for and if they were possibly hiring. He told her he believed they were looking for a PTA. Mom got the contact information from him and gave it to me.

I called the owner of the company. He said he needs a full time PTA in a place called Mountain Side, about a forty-five-minute drive from Balston. He gives me all the information about benefits, pay, etc. Asks how soon I can start. I explained that I would have to give my two weeks' notice to my current employer and that I'm in the process of moving. He says he will email me all the paperwork and set up an orientation. I left out the vital part that I'm facing a hearing in nine days to see if I will be able to receive a restricted license at all. The job being with a home-health agency, driving is extremely vital. I act on faith and move forward.

Another night offers little sleep. I'm trying to figure out the best way possible to break it to Jared that I want the divorce. He has been texting a lot more. He sent several of my favorite love songs. I send him one about saying goodbye, in an attempt to prepare his mind. I'm also dreading facing Jade. She has been my best friend for so long. I've put her through so much pain. I have the sense that she is done with me. How could I blame her? It is as if a dark cloud hangs over me, and no matter how hard I try, it refuses to release me. There is some saying about toxic people, that they are negative and energy draining. I feel like that is what I have been to her for so long. I don't want to lose her as my best friend, but I love her enough to let her go.

An hour and a half of sleep is not much supply when you are looking at a long day. I worked in two facilities, then went to our storage to look for my winter clothes. Going to our storage building brings on many unexpected feelings. Jared has done some work on separating our things. Our things, separate. Visually seeing us going back to mine and his destroys me all over again. Why is every step of this so heart-wrenching for me? Seeing him having sex with other women and placing them in demeaning positions and photographing them should create so much anger and hate inside me that this would be simple. I have had many bouts of rage, but why hasn't that stomped out every drop of love my heart ever felt for him? What is wrong with me? I'm so angry at myself for still loving him.

Christy had canceled life group last night because there is a church-wide bonfire tonight. I would love to go, but it just so happens to be at the firefighter's house that was on scene not even two weeks ago at my DWI wreck. I had found a church in Cobalt I was considering going to. Jackie had text me this morning asking if I was going to the bonfire. I told her about the firefighter and that it might be better for me not to go. She said to pray over it; she feels God has something for me at the bonfire.

When I finish rummaging through the storage unit, I go on over to Jade's. We talk for a long time. She is so angry at me for not getting my crap together. She told me Jared stopped by a few weeks ago asking her advice on how to get me back. He said he thinks if we drink together from time to time, that would satisfy my desire. Mark got all over him for encouraging me and drinking. She tells me I need to completely surrender to alcohol and God.

I agree 100 percent, and when I talk to myself and other people about it, I'm so strong and definite. Jared has mastered his skills, not just with me. I've seen him work his manipulation on so many people. He has studied me so well that he knows me better than I know me. The sooner we proceed with the divorce, the safer I will be.

During the time I spent talking to Jade, Jared had texted and called several times. I told him I was on my way to a church bonfire. One of the themes of my life seems to be finding myself at places I really don't want to be. Pulling up to the bonfire, cars and women are everywhere. I'm horrified to be there. How many saw my arrest on the Internet like Jade did? What if I run into the fireman? It is his house!

Codi, our pastor's wife, is the first person I see. I have never met her, so we visit and have a nice little conversation. Thankfully, I see Christy, my life-group leader, and it gives me comfort. Another lady from our life group joins our conversation and is sharing about her son getting a DWI. I get a big hug from Barbara and tell her what happened. She told me if I need a place to stay that she has a spare room. I told her I actually need somewhere next week!

I make my rounds visiting with several of the ladies. Alcohol comes up many times. I feel like it is following me, like a haunting or another stamp of my identification. As I go to tell Rhonda bye, another lady comes up and talks about two friends that have come to her for prayer to defeat alcohol. She says they have been praying for it to be taken away, the desire. I told her there also has to be action along with their prayer.

As I turn to leave, Tina, the fireman's wife, and the lady that lives here comes to introduce herself. She is so sweet and starts asking all kinds of questions about me. Turns out we have a lot in common. I told her I'm in the process of moving to Balston. She said she grew up in Balston and lived there until she moved here. Her husband is standing not too far behind us talking to another one of the husband's. I'm so nervous he will see me. As I am about to walk away, he looks up and sees me. We wave, and I leave.

I feel like my life is an enormous, unfixable mess. I sit in my car and cry. All the women at the bonfire, they have their lives together. I felt like an outcast trying to fit in, but my scarlet letter burns on my chest and reminds me I don't fit in. I'm a reject. My life, already a mess, is about to get messier. I'm soon to be a woman twice divorced; three DWI's on her record, possibly unable to drive for thirty months; forty and living with my parents and no job.

Swaying like a tree in a hurricane, I feel so rooted in God and chosen, clear on the path he is placing before me. One text from Jared, one sting of my scarlet letter, and all my branches sway. Some crack, break, and fall to the ground. I can't do this again. I can't crumble and lose me another time. This time has to be different. I close my eyes and recall when God reached down and touched my heart. That moment he rooted me in him. Jared, doubt, worry can make me sway; but my roots are planted on new ground, on life-giving ground. No matter how many times the hurricane blows, and I know it's coming, I must focus on where God has now rooted me—in him.

Just as I rejoice in where my roots are planted, the winds of Satan blow. I have missed calls and text from Jared. Did he completely ignore that I said I was going to a bonfire? Ugh! I'm doing my best to put him off because I want to tell him in person my decision to move and go forward with the divorce. We had already agreed to meet on Monday to talk about us.

He keeps pressing. "If you don't want to talk about fixing us when we meet on Monday, just tell me."

The day has been too much. I ignore his message and sleep.

The next morning, in my attempt to prepare him, I text, "Divorce was never what I wanted but may be best for everyone."

His response, "We could be saved if we work together."

I explain to him that our hearts need healing.

He actually agrees, then sadly adds, "Our hearts can't heal separately when half is with the other." He follows that up with several Bible verses, knowing his game well and how to play me.

I needed to stop by the camper for some more of my things. I checked his fridge to see if he had still been drinking. I see a Hooters' cup and leftovers.

"Have fun at Hooters last night?" I message in pain.

He gives one of his well-known smart-aleck remarks, "Yep! Had fried pickles. Missed you. Kent wouldn't help me eat them."

"This is part of what I have been trying to explain to you. That kind of behavior is unacceptable to me. My husband should be guarding his heart and a lot of that starts with guarding the eyes."

He responds by putting the blame on Kent and myself. "That is where Kent wanted to go. You were blowing me off, and I was irritated, so I said, why not? Maybe if you would give me anything other than ambivalence, then we could work together instead of just hurting each other."

That response gives me a clear glimpse of how he works. His "little pawn" was not responding to him last night as he desired. So that gives him justification in ignoring any and all morals and boundaries. Any slip of control gives him free access and rights to his will despite the other person's feelings. He will never accept responsibility for his actions because it is always someone else's fault.

He finishes the conservation with, "I just want you/us and don't know what to do."

It is well past too late for saving us.

*****

Knowing God revealed Celebrate Recovery as one of my purposes, I act out of obedience. I found a church in Balston that hosts one every Friday night. One of the first people I see when I walk in is my cousin, Lacey. Seeing her gives me comfort and assurance that I need to be here. They open with worship music, have a speaker, and then break into groups. I know God revealed Celebrate Recovery to me, but this doesn't feel right. The group is male and female mixed. I have the strong sense that I need to separate myself from all men at this time. Rhonda confirmed CR to me by giving me the Celebrate

Recovery Bible. I know it is supposed to be a part of my walk. I pray for God to reveal to me in what way.

Ashlynn being out with friends and Brock busy hunting, I pick Josie up after my meeting for some one-on-one time. She opens up to me about school, her friends, just life in general. I talk to her about moving in with mom and dad.

"I know it's not our own space, but I'm finally able to get closer to all of you. That has been a struggle for a while now."

She doesn't say anything, just looks at me with a soft grin. I can't imagine the pain I have put my baby through. I hope and pray that one day she will be able to remember the times when I was a good mom. God is giving me the chance to restore what I have broken. I hope she will give me the chance to be her mom again.

Moments like these that may seem simple and insignificant to a lot of people run deep in my heart. Nothing is simple to me anymore. Every moment, every breath is a gift. The girls and I cook together the next day, work on puzzles, and watch movies. Jared has been flooding me with messages, etc. I'm trying to enjoy time with my girls and am also trying to slack the communication with him. The night ends with "Good night, my love. I love you with all my heart and miss you desperately!"

I respond with, "Me too."

*****

One of the most vital parts of me moving is to get plugged in with a good church quickly. I'm so excited and hopeful to find a church that resembles NLC as closely as possible. The girls and I approach our chosen church; and the door greeter opens the door with no smile, good morning, or welcome. We walk in, obviously lost as where to go and are looking around. We find our way into the sanctuary, still looking lost but find seats. I know we are not invisible. We receive several looks and head turns. I look down at my chest fearing my scarlet *R* is blazing. Nope. It remains deeply hidden.

The worship music begins, and it's not bad. I close my eyes to connect as I often do. When they break for all the kids to go to class,

I get excited. This is it! This is when someone is going to greet us and say hello. I sit, smiling and looking for a friendly hello. Unfortunately, we appear to have some sort of plague. No one acknowledges that we are there at all. I need friendly interaction. My eyes get a little misty with my disappointment.

The sermon was good. It was about David and Goliath and about how the people put false hope in Saul.

I whispered to Ashlynn, "That is what I have been doing—putting my hope in Jared instead of God."

As the service comes to a close, I get hopeful again. Now I bet people will greet and talk to us. Sadly, we left without a single word from anyone.

While in church, I had received several messages from Jared.

"You gotta come back and take care of me. My diet has been terrible. Lucy and I don't feel good."

He knows how much I have always loved taking care of everyone. I hope he catches the past tense in my reply.

"Wish I could. I always liked taking care of you."

I'm attempting to enjoy the day with my girls. Jared keeps sending me photos and sayings, even trying to call. He asks if I will come stay with him tonight after the girls leave. I believe he is feeling his grip of owning me loosening. His control and power over me are beginning to fade, and he is getting fearful of the strength developing inside me, the strength to leave us in the past and walk forward on my own.

Maybe he felt the difference the last time we made love. Maybe he noticed my heart was no longer open to him, actually not even present at all. Maybe he was aware that for the first time, he had become my pawn, and it was only sex. He no longer owns my heart the way he used to, but I care for him. I continue trying to prepare him for our conversation tomorrow. I send him an article about sex and how it is spiritual and sacred. How powerful the consequences are when the sacred boundaries are not respected and the negativity it brings into the intimacy, destroying it. The text battle continues, and his irritation explodes as he begins sending negative responses. I don't respond, not feeding the battle any longer. Tomorrow we will face off in person.

Luckily, one of the first things I do that morning is to check my email. Natalie, heading up the Freedom Prayer, has asked all those signed up to complete a discipleship class in preparation for the one-on-one Freedom Prayer session. It happens to be tonight at seven. That is actually perfect because it gives me a reason to leave my conversation with Jared and offers protection from the temptation to stay and satisfy the call of my flesh.

My one-hour-and-forty-five-minute drive to work in Casten gives me time to reflect on many things. The company I'm hoping to work for has me set up for orientation tomorrow. I'm in desperate need of this job, but I also feel like leaving Jared is giving me a clean slate, the chance to begin again and do things the right way. I call my hopeful-to-be potential boss.

"Sir, I need to be honest with you about something. I respect your time and don't want to waste it. I don't know your hiring process or if you do background checks, but I need to let you know that I have a DWI on my record. I wanted to let you know before I take your time with the orientation tomorrow. I really need this job, but I understand if you choose to not move forward with me."

He replies so casually and somewhat surprised. "Michelle, I very much appreciative your honesty. I know that wasn't easy. You're not the first member or our team to have a DWI on record. I would like to continue forward with you in orientation."

I hope I'm good at masking my emotion in my response. "Thank you so much for the opportunity and understanding."

Tears pouring require me to pull over.

"Dear Father God, I know this is you moving in my life. I'm so humbled. All the mistakes and mess I have created, I don't deserve anything good, but you see my differently. You see me clean and claim me as your daughter. We have many more hurdles to climb. Please be with me as I lean on you as my source. Keep me on your path, no matter where that leads. In Jesus's name, Amen."

After work and before my appointment with Dr. White, I have time to stop by Camp for a workout. It is a much-needed release of stress and anxiety. In my meeting with Dr. White I tell him that I have found a job, depending on having a driver's license, and have decided to move in with my parents in Balston. He expresses concern about me leaving my church and life group. It is a concern of mine too, but I feel God is lining up all the steps leading me to Balston.

"The distance will help keep me away from Jared," I add. "I keep picturing God standing in a mansion beckoning me to come, 'This is yours,' while I have been stranded in a broken-down shack with Jared."

He says, "Michelle, you have been in more than a shack. You have been in a dungeon chained down."

Then I tell him about my plans to sit down with Jared this afternoon to tell him about my decision to move and proceed with the divorce. I'm also asking him to stop texting and calling me.

"Why do you think he would do that?" he asks.

"I think he will understand that I need healing and this is best for me."

I feel that somewhere in the middle of his insanity and deceit, that our hearts did truly connect. Our love was deep and real—at one point in time.

He warns me yet again, "I don't see him giving up that easy. Part of his disease is control."

I have had the ability to walk for forty years now, so why is each step forward difficult and scary? Facing Jared and telling him I'm walking a different direction, stepping away from us, floods me with so many emotions, especially with looking at the uncertainty of any provisions. It's terrifying to walk away from the financial support he offers and step into the unknown. Unknown provision, but the promise of peace and healing with God. No amount of financial support Jared can secure me with is worth giving up my peace again.

*****

My stomach lurches with nervousness as I approach the camper. Seeing Jared's truck there, knowing he is waiting, hoping to continue his seduction of my will and feed his hungry high, this will be one of the toughest steps that must be taken. He has been anxiously awaiting me as he opens the door before I fully approach it. I walk in, my nerves making the steps jittery, clumsy, like a two-year-old. I head straight to the bathroom, not because I need to go, but I need to try to breathe and find some composure other than a two-year-old's.

I step out and with sad eyes, look into his sad eyes.

"From the look on your face and no hug, I assume this isn't good."

We sit on the couch side by side with plenty of space between us.

"There is no other way to say this. I want the divorce. I can't be with you. I can't and never will trust you. I can't stop picturing you with those young girls. Jared, I believe you have a serious problem, more than you realize. A strange sexual addiction, and you need help. Maybe you were drawn to me to avoid fixing yourself."

"I have been reading my Bible. I want us to work on our problems together," he replies.

"Jared, I need to be fee to work on myself. God has been telling me for two years now to let you go. I haven't listened, and the consequences of my disobedience have increased. We have completely different beliefs, values, and morals. I have been putting you as my God and letting everything revolve around you. I can't work on me with you. You are a distraction. God has been calling me. It's time I listen."

"It's not what I want, but if it's what you want, okay," he says.

"It's what I need."

He gets in the floor in front of me, lays his head in my lap, and cries deeply. I cry some because I don't like seeing him cry. It's not because this is difficult. My heart knows this is right. As he is lying there with his head in my lap crying, I see a clear picture before me. I literally see God standing there, arms open as I take a bold step toward him.

He pleads for me to stay.

"I really have to leave. I have an important meeting at seven," I tell him.

"If the divorce is what you want, I will draw up papers. If we both sign, we won't have to have lawyers and go to court."

As I'm leaving, I try to think of a nice way to tell him to stop calling and texting.

As if reading my mind, he says, "Want me to stop calling and texting you?"

"Yes, that would make it much easier."

As I drive off, I look in my rearview mirror and see him standing there, watching me leave. I drive straight to church.

*****

Freedom Ministry, I couldn't be more excited that our church had introduced this program and for me at the perfect time. We had started the semester at Christy's life group with a program related and moving toward the ministry. These discipleship classes are to prepare our hearts and minds for the one-on-one Freedom Prayer session. I arrive at the church a sponge, ready and eager to soak up what I know will start my journey to freedom and healing.

In order to seek freedom, we have to go to the source of where bondage started. The speaker of the class talks about the tree of knowledge of good and evil and the tree of life. God gave Adam and Eve free reign in the garden except to eat from the tree of knowledge of good and evil. When they chose to disobey and partake in the fruit of the tree of knowledge, sin entered into the world of humanity.

This caused confusion and questioning for me. I raised my hand with the question.

"Knowing God is all powerful, why allow Adam and Eve to make the wrong choice? Why not make them obey?"

His response sits very hard on me and was life-changing on many levels.

"God gave us free will to choose. It's not love if it's not a choice. When someone is made to do something, it's not from their heart."

This was an enormous "click" moment for me. Love and obedience must be a choice to be real, true, definite, and from the heart. I can't count the many times I cried out to God to remove my desire for alcohol. He did not. I felt unworthy of God because he had the power but chose not to remove my desire. I figured like to Johnny,

Everett, and Jared, I wasn't enough. I was unwanted. Not chosen, discarded. Understanding free will and choice, I realized it was me. God was there, wanting me, but he needed me to choose him. He had already chosen me.

It wasn't until this night that I understood I had a choice. I had power because I could now choose. It also comes with responsibility, because having the choice, we also have the choice to choose wrong. I had been given freedom, but also responsibility. The lesson coincided with the events of my day. I had a choice between Jared and God. I had been trying to straddle the crevices of the canyon and hold on to both. Tonight, I boldly and definitely chose God.

The speaker also spoke about the prodigal son with such emotion and tears. Maybe at one point of his story, he faced the choice too and was also moved with the open arms acceptance back into the fold. I choked back tears as there I sat, just having made the choice and had become the prodigal daughter. At that moment, heaven was rejoicing at my return. I could feel it in my heart and spirit. The peace and joy inside was insurmountable.

Visiting with one of the ladies after the meeting, she was asking about my move to Balston. She grew up and lived there until recently. I told her I wasn't really looking forward to the area, being in the middle of nowhere and was fearful of leaving my church and support group.

She replied, "Maybe God is removing all distractions so it's just you and him."

I agreed, "This will be our bonding time and my growing time," confirming what God had told me.

On my drive back to Balston, I have so much to reflect on. The day has been very eventful. My emotions are like a roller coaster. I told Jared I'm walking away from us, I chose God. Letting go is difficult. Change is difficult, but I know I'm heading to much better things. I roll my windows down, turn my worship music up, and drive toward my wilderness with new hope and excitement.

*****

The hearing with Driver Control is a few days away. Orientation for my new job is today. The people I meet and the job sounds perfect for me. I will be able to set my own schedule, have lots of flexibility. It requires a lot of driving as I will be going from home to home assisting homebound patients back to recovery. I'm fearful of not being able to accept the position. Everything revolves around the hearing on Friday. I act on faith. One step, one issue at a time. God is clearly leading me away from Jared. I must place my trust in him for provision.

I fill out all the necessary paperwork. One includes a background check. Here I sit, looking at a job that would provide for the kids and me, but fear washes over me knowing what they will find.

"Trust, Michelle," I remind myself.

The lady doing all my paperwork asks for a copy of my driver's license. Well, that was confiscated upon my arrest. I have a piece of paper allowing me to drive until my hearing. I told her I left it another purse and will have to fax her a copy, praying I will receive one in a few days. She also needs a copy of my passport. She then takes me down, makes me a name badge and says, "Welcome to the company!"

I'm afraid to get too excited, not knowing what Friday will bring. I sit in my car before leaving.

"Dear Father God, you have shown me the path you need me to take, away from Jared. I have been so hardheaded and stubborn but have finally found you in the midst of the insanity. You have revealed to me in many ways how you have gone before me. I'm so thankful for you rescuing me. I ask that you hold me ever so tightly so that no matter what the future reveals, I keep you as my focus and trust that you know what is best for me. In Jesus's name, Amen."

I check my phone, and Jared has flooded me with text/quotes. I don't respond. It was just yesterday I told him I wanted the divorce and he said he would stop texting and calling. Before bed, he sends another dozen or so quotes and pics.

"This is who I need to be for you. I love you with all my heart and miss you desperately. Good night, my love."

Dr. White has Jared very accurately pegged. He is not going to easily relinquish his ownership of me. A battle is brewing, and I need to be prepared.

When my workday is finished, I go to storage in search of my passport. It's not in the file cabinet where it should be. I'm trying to avoid conversation with Jared, but I have to ask if he knows where my passport is. He has moved so much around I can't find anything.

My message is very basic: "Do you know where my passport is?"

He says he will check his files at work.

Luckily, it is life-group night, which always refills my soul. Instead of doing our intended lesson, we start talking about how God uses trials for purposes. The many ways God lines things up we need before we are aware of needing them. It is as though God is reaffirming to me the need to use my story for the purpose of helping others. I also feel he is revealing to me that he has gone before me and will be with me at my hearing for Driver Control.

After life group, Christy, Barbara, Jackie, and Rhonda, and I hold hands and pray over Barbara's niece Abby. She goes to the neurologist tomorrow. We also pray over my hearing. God has sent these ladies to me knowing how vital they have been and will be in my future storm.

After I return to my car, Jared has sent me a message.

"If you decide to drink, please come here so I can make sure you're safe. I will probably drink with you. I'm not encouraging you, I just want you to be safe."

What a great way to twist, manipulate, and tempt. I'm sure Satan is very pleased as Jared continues to work against me. I now look at him through the lenses of God. It becomes clearer and clearer why God has tried so hard to remove me from Jared's grip. He coated his evil with temptation catered to my specific wants. He makes them appear to be everything I ever wanted and what had been lacking in my past.

It was just last week at the bonfire Barbara offered me a place to stay as I transition. I follow her to her place as we leave life group. We stay up and talk a good while about everything life is tossing at us. She is very nervous about her niece's appointment tomorrow. We hold hands and pray over the situation before bed. I love the heart of this friend with a twist of Southern sass. She is one of a kind and a blessing to me.

*****

While at work, Jared texts me and says he didn't find my passport in his files at work. He believes he put it in an envelope in a box in storage. After work, I stop to get my portion of mail out of our post office box. Included are my arrest report, officer's accounts, and several other pages of information. I detest having to sit and read over my stupidity. Needing my passport, I decide I have to dig through storage again. My heart is still in so much pain looking at the separating of what was supposed to be forever. As if Jared's "spidey" senses were activated and sensed my weakness, he asks if I will go away with him for the weekend. Again, disregarding our entire conservation two days ago.

So my heart and body are weak. The fleshly Michelle needs touch, romance, swooning. The free spirit, adventurous me wants to escape the heartache; breathe as if I was unbroken; feel my heart beat as though it was not shattered. Everything inside me is yelling, *Yes! Michelle, run! Be selfish. Be touched. Be free if only for a weekend!* Then the less-desired voice in me speaks as I roll my eyes. "Enjoy the desires of your flesh and add chains to what God is leading you out of. Your choice."

Choice, that's right. I learned the other night that I have the right to choose. I thought God didn't want me because he was not removing certain aspects in my life. He was waiting for me to choose wholeheartedly and freely. I respond to Jared's text.

"I have plans, and remember, we are divorcing."

Thankfully, I find my passport. I cross my fingers that the hearing tomorrow will allow me a driver's license. I'm spending another night at Barbara's. Once there, I go for a run, clear my head. When I get back, Barbara's in the kitchen with her granddaughter cooking us tacos. She says her niece received a good report, and we rejoice together. Her husband comes in to pick up their granddaughter and leaves to take her home and watch all the grandkids for a little while.

Barbara shares with me that she grew up with an alcoholic father that was also abusive. She went to counseling and finally forgave him. She said it was so freeing, and they were able to reconcile. I know I need to work on forgiving Jared. My counselor pointed out that forgiving does not mean you have to reconcile. I struggled with understanding forgiveness and reconciliation, partly because Jared kept throwing verses at me about love and forgiveness. Reconciling with Jared would mean me stepping right back into the deepest depths of burning hell.

We talk about my hearing tomorrow and pray over it. I have my entire prayer task force on board too. I go on to my room for in depth prayer. I read over the arrest report, etc. I cringe at allowing myself to get into another big mess! I read scripture out loud and pray some more before drifting off to sleep.

*****

The next morning I wake up early to prepare myself for the hearing. I play my worship music and pray. My nerves are through the roof! So much is riding on this. If I'm not able to receive a restricted license, I can't take the job. I may even lose rights to my kids again. As I'm getting ready, something tells me to put all my asthma medication and the police report in my purse. It's one of those strange nudgings. Like, am I really receiving this, or is this me being nuts? I'm learning the voice of the Holy Spirit, so I do it.

I decide to leave extra early, not wanting to chance being late. As I go to leave, Barbara gives me a big hug and reminds me that our group will be praying.

"You are in God's hands, honey. I love you."

The entire drive I'm praying and listening to worship music. I get to the facility extra early. I sit in my car and pull out a scripture book Rhonda had given me. It is separated by subjects such as fear, anxiety, courage, etc. I read verses out loud as I sit waiting, trembling.

My appointment is at eight thirty. At eight o'clock, I decide to go in, to be sure I'm at the right place. I sit, continuing to pray, and read my scripture book. Right at eight thirty, a nicely dressed man, mid-fifties, steps out of his office and calls me in. My shaking is at full capacity, and I'm nearly in tears.

"Sit down, please," he says with an unpleasant look on his face. "I'm afraid I have some bad news. We have to suspend your license for thirty months because it is a second refusal. We cannot give you a restricted license. There was a new law just passed in June, actually I'm not sure you can ever have your license back."

I think all the blood drained from my body as I sat there completely dumbfounded. I can't even comprehend what all he has just said because my brain had passed out but my body was still holding me up. Thankfully, something inside me kicks in.

"Sir, this is not my second refusal. The first was thrown out."

"It's still in the system," he says.

I took the police report out of my purse. The officer's account says I took the breath test but was unable to blow hard enough. He stated I tried three times. I also show him the consent form I signed agreeing to take the test. Then I proceed to take out all five of my asthma medications that I had tossed in my purse last minute.

"Sir, I was really trying to cooperate," I said with an intense, tearful plea in my eyes as my entire future path is at stake.

He looks over everything I have just presented to him. As if he is surprising himself, he says, "Well, I really wasn't expecting that. I'm going to contest the suspension and give you a restricted license."

With all my strength, I could not have held back the tears. They began to slip out, then pour. He handed me a tissue.

I told him, "I really have been working hard to get my life together. I let some things slip me up."

"I hope you do, ma'am. You have been given another chance. I really didn't expect this today."

He fills out the proper forms and hands them to me. He also gives me a look I will never forget—one of surprise, wonderment, and hope.

Luckily, I make it to my car before the entirety of me collapses. I cry my heart out to God in thankfulness. I feel so humble and undeserving. I cry and praise for at least fifteen minutes before I'm even able to update Christy, Barbara, Rhonda, and Jackie about the amazing news. They all rejoice with me.

*****

I'm working in a different area today, and it's about a two-hour drive, so I have time to reflect. This is an absolute miracle! There is no other word for it. My license will be restricted for 2.5 years, meaning I will have a breathalyzer in my car. It will be annoying, but hello! I can drive! To wrap my head around the enormity of what happened this morning, I think how it would be if Driver Control had suspended my license. I would not be eligible for the job I was just hired for, meaning I would have to have a job I could walk to from my parents', like Walmart or a gas station. I would not be able to pick up the kids, and Everett and Lilith would most likely attempt to revoke my rights. It continues to go downhill from there. And that is when my praise gets louder! God has gifted me with favor and mercy. It amazes me that he would be that good to someone so undeserving. But God is above human understanding. He is making a way for me, and I must follow.

My thoughts are interrupted with a text from Jared.

"Did you find your passport? I'm about to fly out. I love you, baby!"

Shocking! It looked like Jared the other day when we had the conversation at the camper. I firmly told him I could not and would not stay married to him. He was even the one that asked if I wanted him to stop texting and calling. I know my yes was not mistaken for a no. Getting Jared to let go of me will be an uphill fight. Because of my love for him still, it will be extremely difficult and painful. My focus is set on God's best for me, and as unworthy and unwanted as I have felt for the past nineteen years, God sees me as a valuable treasure.

Complete change is hitting me hard like bricks knocking me upside the head. Following my work day, I go to my residence. I am beyond privileged to have a safe place to go, my parents'. It's also tough on the ego to be forty and moving back in. I start to unload my clothes and shoes and begin to organize what will now be my new room. I'm already worried, afraid I won't make any connections and will lose myself again. God revealed to me his reasons for bringing me here. I must let my faith overpower my fear, especially seeing the miracles he lined up in only the past week: the ability to drive, a new job, and a safe place to live.

Being given a second chance, who am I kidding? Way beyond a second chance, but a clean slate, the chance to do what is right, my desire is to walk in radical obedience. Knowing Celebrate Recovery was one of my revelations, I go again. I have the same sense as last time. Having the mix of male and female is not what I need at this time. They break into separate classes, but it's not fulfilling what I need. I pray that God will reveal to me the proper way he needs CR to unravel its importance in my walk with him.

It's so apparent that I am needed and meant to be here. Ashlynn comes to spend the night with me. We get to hang out in a way that was not possible only a week ago. I have put all my kids through so much. Ashlynn is shining mercy and grace on me, not even knowing it. My choosing God and walking away from Jared is already opening doors of restoration and blessings.

As much as God is rejoicing in my choices and obedience, Satan is flaring with anger. He had me for so long, but now I have turned my back to the dark and am heading to the light. As typical, he ups his game.

Jared text me at 1:07 a.m. "I need you."

*****

When I wake up, the next morning, I reminded him again that I am moving forward with the divorce.

Jared is not a man used to or one that settles for losing. He sent several pictures of us and a quote, said he would like to see me today.

I did not reply. He was burning inside as he could almost taste the toxic high brewing deep, deep inside. My resistance was only fueling his poison. He knows how good he is. He has studied people, me in particular. My challenging his skill was increasing his insanity to win.

I had plans Saturday evening with Jade and her church group. Dinner and a paint party. I was attempting to keep my Cobalt connections and also fill my kidless weekends with plans to avoid loneliness.

Jared called several times, which I ignored as God and Dr. White had repeatedly said was best. At dinner he called and left a voicemail stating his "concern" for my well-being.

Irritated, I text him, "I'm fine."

He replied, "It would be nice if you would at least respond."

"I'm out with friends, and you keep ignoring the fact that I asked you to stop calling and texting."

As if I cared in the least, he responded, "I'm out with friends too."

Probably scouting out a new conquest, I thought with my automatic eye roll.

*****

Thank God for Sundays! I'm running late so instead of looking for a friend to sit by, I slip into the back. There's a guy sitting there by himself too. During worship, he sings and raises his hands. Several times during the sermon, he says, "Amen." I'm nowhere close to being interested or ready for a man in my life. Seeing the way this man is worshiping and praising God makes me realize how badly I desire a godly man in my future. I can only imagine how spiritual and connecting that would be to experience with a man I'm in love with.

The rest of the day I shop for supplies for my upcoming ladies' wilderness weekend. I meet a friend at the gym for a workout, then go back to Jade's. Mark grills burgers, and we all enjoy dinner and conversation. It feels so good to spend time with my best friend and her family. Jade and I sit up, talk, and laugh.

SHED

Jared text at 5:00 a.m. "Miss you" and some quote.

Later, while I'm at work, he says we need to meet to swap the rental car. The company says we have had this one too long and it needs to be exchanged. Lovely! That means I'll have to see him, but I'm much stronger and don't ache for him like I did. Yes, it bothered me the other night when he was out, but hey, that is human to feel that way.

Since the car is in his name, we meet at a parking lot close to the rental place. I sit in his truck while he takes the care to swap. He is gone about twenty minutes and comes back with the same car. He says they didn't have the other ready, got mad, told them off, and left. He tells me he is going to call the manger and our insurance company to complain. He loves using his power and authority over people.

While I'm sitting in his truck, he says, "I know your birthday is coming up soon, and I would like to take you away for the weekend. Maybe go to Hot Springs, eat at our favorite German place, and hang out. I know we both love spending time together."

"I already have plans. You do know we are getting a divorce?"

"Well, maybe you don't feel it right now, but we can still have a life together."

I say with severe firmness, "Jared, I can't believe anything that comes out of your mouth. You want us to work on being together, but you still can't tell me the truth. You have only owned up to the things I have undeniable proof of what you were doing. What you do not know is that I know more. I spoke with Ellie. She finally admitted to me that you two had been sleeping together. I also have no doubts the dates on the files are correct, and you were having sex with Valerie that day at the camper. You continuing to lie to me makes me feel like a fool, and the pain throbs sharper and deeper. You want me to put it all aside although you still lie and manipulate me. Even before when we were trying to work on us in counseling, you lied to me and the counselor. Nothing will be different now. You have lied to me and cheated on me our entire marriage! Everything with you is a lie!"

He replies with no apologies in his tone, "I lied because I love you so much. If you knew the truth, we never would have gotten back together."

I am rarely speechless, but that comment left me unable to utter a syllable. Did he really just say that? Slowly and painfully, the words begin to ease their way out.

"If you really loved me and stood by me to help me like you promised, you never would have done any of that. You are so deceitful, like someone I don't even know. You're not the man I married. My Jared would never have touched another woman!"

"Michelle, I'm still the man you married. I feel like I have to be so many different people. I have been trained to put my emotions aside. One saying in the military is, 'You have got to be able to look a guy in the eyes while shaking his hand and strangling his daughter with the other behind your back.' I know I messed up, and I'm sorry. I want to do things right this time."

Now with shock and trembling, I utter the words, "You really have no idea the impact of your actions." The tears leak out of my eyes, small, clear symbols of my pain.

As if oblivious to the damage, he asks again, "Please let me take you out for your birthday. Doesn't even have to be on the weekend. I can take off work."

I imagine he feels his grip on me loosening more, increasing his panic. I look at him with disdain for the man he has become to me. "I have to go."

The twenty-minute drive to church gave me time to dry my eyes and compose myself for the discipleship class. Natalie was teaching tonight, and she was good, inspiring. She taught about spirit, soul, and body in depth and how some of our choices remove ourselves from God's umbrella (protection). She was able to speak and pray with such confidence.

After the class, I tell her how I hope to be able to speak and pray like that one day. I can't even pray out loud in front of people. I cry so much just thinking about trying. She said she used to be like that too, and it took a lot of work. I told her I had signed up for Freedom Prayer again.

"This time I'm ready. I have let go of Jared, my will, and have fully surrendered. I'm not happy about moving to Balston, but God is leading me there."

"Michelle, I was stripped of everything at one point too. For four years, I learned and grew into my purpose. Now that you have let it all go, God will start pouring into you."

Driving so much leads to thinking too much. Last night I felt so hopeful and at peace. Now on my drive to work, my conversation with Jared washes intense anger all through me. I really had not spoken to Ellie. I made that up to get him to finally admit to a sexual relationship with her. I had always known it in my gut, but having it confirmed made my head hurt, catching up with reality. All those times being around her at Lucy's events, and she would give me that look. It's all been true. All the times I had felt like such a fool, now I realize how much of one I have really been.

As if touching a hot stove, the hurt and anger burn again due to Jared's actions. The scenes will not stop trampling in my mind. How did it start? How did he take her to the bedroom? Did he look her in the eyes as he began touching her? Did he think of me at all? How could he forget what we shared? Does he have any real feelings at all?

Fueled with anger and pain, I text Ellie. I'm tired of Jared's lies and him blaming me. I told her that Jared finally confirmed to me their sexual relationship. I told her the real reason we separated was because of the files I found on his phone, one of them being of her. I'm not sure why, maybe for Lucy's sake, but I warned her, "I have left him for good and am pursuing a divorce. He will probably attempt to come after you again."

Surprisingly, she replies, "I guess I should thank you, but I have already learned my lesson. I have no intention or desire to ever get back with him. I do wish you well."

I suppose we oddly developed a mutual respect for having walked through the hell of Jared and surviving the flames.

The burn continues inside me, and again, I'm a balling mess. The truth continues to penetrate, a blazing red coal searing into my heart. I feel the need to lash out at Jared. I want him to know how painful his lies are, if he is even capable of feeling.

"I can't even explain how painful it is you having confirmed sleeping with Ellie. How could you? You looked into my eyes and flat out lied to me! Did I ever mean anything? I thought we connected on a soul level. You knew how difficult it was for me to let you in, but you pushed. Only a few months after saying your vows to me, you were sleeping with her and giving her your heart. You two had your own secret. And me, your wife, was left out of it. I felt it when having to be around her, but you love the sick little game. You have cheated your whole life. Why marry me knowing you were incapable of being faithful? Look at your past. Your lies and cheating hurt everyone that has ever loved you!"

His response only makes things worse. "I'm hurting too. I'm done arguing and discussing anything. I love you! If you need help with anything, let me know, but I am done arguing."

My meek, pleasing answer: "I'm trying to understand so I can heal."

He was professionally trained to hide his emotions. I believe they no longer exist. Love, sex, and people's hearts are only pawns in a game to him—a game he will deceive anyone to win.

*****

At our next life group, Jackie and I talk about churches. Jackie also lives several hours away and attends NLC and life group as often as possible. She said she is not fully satisfied with her church but feels God wanting her there for some purpose. I told her how afraid I was moving to Balston and leaving NLC, but God wants me in Balston.

Following life group, I go to stay with Barbara again. She sits with me in my bedroom and asks how everything is going. I told her about having to see Jared the other day and him confirming he was sleeping with Ellie.

"I feel like every step forward I take is laced with pain and peace. Transitioning from the dark to the light is threaded with so much adversity, but I know I'm going the right direction because God fills me with peace to ease the suffering. I'm going to miss NLC, but I know God needs to separate me, to heal me. I just don't want to miss out."

In her sweetest Mississippian accent I love so much, she tells me, "My momma used to tell me this all the time, and it is truth—this too shall pass." She gives me a big hug, tells me she loves me, and heads off to bed.

As though Rhonda had heard both my conversations with Jackie and Barbara, when I climb into bed, she texts me.

"Even if you are in Balston, you can watch NLC live 24-7. Don't ever feel like you are separated from us. This time is all about healing, Michelle. NLC will always be here for you. Always!"

That is the Holy Spirit in action.

*****

Lane flies in from LA for his best friend's wedding. It is always a huge blessing when I have all my kids together. Lane and I stay up late talking about all things life brings. We have always had a special bond. For a while it was just us, and even after marrying Everett, it was just us before Ashlynn was born. I have always been very open and honest with him, and he has always been a big support to me. Lane leaves early the next day for the wedding preparations.

While the kids are still sleeping, I use my time for devotional and wrapping my head around the last two months. I'm very thankful to have Mom and Dad's house to stay, but I want my own space. I'm unsure if I should buy a house or get an apartment. Getting to be around my kids is huge, but I'm afraid I won't fit in or be happy here. I know God has led me here, and I'm trying to get happy about it, but my attitude stinks. I pray, not about God changing my situation but my attitude.

In quiet stillness of my soft prayer, God gives me a verse, one very unfamiliar to me. When I turn the pages of my Bible and find the words, my heart beats with understanding.

Hosea 2:14–15, "Therefore I am now going to allure her; I will lead her into the wilderness and speak tenderly to her. There I will give her back her vineyards, and will make the Valley of Achor a door of hope. There she will respond as in the days of her youth, as in the day she came up out of Egypt."

How simply precious that God is being so tender with me. He sees the wreckage in my wake. Like he parted the Red Sea, he is cutting through the ripples of my sin to reach me. He brushes them aside as he does not define me by my past. His love is alluring me home. Tender. So tenderly he speaks to restore my soul to its youthful innocence.

I wonder if I will ever get off the roller coaster of emotions.

Saturday is full of blessings. Ashlynn and I attend Lane's best friend's wedding. That evening Ashlynn has friends over to carve pumpkins and includes Josie and me. These are precious moments that I have been missing out on. I get to pick Brock up from a school trip. We sit in the living room at Mom and Dad's puzzling and watching *Fallen*.

Sunday, we try out another church. The atmosphere seems okay, but I don't feel like I fit in. Forgive me, but the people do not seem like my type of people. How will I ever fit in here, in this town? I lift up a prayer to God.

"I know you want me here. I have so much healing, learning, and growing to do. God, please help my attitude and please help me find my place."

After church, I go pick up Brock's girlfriend, Faith. Crystal and the boys are coming for mine and Jacob's birthday lunch. We all play Guesstures. Everyone is laughing and having so much fun. Sitting on the couch, I pause to breathe in the moment, and my eyes tear up. I have only been here a short time, and God is already blessing me with more time with my kids, and they are so happy. It's like they are welcoming me back with open arms, the prodigal mom.

We talk about old times, things they did to each other as kids and laugh. We make one of our favorite snacks and watch one of their favorite childhood movies. Brock and I leave to take Faith home.

On the way back, I told him I wanted to drive by a house I have been thinking about.

"I'm not sure if I should get a house or an apartment."

"You mean you are staying here for a while?" he asks.

"I have been wanting to be closer to you guys. I finally have nothing pulling me away."

That night Jared texts me.

"I have the papers ready. I really want to see you, spend some time together. I know you are making me out to be a monster in your mind, but all I want to do is love you! I love you and miss you, baby!"

I reply, "You really don't understand how messed up the things you did are."

"I'm sorry. You're blowing it all way out of proportion."

The next morning I have an opportunity I have not had in way too long. I cook the kids breakfast, wake them up, then send them off to school. Some of the tasks that I used to dread are now special gifts. Joy begins to grow inside me at the simplest normal things.

I have an afternoon appointment in Nashville with Dr. White.

"I told Jared I want to go through with the divorce and to stop texting and calling me."

He shook his head knowing he had not.

"Jared finally confirmed to me he was having sex with Ellie, then denied he confirmed it. I don't understand?"

Dr. White answers, "It's part of his control and to minimize what he did."

"I am nowhere near wanting another relationship. But visualizing a healthy, God-centered relationship versus what I have had with Jared gives me hope and helps me to see how wrong he is for me."

"Michelle, you really need to focus on healing. It could take two years or more. If you stay with Jared there is a 90 percent chance this would continue. He is probably already talking to several women trying to line up the next one."

Sadly, I reply, "I already figured he was."

Tonight is Lane's last night, so I asked Everett if he would let the kids come for dinner. Thankfully, he says yes.

On my way home from Nashville, Brock calls and says, "Dad won't let Ashlynn drive, you will have to come get us."

In the background, I hear Everett yell, "If she wants y'all to come that bad, she can come get you!"

I told Brock that Lane and I were on our way back from Nashville, but I'm sure Papa wouldn't mind picking them up.

My dad is always so willing to help. He arrives with the kids about the same time Lane and I pull up. Mom has a delicious dinner fixed; and as usual, we all talk, laugh, and enjoy. We watch a few old videos from when Lane and Ashlynn were little and enjoy several rounds of Ping-Pong. Lane offers to drive the kids home. I'm glad they will have some one-on-one time together, but the thought of Lane pulling up to his "dad's" house saddens me. I believe they have had one conversation since the divorce, and he has never invited him to any family gatherings.

*****

The December before the final explosion of Everett and me, Lane asked if he could tell me something.

"You can always come to me with anything," was my reply.

He told me he thought he might be bisexual. It's something he has struggled with for a long time, not understanding, and not wanting to be different.

I smiled and said, "Lane, I love you. I've watched you grow up, I've always known."

"Why didn't you tell me?"

"It's not my place to define you. Only to love you as you are."

It was about a week later that Lane told Everett and the rest of the family. Everett blew a gasket. He yelled and cussed for days. As if he didn't treat Lane badly enough, it got worse. It was easy for me to add another layer of hatred toward him.

Beyond anything my kids could ever do or be is my deep, unconditional love for them. I was raised believing homosexuality is a sin. I also witnessed raising my son and having a clear, internal knowing that he was gay. Making sense of this in lining up with scripture is unclear to me. I know God is love, and he is the perfection of love. He is the definition, foundation, and creator of love. How do I define my son's homosexual making? I can't. Only God can define anyone.

Jared texts that evening and says, "You never replied about meeting to look over the papers. I really want to see you. When can we meet?"

"I have a CPR class tomorrow, plans Thursday and all weekend. Just drop them in the PO box, and I will pick them up."

That infuriated him.

"Really? You don't want to see me at all?"

I did not respond. I cannot believe nothing I say sinks in, not even a drop.

*****

Tuesday afternoon Mom takes Lane to the airport for me so I can go to my CPR class. On my way, the lady from the body shop calls. She says my Pathfinder was ready early. My deductible is $500. She said Jared ordered a fog-light kit and that would be $400. What? Why would he do that? I had been praying the Pathfinder would be ready early because my temporary license runs out in a few days. In order for my restricted license to be valid, I would have to have the breathalyzer installed. That would have been impossible without the Pathfinder! Look at God's timing! Delivering me again at just the right time. I schedule to have the breathalyzer installed Friday. Monday will be my first day at my new job.

I need to text Jared and make plans to meet tomorrow to pick up the Pathfinder. I don't want to start a conversation with him, so I ask God to take care of the details. I focus on praising God that the Pathfinder is ready early and he has lined it all up. Amazing! I have papers allowing me to get a restricted license, miracle in itself. Pathfinder ready early, breathalyzer install on Friday, getting my restricted license made immediately following, and my new job starting on Monday—that is a whole line of miracles! I continue on my drive to CPR class, blaring praise music and singing at the top of my lungs!

That night Jared sends a message saying what time he will meet me at the body shop.

He says, "I know it is only business, but I'm excited to see you. I miss you terribly!" Then he sends one of his favorite pics from our wedding.

I do not reply.

*****

I see Jared today, and I dread it. It is undeniably clear that I must walk away from him and avoid him as much as possible. It is also undeniably clear that he still affects a small portion of me that loved him before unveiling the real Jared. I'm so much stronger now, only a little over two months since leaving him. I have filled my inner being with prayer and positive spiritual books. Understanding I still have weaknesses, I prepare with reading.

I read my favorite part of Joyce Meyer's book *You Can Begin Again*. "Plan B means better. The reasons plan A did not work: God is (1) protecting you from something, (2) producing something in you, (3) preparing you for something greater, (4) teaching you that all things really are possible with God." I believe he is doing all four in and through me.

On my drive to meet Jared, I listen to the Free Indeed lesson "Wounded Warrior" about emotional healing. I relate to everything he speaks about. The last wounds he speaks of is from the spirit of control/manipulation. Jared's characteristics resemble his description with complete accuracy.

As I arrive at the body shop, Jared is already there checking over the Pathfinder. He sees me pull up and walks toward me with a look of love and longing in his eyes. We hug, and it feels so good. He tells me how beautiful I am, many times. We drive down the street to return the rental car. Walking in, he puts his hand on my back. Why does that have to feel so good? I so miss being touched. We get in the Pathfinder to drive back to the body shop. He kisses me. He tells me how much he misses our cuddling, waking up with me next to him, making love. I force myself to hold the tears back that are on the verge of busting out.

We go into the body shop to complete our payments and paperwork. When we step outside, he says he brought the papers so we can sit in the Pathfinder and go over them. Number 4, the reason for divorce, brings that burning fire up out of my gut.

It reads, "During the marriage, Defendant (me) has offered such indignities to the person of the plaintiff(him) as to render plaintiff's condition in life intolerable."

My blood is at boiling level! After I finish reading all of it, he says, "Okay?"

"No! I have a problem with number 4. You are putting all the blame on me, and this is not true."

"Michelle, we are getting a divorce because of your drinking."

I believe my head spun 365 degrees at least fifty times while smoke blazed out of my ears and nostrils! I have never spoken with such despise and grit in my voice.

"Jared, I left you because of the photos and everything I discovered. You have incessantly been begging me back, so obviously, I have not made your life intolerable! Number 4 needs to say adultery!"

"I'm not putting that!" he replies.

"Well, it's the truth!"

Again, he says, "I'm not putting that. That will open me up to all kinds of legal issues."

Confused, I ask, "Why?"

"It's illegal."

"Huh?"

"Adultery. It can get me into a lot of trouble."

"Well, it aggravates me! It's once again you minimizing and not owning up to what you did. You obviously have no idea the hurt and torment this has caused me. You want to cover it all up and have everyone think you are some amazing guy that got screwed over, leaving you looking squeaky clean. No, it's not the truth."

"I'm not putting it. We will have to both get lawyers, go to court, and fight for what? A word on a piece of paper? It will drag out for a year or more and cost us each at least $4,000."

"Okay," I respond.

"I do understand how hurt you are. It kills me. This is what I was trying to prevent, why I lied. I was trying to prevent losing the most important thing to me—you. I have nightmares at night. I wake up and miss you being there. I don't want to lose you!"

I'm sobbing now, but it's not at losing him. It's at the loss of what I thought I had. My feelings toward him are so different. I'm fine with letting go of this person beside me. I'm mourning the memories that were so special to me; but now they are tainted, contaminated, corrupted, and none of it was real. It was all an altered reality. The last three and a half years of my life were nothing but lies, insignificant events, and meaningless moments.

"I really need to go," I speak in a haze.

"Michelle, please let me take you out for your birthday." He hands me a card. "I love you so much. I remember exactly when I fell in love with you. You weren't there yet, you didn't see it, but I remember everything about it. Where we were, how you looked… well, you'll read about it in the card." He gives me a kiss. "I never know when I kiss you if it will be the last. I love you. Please think about your birthday."

Unbelievable! The level of this man's insane behavior shocks me. I drive off stunned and sick of being sucked into his madness! He is begging me to stay, but since I am demanding a divorce, he situates the papers to his liking and protection. The back and forth, up and down is keeping me at an unhealthy crazy level. I would love to cut contact with him, but there are so many things needing to be settled. I want to punch every square inch of him, scratch his skin to blood level, and kick him to his knees. At the same time, when he holds me, I get intoxicated with his fumes, and that burning flame of desire dances toward the insanity of our lost intimacy. I need to get out of this. Fast!

When I stop to eat lunch, I bring his card with me. He has a letter and photos from our wedding inside. Those photos seem like yesterday and ten years ago with all the mess we have gone through. I was beyond elated that day. I couldn't wait to marry him, I thought I would bust with so much happiness inside. Reading his letter does not evoke the emotions in me that I expected. He told me the very night he realized he was falling in love with me: when we were walking the strip in Vegas and I latched my arm around his. He tells how deep his love is for me is and how he is afraid neither one of us will ever find that again.

My feelings are a combination of opposites. I loved him deeper than anyone ever before, but I hope I never find his kind of love again. I never want to scale that level of betrayal ever, ever, ever again. I have to find my sanity. The wounds are deep and healing will be long and painful, but I'm choosing to step forward. I think about the papers and what to do. I want to ask Jade and a few close friends for advice. Mainly, I want to pray about it and see where God leads me.

*****

It's beautiful outside. I go to the gym on camp, have an amazing run, lift and shower to get ready for life group. Ugh! While I was working out, Jared text a bunch of quotes and pictures. He said he talked to Allen and he recommended someone from church for counseling. He asked if I would go. He thinks a Christian counselor would be good for us. I told him Dr. White is a Christian counselor. He replied that he never liked him and didn't think he tried saving our marriage. All I said was, "You really liked him when we first started." If anyone begins to see through Jared's lies and deception, he does his best to remove them.

Life group at Christy's is always so powerful. We continue in our Free Indeed series. We watch the video, *Wounded Warriors*, the one I listened to on my drive to meet Jared. At the end, Robert Morris asked us to close our eyes, focus on healing, let the Holy Spirit bring up a memory. My heart was full of fresh pain due to my interaction with Jared earlier. Surprisingly, the Holy Spirit cut through my focus on Jared and brought up a painful memory from years ago. It was a memory of me leaving the kids at Mom and Dad's, driving back to Cobalt to Jared. I was crying intensely for leaving them; it was always agony with no relief. God revealed to me he was reversing the process of my choices, restoring what I had messed up. He gave me deep confirmation that the road he had placed me on, into the wilderness, would lead me into healing. He also highlighted that my path to Jared only created more wounds. It was so intense and powerful!

Rhonda and I talked after we completed our study.

"You seem weighed down tonight, friend. You okay?"

I explained about my day with Jared, the card, him asking me to go away with him. "Part of me slightly considered it, but I know I can't."

She tells me, "As you lean into God, you develop discernment. You are able to see right through him now. You're seeing his lies and deception. That is a good thing. Stay strong, and if you ever need me, you know where I am."

Driving back to Balston gives me long conversations with God.

"Dear Father God, thank you for bringing me the memory I needed, although painful but confirming your path. I choose you. I trust that you have an unbelievable plan in front of me. I can't see it. I have no idea what you have in front of me, but I know you. I know it will be more amazing than anything I could have come up with on my own. I have had nudges of writing a book and visions of speaking. I'm not sure if that's from you. If it is, I can't do it. I need you to fill me strength and wisdom because I lack the capability. Please give me the ability to embrace my situation. You are sending me to almost the last place I wanted to be, but oddly is becoming exactly where I want to go because I know it's you sending me. May your will be done. In Jesus's name, Amen."

I think about the story of Peter, it has been a recurring thought the last several weeks. I know he was chosen and followed Jesus. He walked with Jesus, even on the water at one point. When taking his focus off Jesus and looking into the storm, he began to sink. When he called to Jesus for help, he held out his hand, and Jesus pulled him to safety. He denied Christ, but Jesus loved and forgave him. What I recognize most about Peter is whenever he fell, he got up and tried again.

*****

SHED

I wake up my birthday morning alone, longing to be in the arms of my husband. He sends me a Happy Birthday message and asks if he can call me later. Painfully, I ignore him and get ready for work. I'm still transitioning, so it's a long drive there and back. As I'm driving home, my phone rings. His name flashes on the screen, and out of automatic reflex, I answer.

"Happy birthday, baby! I really want to see you. Will you please spend time with me?"

I get very upset. "You just don't get it. I'm hurting."

He begs for me to spend time with him, but I repeatedly turn him down. Why does lonely on your birthday intensify the feeling? At least I get to see Ashlynn when she stops by after work.

Friday will be busy and the weekend exciting with the Wilderness Women's ministry. Monday is the start of my new job once I get everything lined out with my breathalyzer and license. While the guy installs the unit in my vehicle, I go for a run. When he is done, I'm able to get my approval from Driver Control, verifying installation and get my new restricted license made. I find a place to make copies and fax to my new job. It all lined up perfectly.

Camp is conveniently close, so I swing by to shower before I meet the girls to out into the wilderness. He must be able to sense my closeness. As I'm loading my things to leave, Jared pulls up.

"You look really cute. I really want to take you out for your birthday, spend time together."

Rolling my eyes, I say, "We're getting a divorce!"

He leans down, hugs and kisses me. "This feels so good, Michelle. I want you so badly."

It does feel good, really good. I kiss his neck as he is holding me. Breathing him in cuts my resistance with simple ease.

"We can go to the camper for a little bit," he suggests.

"I'm meeting some friends and really need to go."

He pulls me in tightly. I feel his heart beating and hear him breathe me in. I feel his poison releasing inside me, melting my heart and self-control.

"I have to leave right now," I say in desperation to slip out of his claws.

I cry as I drive away. *When will this ever get easier?* I question myself.

Thankfully, I have a weekend in the wilderness to look forward to. I meet with Alicia and Crystal, girls I met in life group, and we take off to our destination, where we will meet with the other ladies. When we stop for dinner, it just happens to be across the street from where I ate with Jared a month ago on our way to the cabin. Why is everything with him so much fun? Will visions both good and bad ever quit haunting me? I force myself to put him out of my mind.

The drive into the wilderness is giving us a glorious welcome as the sun sets on the mountains. Those delicate little gifts from God remind me of the majesty of his plans. As I shift my focus, he fills me with joy, hope, and excitement.

It's cold and dark as we arrive at the campsite. The other ladies haven't arrived yet, but we set up what we can. Due to a recent rain, we are unable to start a fire to warm up. Alicia and I huddle close in our tent. She sleeps as I read my Bible. A few hours later, the other ladies arrive. I had met most of them at the meeting I went to with Crystal.

The leader, Tori, gathers us all for introductions and announces she has paired us to tent with someone we don't know as a way of branching out and making new connections. She also has separated us into food groups, meaning the group we will cook with and split carrying supplies. It's a pretty cool idea. She leads us in prayer, then we all separate with our tent partners for the night.

Morning comes quickly after not going to sleep until midnight, but I'm facing this weekend with anticipation and excitement. There is no phone service. I'm in God's beautiful creation with godly women. Finishing breakfast and packing up camp, it's time to enter the wilderness. By the way, my backpack is about three-fourth the size of me. I'm only four feet eleven and a half, so if I tip slightly backward, it's downhill for me. Really.

Maybe half a mile into our hike, we cross a creek, which is pretty exciting and one we were prepped for. I zip off the lower section of my hiking pants and put on my creek-crossing shoes. It's a cool experience when you've never done it. Several more hours into our hike, we come upon one of the highlights of our trip: a double waterfall. I love water. It represents life to me.

Tori tells us it is TAG time, time alone with God. She instructs us to take our Bible and journals and spread out. Overlooking the waterfall, I found a tree carved out like a recliner. It fits me perfectly, like it had been waiting for my arrival. I didn't feel like writing in my journal because I had been doing that every day. I decide to read one of the Proverbs. Then I wanted to sit and listen, to hear from God. My mind was difficult to quiet. All day thoughts of Jared had found me. I miss him so. Why did he have to do those things? Why couldn't he have been faithful? I'm trying to quiet my brain chatter as images come to me.

It's dark. My head is covered in a red hood, and the cape wraps around my body. I'm running through the woods, trying to find my way out, to the light. I'm running, running forward and fast. Occasionally, I look back because I know the wolf is there, somewhere, chasing me. Trying to catch me. As I'm distracted, he pops up in front of me. Instead of running faster, I slow down. I start to lose my way. I can't find my path. Fear and confusion start blinding me.

Suddenly, someone taps my shoulder. One of the girls has come to tell me it's devotional time. I was completely in another world and didn't hear them calling. During devotional time, some of the ladies really open up, raw and real. I'm full of heavy emotion, so the tears run freely down my cheeks.

We load up to hike further on and look for a good spot to set up camp. As I'm hiking, I'm processing the vision I just received. Then God gives me clarity. Stop slowing down for Jared. When things with him arise, run faster. My head and Spirit know this 100 percent. It's my heart and flesh where the struggle lies.

Countless times I have camped in official campsite facilities. Here, I stand in the middle of a wilderness with a group of godly women, on top of a mountain, looking for a good spot to make camp. Just God, nature, and women with backpacks. We all decide the area around us would be sufficient. All tent-mates choose their own area. Josie and I get ours set up rather quickly. She is a sweetheart, and of course, I love her name.

Luckily, all of our food groups are able to get dinner cooked before the sunset. As expected, the sunset on the mountain was once again spectacular. We gather wood for a campfire, which feels amazing because it's in the thirties. Tori and one of her cohost had put together a wonderful lesson, scripture reading, and then opened for sharing.

Several ladies began sharing a variety of experiences, some very emotional. The Holy Spirit would not ease up on me. I had that feeling in my gut, the racing in my heart, and the words sitting on my tongue.

No, I don't want to be raw and vulnerable. Please let me off the hook, I said in reply to that nudging feeling. When it increased, I knew I had to choose obedience.

I love talking to people and am always very friendly, but to open up and share personal things is very hard. I can't control emotions well. So when I started speaking, I warned everyone that my wounds were flesh and the brokenness would likely pour out of my eyes, and they did.

I explained about leaving my husband a little over two months ago for infidelity. I'm moving in my with my parents, but it will be closer to my kids. I gave a quick background on that situation. I told about my fears of the move, new job—basically a new life. I shared about the pain of saying goodbye to the life I thought I had with Jared; his continuation of lies, deceit, and manipulation. Then I shared about what I had recently learned about loving God and obedience needing to be a choice. God had been revealing truth to me about Jared for two years now, but I wasn't following in obedience nor surrendering to his will. I explained how I had come to the end of myself and have now chosen God—fully, all in, 100 percent. I declared my faith in his will and path for me.

After sharing my story, several of the women were crying. One of the ladies sitting next to me said, "Your words have really spoken to me. I'm separated from my kids too and have been struggling with obedience in similar areas."

Later, she and I were able to speak privately on a deeper level. The Holy Spirit has reasons for nudging. We may or may not know or understand but are called to act.

Sunday morning, after breakfast and packing up camp, we hike to a beautiful area called Sandstone Castle. Among the enormous rock formations, on top of the mountain, we have worship. Sweet songs of praise lifted up in the middle of enjoying God's creation. Don't you know he was looking down at his daughters smiling!

It was a long, glorious, giggly hike back to our starting point. We had given our time and devotion to God this weekend. He supplied each of us with blessings, revelations, and new friendships. A smile was on every face as we concluded our wilderness trip. I still treasure those moments.

New beginnings are often difficult to appreciate because of looking back at what you had. If I was ever going to see the good things in the wilderness, I had to stop highlighting the bad, choosing to focus on the good. To be accepted as an employee for this therapy company was nothing shy of another miracle. I was given the territory of a small, musically inclined town in the hills of Tennessee, Mountain Side.

I met with Lisa, the lady doing my training, to ride along with and work beside her as she introduced me to the process. She was very sweet and patient with my learning and apprehension. Mountain Side is tucked away and scattered throughout the hills of the mountains. It's very hillbilly, surrounded with natural beauty and glorious views.

As soon as our therapy visits are completed, I drive back to Cobalt for Discipleship Class. To think, a week ago I was stressed about having a job, more so the ability to drive. Now I'm driving as part of my well-paying job.

After Discipleship Class, I ask Natalie for advice on how to hear from God about proceeding with the divorce. She suggested I write each scenario possible on paper and pray over each option.

"God will lead you," she said, adding, "Call if you need help."

Another night with my favorite Mississippi girl, Barbara, asks how everything is going. I gave her a quick as possible update on the Michelle saga.

"I really want number 4 to say adultery. I want him to have to own up to what he did, see how messed up he is. Maybe then he will get help," I say with frustration.

Knowing the details of my struggles, she answers in that sweet-as-honey accent, "Michelle, you can't fix him. It won't matter who finds out. He is sick, and he will continue to do what he does. You need to try to get some of your money back in exchange for not turning him in. Be firm and direct. When he starts his pleading, stop him and say, 'No! I'm not going to hear it!'"

She shared about her friend's daughter having a personality disorder. She has tried and tried to help, but it does no good. Dr. White has told me the same thing. He has to want to be fixed. Even if I turn him in, he will find a way around it. Barbara has helped me see this another way. Yes, God can change people, but he has no desire for that. Have I had too much pride in myself, to think that the loss of having me would be enough to make him see?

So finding out my husband has been lying and cheating our whole marriage; DWI number 3; letting go of all I had in this town, in this marriage, a few different doctor's appointments pile on two more things to my long list: two surgeries. One for bladder issues and another for skin cancer. At this point, adding a thorn to an already wilting rose does not prick so sharply. It's hard to break broken.

Laughing is not what most dermatologist hear when they say those dreaded words, "You have skin cancer." As I waited on the biopsy to test which kind, I slowly wilted in my chair. I told myself I could handle anything. Picking up the pieces of my broken heart and turning from my dreams to an unknown path was internally painful. But I did it. As I figure, the heart and brain are two of the most vital organs in the human body. If I'm able to function with damaged internal goods, the external should be manageable. Not easy, but doable. Especially now that my focus had shifted.

I released a puff of air when I was told it was basal cell carcinoma. As the doctor said, "If you're looking at skin cancer, this is the one you would rather have. It's doable to remove with no other treatments necessary."

The surgery was scheduled for early January. The red dot from the biopsy was front and center on my forehead. He said they would remove the cancer in layers until they were able to get all of it. I would be left cut open and sent down the hall to a plastic surgeon, who would then fix the opening. The bladder surgery was set for early December.

In the midst of holding these heavy loads, Jared did not ease up. He had sent roses for my birthday and was constantly sending me photos and quotes pleading for us to start over. I kept ignoring him. My focus was on proceeding forward with no more mistakes. The first and most important was to cut myself loose from Jared—in all ways: legally, mentally, and emotionally.

Gathering the divorce papers as Jared had written them up, I sat down with my pen and paper to write down the options: (1) Number 4 says we both have caused life unbearable. Him, plaintiff; me, defendant. Immediately after writing this, I have a bad feeling and cross it out. (2) Me file; him, not knowing. Me, plaintiff; him, defendant. And number 4 says adultery. He probably would not agree to sign that, and we would end up in court. (3) Me, plaintiff; him, defendant; number 4 saying we both caused life to be unbearable and for him to restore part of savings in exchange for not turning him in.

I was very confused as to which way to proceed was the right way. I was married to Everett for fifteen years, helped to build our land-leveling business and farm, but only walked away with about $115,000 and no rights to my kids. I was so wounded I just needed out. I didn't seek a lawyer because I felt unworthy of any one standing up for me. I wanted to stand up for me this time, yet I also did not want to take action out of anger by seeking revenge.

Pursuing vengeance scared me. I knew God's stance: "Vengeance is mine" (Romans 12:19). My entire system was filtering through anger and intense pain. I knew I couldn't see the answer clearly. My love for Jared remained under the layers of hurt. I didn't want to see him go down or harm his children. My heart, as wounded as it was, thinking about turning him in made me ache. Again, I just needed out, but this time, the right way.

God provided and guided the Israelites as they wandered in the wilderness. Unfortunately, they didn't obey, and their trip became longer and longer. Wandering had become exhausting for me too. Seeking more and more of him, not just ideally but actively, full force, no holds barred, hands empty, fill me with Jesus, wandering but ready to be transformed became my new attitude as I sought my promised land flowing with healing and joy.

Knowing the path before me would be full of bumps, curves, plummet to extreme lows, bounce to soaring highs, I had to keep myself tethered to God. Jackie, Rhonda, Barbara, and Christy became my life-support system, even an hour and a half away. They continued to pray and pour life into my dry, empty soul as I was beginning to learn to walk on God's path.

The opportunity before me to be unchained from my demons, wash my slate clean, and unstitch my scarlet *R* held an ocean of responsibility. To have the chance, after all the destruction in the path of my steps behind me, was humbling. It was also frightening because Michelle screws everything up, at least that was the train wreck of my past. I couldn't rely on myself to make decisions.

It was most important to step outside of myself for guidance. Looking over the ways God had boldly led me away from Jared, although it took a while to get through my hard head, it was evident he was leading me, if I let him. I could not deny how in a week's time, he opened doors for me to move, brought me a new job, and the ability to keep my license. My hunger for his way became insatiable.

In any relationship, communication is of extreme importance. Knowing prayer was my link to God and the Holy Spirit my connector, I studied about prayer and the Holy Spirit. I also wanted to understand more about who God really is, because all I had ever understood about him was pretty much scary. I saw him as somewhat mean, a cruel rule maker with no compassion, only domineering and scowling. My days were full of studying during any spare moment time offered.

Life was moving forward at last. My past was still in sight but no longer my focus. It was my jumping point. Time to call it for what it was: events that molded me but no longer define me. A point of reference, not residence. The beginning of a new beginning. The more I studied, something beautifully uncontrollable began to bloom deep, deep in the dry crevices that once screamed to be parched. The pure hope of new life was explosive.

As I drank in more of who God really is, all areas of me were given life. Feeling God save me was so intense. It was not containable. My gratitude was fierce as he replaced my scarlet *R* with redeemed and wiped the existence of rejected and replaced. He wanted me, and I wanted him.

I leaned into God to guide me in finalizing my ties to Jared. I wrote down the two plausible options for the divorce. In my studies of prayer, I had never understood this before; but now, willing to do all I could, I set myself on a prayer and fast. I decided to fast TV and devote my evenings to prayer. I also set my alarm thirty minutes earlier in the mornings to give time for devotional and prayer.

Jared presses me hard in such a strange way. He begs for me to spend time with him, then lashes out in anger.

"Please spend the weekend with me. I miss holding you all night. I will take you anywhere you want to go, I just want to hold you."

My body is starved for it all. His temptation is an enormous struggle to overcome. The old me would have jumped in eyes closed. God has been supplying me with wisdom and discernment. Jared offers a temporary satisfaction to my flesh but wounds to my soul.

"It will only make things worse," I explain.

Then he hounds me about getting together about the papers.

The papers. Doing the papers—the right way, as God sees fit—has been the focus of my prayer and fast. I have been putting Jared off because I had not been led to an answer yet. I offer up more time in seeking an answer.

One evening, as I was lying in the floor, praying myself to tears, the answer came to me. Ask for $65,000 back. It was not an audible voice. There was no vision or angel to appear. It was a thought impressed into my mind from an outer source. I knew it was not of me.

Knowing that is a large sum of money, I wanted confirmation. I wanted to be sure. I had left with $45,000. After paying some of our mutual debt and living off it, that amount was dwindling quickly. I would not make a definite move until I was 100 percent sure God was leading me. I persisted in my fast and prayer, seeking assurance.

Jared presses me again. "When can we meet to go over the papers?"

Knowing I don't need the temptation of having a weekend with him, I answer, "Maybe Sunday."

Then he starts in on me. He overloads me with photos of us, scriptures, plans of how amazing a night together would feel. I try my best to ignore it all. Inside, my desire is scorching me, and through all the hurts, the good memories find their way to add to my torture. It should be impossible for eyes to continue to produce a river of tears, but they flow and so does all the hurt.

He ends my silence when he attacks with me being at fault.

"If you loved me enough, you would try to get through this."

He will never understand.

"Loving you enough is not the issue. Trusting you is."

I'm sick missing him so much. Daily, I have to talk myself out of running back to his arms, painfully aware that it can never be.

Needing to combat the hurt, I put my phone down and pick up a book *30 Days to Becoming a Woman of Prayer*. I'm not sure which chapter to read, so I ask God to give me one. I open right up to "Live in the Freedom God Has for You." Sounds great but I'm not free yet, so much to still deal with. I glance at the first few sentences.

"Finding the freedom God has for you means separating yourself from anything that separates you from God. It means getting free of whatever holds you back from becoming all he made you to be."

It's as if God had book marked and highlighted the chapter for me!

Stuck in the middle of the duel for my heart, my soul, my life, the mistakes gaze intensely on me as I look back. The future shines ahead: blank, unknown, clean, full of potential, awaiting my footprints as I step forward. It is like standing on the edge of the canyon knowing I must jump. The breath of the wolf blows across my neck, causing each hair to stand in fear. Looking over the edge, the clean, white fog hovers over all the answers that lie beneath. The air whispers assurance softly and tenderly, familiar yet undefined. I close my eyes and soar into its majestic grasp.

"Where do my tears go, Lord? I know you catch everyone. You are near the brokenhearted and I exceed that. I feel you here, beside me. You gift me with glimpses of your touch. May it be in the sunrise, a warm smile, a beautiful purple rose, sweet words from a friend, or the rush of your Holy Spirit. I ask that you release me from pain's hold on my heart. But if that is not your will, give me the strength to endure the intensity. Bring usefulness out of my tears. Where do my tears go, Lord? Do they nourish the glorious purple rose? Give me eyes to see your hand working for my good. Amen."

Visually, I see myself pushing with all my might the enormous metal, rusty door to all things Jared. He is forcefully pushing back, cracking its opening to his darkness. He casts shadows of doubt on my freedom. Out of desperation of falling victim to his pleas, I message Jade.

"I need you. Can we spend the weekend hanging out?"

My heart beats faster as his pleas ebb the firmness on which I stand. I know I need to guard myself. Unfortunately, Jade is busy with family. Following my work day, I go to camp for a workout. I play "Set Free," another lesson on the Free Indeed series. The lesson ends with a prayer to be set free from bondage. I repeat it out loud, as instructed. A few minutes later, Ashlynn texts and asks if she could spend the weekend with me. In excitement, I tell her she has just answered two of my prayers: to fill my weekend and to receive more time with my kids.

*****

Sessions with Dr. White would soon be ending. Once I'm completely transitioned to Balston, I would not be able to continue. Health insurance would also end with my marriage to Jared. I'm facing the right direction now, but my heavy load has not eased. If he would have started any other way, I may have been able to contain it.

He asked the dreaded three words: "How are you?"

The loaded question received a barrage of answers dipped in emotion.

"I don't think I can do this," I winced. "This last week has been horrible! I'm now at my parents', and I'm trying to figure out how to proceed with the divorce, but I can't focus. I miss him so much. I want him to hold me, love me, and simply be with me. He has been texting me nonstop and sending pictures of us. I don't know how to do this without him. I miss him so much it hurts!"

"Michelle, these are all thoughts. Stop. Breathe. You need to get to the root of the thought."

I pause, close my eyes. Deep breath in, exhale. Tears respond first. Then my broken answer ripped from within.

"I'm so mad! I have to let go of all we had. I have never had anyone to do stuff with, workout together or just hold me. I'm mad at him for screwing up our chance to be together, for doing something not repairable. I'm mad that he got me to let him in. I'm mad that I let him in! I'm mad that he made me think not trusting him was all my fault. I'm mad I believed. I'm mad he made me a fool!"

Dr. White responds as I dab my tears, "Everything you are missing was built on lies. It wasn't real. Could you ever trust him?"

"No!" I clearly exclaim.

"I don't think so either. I'm all for healing marriages when I see potential, and I would tell you if I thought it was possible, but it's just not. Jared is only out for himself. He was never honest in marriage counseling, and he can't even respect you enough to leave you alone."

I have never thought of it in that manner. None of my life with him ever existed. It was all fake, pretend, nonexistent. That made me even madder at the moment. The heart I blindly gave him was real. The wounds he inflicted were immensely real. The life I was living had already crashed. Now the fact that I had lived the intimacy and passion alone in that world sunk even deeper. Him walking out unscathed while I lay broken in his wake burned me with anger.

Drowning myself in the bottle would make the inflictions numb. I could bear numbness, to cloud the reality of my life, the man formerly known as my best friend, soulmate, to enter back into my fairy tale. Moments. They would be temporary, unsatisfying moments. Entering daylight with a fog, headache, and sobering realities would smack me with disappointments. I gave him my past and present. I claim my future in God's name. I'm taking me back.

Gathering more of my brokenness, I leave Dr. White's to go straight to life group at Christy's. The drive takes me by several liquor stores. Their neon signs flash the temptation. I don't even turn my head. I know where I'm going.

The love is nearly palpable as I enter Christy's. It's a comforting, safe place. We continue the Free Indeed series by watching the video I watched earlier in the gym, *Set Free*. Christy asked us to stand, close our eyes, and say the prayer out loud. Begging for release, for freedom. In my darkness, suddenly light appears. I feel him envelope me as he lets me know he is near.

Not for lack of trying, but nothing can be put off forever, certainly not Jared. He is consistently calling and texting, asking for me to spend time with him. When I ignore him and he gets mad, he presses me for time to meet about the papers. I know God answered me. It's an assurance you feel that is difficult to find human words to explain. It really is on a level out of our scope. It just is. My fear of making another mistake is wanting more time. I want time to stew on God's answer until my peace drives out all wondering.

Ignorance acts on impulse. Jared will not let up. He demands I meet with him or he will just show up at my parents'. To soothe his demanding nature, I tell him I will meet him in a public place on Sunday after church. At first he says okay. Then hours later, to toy with me and grasp control, he tries to change the time around. Sick of his games, I stop responding. My intent is to not feed into his games. He continually attempts to interfere in my time with Ashlynn, taunting me about meeting him.

"Please understand how hard it is to see you. The photos are so fresh in my head," I tell him.

"I told you that was not me in those photos," he responds.

Now he has me boiling! "Are you trying to tell me you did not admit to me that night I came to the camper that it was you?"

"No, it wasn't me," he says.

This guy is some piece of work. He wanted to get to me, and he did.

Fuming, I tell him, "Don't mess with me! I have some undeniable proof that would knock you to your knees."

He responds with calls, texts, and, at last, a "So twelve?" message.

Anger is drilling a hole in my gut. I have never come across such a narcissistic, manipulative person. I don't know how to deal. A large portion of me is questioning all I have seen and heard. As difficult as it is, I look at the photos to once again define his deception. I replay the entire ninety- minute conversation, rewinding several parts where he clearly admits to his sexual acts. I'm lost in a swirling sea of heartache and insanity. It shocks me to revisit these facts, but I do in order to squash the doubts he targets at me. He has me so shaken on what truth is, but thankfully, God supplied me with evidence. Not so much to use against him but to use against my desire for him. The truth hurts, but it's also setting me free.

*****

Sunday morning, feeling more grounded, I tell Jared I will meet him at noon. I have alerted my girls, Rhonda, Christy, Jackie, and Barbara so they can be praying over this meeting. The hour-and-fifteen-minute drive to NLC is filled with my prayers asking God to surround me. The doors of the church open like loving arms welcoming me back.

I have prayed for many things the past few months. One of them being how to use 10 percent of the $45,000 I left with to honor God. Pastor James announced a trip to Israel would be coming up in the spring. As he was sharing information, my heart was heavy with the desire to bless someone by fully funding their trip. This someone needs to be chosen as a future influence for God. Someone that is searching for direction and needs to know God is needing them. While I was zoned out listening to the Holy Spirit, a silhouette came into view.

Coming into clarity, I identified the silhouette. Paul, a high-school student I had met on the mission trip to Haiti. I know Paul has a big heart for missions, and I assumed he would be interested in this trip. I tucked the moment into my back pocket to be prayed over and for further revelation.

I was able to see Christy, Rhonda, and Barbara before leaving church and heading into "the mouth of the lion." They prayed over me for strength and clarity. The Michelle—daughter of God, powered by prayer and the Holy Spirit—is going into this battle. Satan's version of Michelle—weak, unworthy, and forgotten—was now in her shadow. Still there, but diminishing with each purposeful action forward.

I imagine my movements forward to be like that of a baby giraffe taking his first steps. Clumsy, awkward legs attempting to navigate ground and gravity while balancing a tiny head atop a long neck. The weak, lanky legs give way time after time, but he knows he was born to run. He knows by looking at his father he has twenty-foot potential. I lean on that image as I walk into the "lion's den." I look to God and see my twenty-foot born-to-run potential.

The coffee shop I wanted to meet at was closed. Jared suggested a little Italian place we had frequented. Luckily, I was first to arrive. I'm sure I maneuvered awkwardly to a table in the back. I was sure terror and brokenhearted was echoed in my footsteps. I had to pray those thoughts away.

Why of all days is Jared wearing the face of the man I fell in love with? He approaches me and asks for a hug. He is clearly mental. I don't even feel like looking at him. I wish this was over. He begins to drip those honey-soaked words into my ears.

"Stop. We are here about divorce papers," I say as I hand them to him. "There's one part you will most likely have an issue with. I want $65,000 of my savings restored."

"So you're trying to extort money from me? That's not even me in those photos."

Thankfully, my face did not freeze in that moment.

"Jared, I'm not doing this again. You admitted to me you participated in several affairs. I'm not allowing you to take advantage of me anymore. After paying off some of our debt and living expenses, you returning $65,000 would restore my savings to what I had before the storm of you. I don't want to turn you in, but I will not be manipulated anymore."

"If I don't sign these, we will have to go to court," he states.

"I'm ready for the fight," I reply.

"Let me look over them and get back to you after the holidays," is his final statement.

*****

One afternoon I'm in my parents' kitchen finishing painting some trim. Thoughts enter my mind again about sponsoring someone for the Israel trip. The cost is $4,200. I want to give $4,500. That is God's portion he returned to me. This person needs to be one that will lead others to Christ. One that is struggling to see who God really is, like I have been. This person needs to see how real God's power is and the power he has given us. I don't want this person to know the source of my gift until afterward, if at all. I'm hoping to find a way that I can go too. I don't want a sense of awkwardness on the trip. I decide to contact the church about my decision and to ask for help choosing the person. And I pray.

When I control my thoughts by reading scripture or listening to worship music, I stay fairly positive and hopeful. My Thanksgiving is filled with family, food, and laughter. Unexpectedly, the destructive seeps in. I had blocked Jared from my Facebook, but somehow he liked an old photo of us, and I received a notification.

I went to snooping. It showed he recently became friends with Valerie. *That* Valerie. A rush of all the excruciating pains I had been packing away are dumped on my heart. A U-Haul load of them! I hesitate for all of a split second, then text him.

"I see you added Valerie as a Facebook friend. I guess the temptation just won't go away."

"Why would I not add her? Good to see you are still watching close."

"Why would you not add her? Maybe because you were having sex with her while married to me? Or maybe because she is one of the subordinates you were sleeping with while you are a superior officer?" And I go on.

Then he claims she sent him the request and he accepted because he was afraid I was harassing her. He's not sure where I'm getting my information, but there is too much coincidence, and he is concerned. This is an enormous slap in the face. I allow my anger to respond. I say a lot of things to him that are out of character for me. I go to bed mad and hurt again. He is probably scrolling through all her photos and imagining things. It's as though he is saying what he did was not wrong.

I cannot believe I let someone like him infiltrate my life. I'm so thankful I'm out of the relationship, but why do I continue to allow the pain to fester? I contact Jackie for advice to move through this.

"Let go and let God fix you. If God shuts a door, quit banging on it! Trust that whatever is behind it is not for you. You are allowing it to hurt you. Stop focusing on Jared and things that hurt. Think on people and things that bring life." She sends me verses and quotes to help redirect my focus.

The Holy Spirit woke me up early this morning. I needed to apologize to Jared for the things I had said. The idea of that bit my pride deeply. I'm learning to listen and obey, so I follow through. In the process of my text apology, as I humbly admit my wrong, I receive something unexpected. The power I had given Jared to control my emotions comes back to me.

You are not worth it, my thoughts tell him. *You will never be any different. Anyone you are with, you will continue to lie and cheat on. I'm better than that.*

The night before my bladder surgery, I stay at Jade's since she will be taking me in early. I'm so fortunate to have her here for this. At the same time, I ache to have my husband with me during this process. Jared doesn't know about my surgery. He texted me to remind me of my court date tomorrow and says he will go with me if I needed him. He also does not know that it has been postponed.

Preparing me for surgery, the anesthesiologist asks a bazillion questions. No problem, easy breezy until he gets to one.

"Any heart problems?" He has no idea how loaded that one is.

Yes. It's broken. Completely shattered. It aches and cries all the time. Like the scarecrow needs a brain, I need a new heart.

My doctor comes in to check on me and says, "Remember the biggest precaution."

"What? I'm not sure what you mean?"

"No sex."

"Yeah, that's not a problem," I respond with tears in my eyes.

"I am so sorry, I forgot you are going through a divorce." He pats my leg. "That is one of the toughest things to go through, but you will be okay. You are a beautiful woman."

I could not hold them anymore. The tears roll out of my eyes.

"I'm sorry. Do you need anything?"

Hmmmm. How about while you have me under and are fixing my bladder, you stitch this heart of mine together again? I know it will never be one piece but something closer to its original form and function would be helpful.

If only it were that easy.

One surgery down, one more to go, plus court for my third DWI and a divorce to complete. Sometimes the woods are so deep, I wonder if sunshine still exists. It must somewhere, although not on my face at this time. But people are still moving and living as if there is a reason to.

While juggling these hard situations, my prayers have continued for God to show me the right person to sponsor for the Israel trip. My current devotionals have been on Paul. The Paul from NLC had posted on his Facebook his desire to go on the Israel trip. His silhouette from that one Sunday is pressed into my mind. I'm sure he is the one.

In town for my second surgery, I stop at NLC and meet with one of the leaders to give him the $4,500 to sponsor Paul. As I'm there, he calls Paul to share the good news. He is basically speechless but, through his broken voice, expresses a deep thanks.

*****

One of my stops includes the storage unit Jared and I have. I was only planning to pick up some of my things, but front and center is a gift and notebook. Without opening either of them, my heart sinks, and tears erupt. He said he wanted to explain because I keep asking how and why. All his answers revert back to blaming me. What he fails to recognize is that no matter what another person does, we each are responsible for our own actions. This is a truth being highlighted in my learning process.

Surgery to remove my skin cancer leaves me with a cut, bandaged up, smack in the middle of my forehead. If my internal scars required the same, I would be mistaken for a mummy. Good thing they are not, because I would send thousands of humans running and screaming.

Or maybe that would be a good thing. Less of an audience to face in court. Sentencing for my DWI is the day after my surgery. Facing the consequences of stupidity is hard to walk through. I wish I could pray this out of existence. I wish there was a miracle to erase it, but it happened. I pray for the best possible results.

This is another moment I have to make a conscious decision to breathe. I'm sitting alone in the courtroom with a bandage strapped across my forehead, marking me like, yeah, this girl is not normal. She is loaded with issues. At least my scarlet *R* is not stamped boldly on it. Or is it? All the eyes peering at me make me shrink in my seat. Directly across the courtroom are the firefighters and officers that were on scene.

Momentarily, I slip into the torment of the Michelle that keeps a bungee cord to the Michelle I am becoming: "You will never be worth anything good. You will always make the wrong choice. No one can love you the way you desire. You are broken. Broken is broken." She's right. In all human aspects, she's right. But humans don't define me anymore. The hand I chose to grasp those two years ago was God's. I squeeze it now. "Help me deal with this situation, Lord."

My lawyer is back and forth with the judge and others in the courtroom. Technically, this is my third DWI. They marked both my first two as DWI one. My lawyer is able to get them to merge charges and set this as a DWI two, no jail time. Driver control is a separate entity, and my punishment follows the DWI three criteria. I'm required to do an outpatient treatment program and the interlock device is mine for thirty months.

That will be a pain to deal with, but wow! I'm so fortunate. No jail time. They counted the night I had already spent. And I'll be able to keep my job! Before I head back home, I stop by the storage unit again. I leave Jared a letter of apology. I own up to my mistakes and ask his forgiveness.

As hard as I'm trying to close doors to my past, Satan is trying harder to crack them. It feels like each step forward pulls me back three. Jared continually sends me texts, calls, and even drives to my parents' and leaves gifts on my vehicle. He has his daughter contacting Josie, he sent my kids Christmas presents, and he has gotten in touch with Jade.

A weekend I had planned with a longtime friend is canceled last minute. I was already in Cobalt. I end up spending the entire weekend with some girlfriends…and drinking. I guess the Holy Spirit alerted Rhonda what I was up to. She tried calling me Saturday night, but I ignored her.

Rhonda and Jackie ministered to me all week about repenting. God had placed a strong desire for him in my heart. I began the process of repenting. I say deep, emotional prayers and read, meditate on his word. I battle the feelings of shame and unworthiness telling me I don't deserve it. I don't. But Jesus's blood says I do.

*****

A major step forward is my Freedom Prayer session. Today is the day, and I'm ready. I need this. I so badly want to be unchained. As I'm driving to work, I'm crying and praying, "Lord, how am I going to do this? I keep seeing visions of me writing a book and speaking, but is that real or just wild thoughts?" As the words leave my lips, I look up to the sky. The clouds have a perfectly formed cross. A song comes over the radio, "Just look up, know you are loved."

Trembling, I pull over. God has just confirmed his plans to my heart. He has already accomplished so much. This is big and impossible and completely him. I finish my work day, then drive to Cobalt for my Freedom session.

A year and a half ago when I attempted Freedom Prayer, I was not ready to fully surrender. Today is different. My heart is no longer divided. I despise the fact that I continue to make mistakes, but Jesus is my source for everything now.

Andrea and I had met when I first started life group at Christy's. She was also on the Haiti mission trip. I knew she had come on board with Freedom Ministry and that she would be leading my session. I did not know, until I arrived, that Christy would be the prayer intercessor. She was the perfect choice.

Andrea told me this would be very powerful for me.

"You have some strong soul ties, and we are going to break them."

I had filled out pages of information months ago. There were questions about soul ties and inner vows. Natalie and I had worked through my childhood issues. Now the focus was Everett and Jared.

As I was saying the prayers and inner vows out loud, I stumbled over, "I will not trust/forgive myself." This one was especially difficult because I had never felt worthy of forgiveness. We moved on to the soul ties. I read the prayers, and then there were prayers where I had to insert names. I paused because I could not speak. The words were stuck in my throat, trying to make their way to audible words. The tears had no trouble finding their way out.

Here it is. I'm telling God and the spiritual realm that I do not want to be tied to Jared anymore. That broke my heart. I love him but choose to release him. I do the same with Everett and others. Andrea is crying with me.

"Sorry, I usually get teary eyed but don't cry. I can feel how powerful this is and that God really wants you to be free."

The session was emotional and intense. She told me to envision the cross and laying it all down. As I bent down and emptied myself, God said, "This is mine now." As if he was kneeling beside me, he reached over and physically removed the heavy weight holding me down. Then he softly blew his breath over me, restoring the new space with himself.

As we concluded the session, Christy said she was given two verses: Psalm 37:24 (NKJ), "Though he may stumble, he will not fall, for the Lord upholds him with his hand," and 1 Peter 1:3, "Praise be to the God and Father of our Lord Jesus Christ! In his great mercy he has given us new birth into a living hope through the resurrection of Jesus from the dead." God showed me to her as at tree. He was pouring fresh water into me, reviving me.

My second and final session was scheduled for the following week. Andrea warned me that Satan would try to steal the moments from me that had taken place. "Pray and hold them tightly."

Aware that God was trying to move me forward, I knew I had to step into stronger obedience. I had befriended the daughter of one of my patients. She was experiencing some extreme health issues. One day, while treating my patient, her daughter was laid heavily on my heart; and I was told to kneel and pray for her with her mom.

That is a simple task for most, but not me. I had never done this before. I fought the desire to ignore the instruction and just leave. After asking her permission, I kneeled and clasped her hands. My tears began to flow ahead of my words, but then they found their way. Before I knew it, beautiful, heartfelt words were being strung together, and she was crying with me.

After getting in my car to leave, I said a prayer to God, thanking him for giving me the strength to follow through. Then I asked him a question, "Why me, God?"

His reply was gentle. "I need you."

"Me? Why would you need me, God? I need you. How can I be of any need?"

"Because you have the heart."

I took many steps forward the week between my Freedom sessions. My cousin Lacey and I spent time working on the divorce papers. She mentioned a step study that was about to start. It was all women, and it was through the Celebrate Recovery Ministry. She didn't have to tell me twice. As soon as she mentioned it, I knew it was for me. Celebrate Recovery was one of the three things the Holy Spirit revealed to me while I studied "Your Beautiful Purpose" in Christy's life group.

My desire to be completely free was so strong it was bubbling inside me. I had no idea what this last session entailed. I knew God would meet me there, and my heart was ready to continue the process necessary.

Andrea and Christy met me with hugs, and they both seemed as excited as I was. Andrea led us in prayer then asked me to get very comfortable, either sitting or lying down. I chose to lie down so the only thing my body was responsible for was breathing.

"Close your eyes and take several deep breaths," Andrea instructed. "Go to a place of comfort, safety. Envision yourself there."

I took myself to the beach. The sun was perfectly warm, not hot, a tender hug from a soft, oversized sweater. A hammock lay empty waiting for me. It was a soft white, looked like a pillow against the wooden porch where it was stretched out. As I lounged into it, I could see lush green tropical trees: light greens, dark greens, and yellows. Splashed ever so perfectly were brilliant flowers, some in colors I had never seen before. A few birds soared in the air, boasting their brilliant colors. The sound of the waves deepened my comfort. As I looked across the shimmering ocean, Jesus was walking on the water toward me.

When Andrea asked me to describe where I was, I did. But I left off the Jesus part. I didn't want her to think I was utterly nuts, and I didn't want to ruin whatever she was trying to do. Then she told me to invite Jesus to where I was.

I giggled and released a few tears. I didn't have to ask him; he was eagerly seeking me. I told her he had been walking on the water toward me.

"Where is he now?"

He had taken my hand and led me to sit beside him on the steps.

"Tell Jesus how you see yourself."

"Jesus, I see myself as unworthy, incapable."

She asked me to look at Jesus and ask the truth. I didn't audibly ask. I looked into Jesus's eyes, and with an understanding between us, I asked Jesus to show me the truth of who I am. He kept my gaze as he told me, "You are worthy, capable. I accept you. You asked me to take your life and use you. You are enough. Forgive yourself."

Andrea then asked if I could identify any walls I had placed around me.

"Fear of rejection," I answered without hesitation.

"What would it look like without that wall?"

Instantly, I saw the purest of white wings flying, like freedom. There was nothing to be afraid of. Thoughts and opinions did not matter. Wrapped in his wings, I would always be safe. He would see my heart and love me no matter what. To him, I would always be enough. He looked at me as he still had my hand clasped in his. "You are my disciple."

More than hearing his words, I could feel his impassioned love for me. I relayed to Andrea the events I found myself in as best I could. This love is beyond the capacity of human words.

"Now ask Jesus to take you to God."

Holding my hand, we walked out on the ocean together and up to heaven. He introduced me, "This is your faithful servant."

There was not a designated being but an all-around presence that felt like peace.

"This is where you belong. You are on our side."

"But I don't feel capable."

"I made you. I equipped you. I love you and need you. I made you to empower."

I didn't need to question what he was telling me. His words carried power that dissipated my doubts and hushed my fears. I respond with conviction, "I love you and want to follow wherever I need to go. Whatever I need to do."

Andrea then asked me to invite the Holy Spirit. He was already present, the four of us, in a circle, holding hands. I had a fierce calmness all throughout me. She asked what the Holy Spirit was showing me about his love.

"Unconditional. It's completely unconditional and without limits."

"Ask the Holy Spirit if he has a gift for you."

He answered when I asked, but it didn't make sense. So I kept asking.

Andrea could see my confusion. "What is he giving you?"

"I don't really understand, but he keeps gifting me discernment. I don't know what that is."

"That's awesome. That is a spiritual gift. The Holy Spirit is our protector. How is he protecting you?"

At once the Holy Spirit showed me a bubble. He has a bubble encircling me. Everything in the world coming at me, he is filtering, guarding me.

She then asked me to picture Jesus-God-the Holy Spirit circling me. It was then I told her we were all already holding hands and they had made me a part of their circle. I am accepted.

During the session, Christy kept receiving images of me dressed in a white gown, glowing and beautiful. She realized it was me glowing with God's glory, becoming the bride of Christ.

Andrea didn't have to pray the enemy away. I was able to see and hear clearly. She said that has never happened in her sessions before.

Wrapping my head around the visions and words I had received was difficult to digest. I have never been the chosen one, the desired one. I was always the "extra," the third wheel or the one not included. The visions and words were more than I would have given myself; I knew they were authentic. I had been worried that God wouldn't show up or that I would be incapable of receiving. This day, not only did I see him, hear him but I felt him. There was a presence outside of myself that infiltrated me to my core. I thirsted to never be quenched, to always hunger for more.

I drove home on a definite "high," feeling validated and chosen. This was real! The new world I was stepping into held promise. I was learning to battle and stand up for myself. Little did I know the excruciating battles to come.

First thing I see when I get home are gifts from my unwanted Valentine. A dozen gorgeous red roses, chocolate-dipped strawberries, and adorable little cheesecakes. Talk about timing! I went from feeling empowered to feeling like freedom was only a "good idea."

Then I remembered what God told me: "I need you." I knew his words were genuine, and I was safe in trusting him.

*****

Valentine's Day this year fell on a Sunday. To lighten my lonely heart, I decided to attend church at NLC and have lunch with my girlfriends. As I'm getting ready, an uneasy feeling strikes me. I'm trembling and get sick to my stomach. I have a passing thought that Jared would be at church. He never goes to church. I brush it off.

He had text me early morning.

"Happy Valentine's Day, my love. Can I see you today?"

I didn't respond.

My excitement to be at church is squashed as soon as I step inside. One of my friends tells me Jared came to early service and is inside. I shrink with fear of seeing him. It has been two months that I have been detoxing from last seeing him. Before I can formulate a plan of action, he approaches me from behind. I can feel him.

He touches my arm, causing the lava to erupt in my heart. Memories of last year's Valentine's cycle through my mind. He hugs me as the lava scorches deeper into my desires to be romanced.

"Can I sit with you? I promise I won't talk." He meticulously aims his poisons at me. He knows he doesn't require words to inflict me.

"No!" I respond as I take off to find my friends.

I go straight to Rhonda's arms and break down. She grabs my arm and walks me out. I tell her about my "episode" this morning and then seeing Jared.

"That was the Holy Spirit warning you. You've got to learn to recognize him and listen. Keep following what God has shown you. Maybe you are meant to use this and be a motivational speaker."

I had not told anyone about my revelations.

69

The Freedom Ministry blooming at NLC has been adopted from a few sources. One, a church in Dallas, holds two big conferences a year called Kairos. *Kairos* means "an appointed time." I had been wanting to explore deeper into Freedom, and this conference has been on my list. During lunch, Rhonda mentions going. That's it! We decide to register and make plans. Another step into freedom.

As I leave lunch with the girls, I check my phone. Jared has flooded me with sweet messages and photos of us. He asks me to come see him. In slow-motion *Matrix* style, I picture myself walking the rope across my canyon. As I stand in the middle, part of me steps to the left, toward Jared. The other moves to the right. I can't see the destination to the right. The left catches my gaze, so I step closer. I begin to feel intrigue and warmth. My curiosity peaks, inclining me to come closer. I look down as I'm about to leap forward. The rope I am standing on disintegrates into ravenous flames.

I choose the direction away from the burning intrigue. My flesh aches the entire way home. I take advantage of the aloneness in my vehicle. With tears and power, I yell at Satan to leave me alone.

The divorce papers are complete, awaiting my signature. I'm sick to my stomach. This is an obvious step, and I must push through. I feel like a tiny speck facing a victorious giant. This path clearly leads to freedom and toward God. I thought it would be easier. As I leave the post office, I have another crumbling.

"God, I know you have guided me to this very moment, and it must be done. Why does it hurt so badly? You need me to do this, so why aren't you removing the pain? You see my tears. You see my heart attempting to function through shattered pieces. Please take away this pain and temptation."

Prayer, worship music, Bible verses—there is no relief.

"God, I'm the girl you lured into the wilderness. You led me here to speak to me, tenderly. Where are your tender words now? Why aren't you near my broken heart?"

The pain is a relentless flood. Seeking answers, I turn to Christy for advice.

"I feel you are not truly surrendering this to God. Ask him why the pain and temptation is not being removed. He has to bring up the hurt for you to face, sometimes to dig deep and really be healed."

I have done so much surrendering. What am I not understanding about true surrender? I dig deep into research. What really stuck out was Jesus's surrender. He prayed, "God, if it is in your best interest to remove this suffering, please do so. But if it fulfills your purpose, that is what I want too."

There it is. Like Christy was saying, for some reason God needs me to feel this pain. I lay on my bed and poured my heart out for answers.

"God, I'm tired of hurting. I know you want me out of this marriage, but I don't understand why you're not taking this pain away. Some days I can barely function. I miss him. I miss his touch. I miss being held. I miss all the things we used to do together, even nothing. I'm trying my hardest to do your will. I have been denying my flesh. Why can't you make it easier? If it is your will for me to suffer through this, give the strength. Please give me understanding. In Jesus's name, Amen."

I hoped for answers. Either way, my shattered heart had to press forward. I sat still to listen, but God was silent. He had no tender words to whisper to me. That hurt my heart; but I knew, deep down, he had purpose. Laying my weary head on my tear-soaked pillow, I uttered the day's final prayer: "If it be your will, remove this pain and give me understanding."

70

On my way to work the next day, a vivid scene flashed to my memory. Last night as I was sleeping, Jesus came and sat beside me on my bed. I asked him why he's not taking the pain away. Then I heard his tender words.

"If I took the pain away, it would be easy. I need you to battle this. This is when you will gain strength and learn to trust in me more. I need you to fight this temptation. It is your choice to overcome it. By choosing me over the temptation, you are showing true surrender to me. You are also showing Satan that his evil has no power over you and he is defeated. If I cannot trust you to overcome this temptation, how can I trust you with the gifts and power I want to give you?"

Then he gave me Psalm 1:1–3. I pulled over on the side of the road to look up the verses.

"Blessed is the one who does not walk in step with the wicked or stand in the way that sinners take or sit in the company of mockers, but whose delight is in the law of the Lord, and who meditates on his law day and night. That person is like a tree planted by streams of water, which yields its fruits in season and whose leaf does not wither. Whatever they do prospers."

This was not a vision. This was a memory. I remembered feeling him there. I remembered opening my eyes and seeing him, sitting beside me. I looked into his eyes as he spoke. The understanding coursed through my heart. His purpose was deeper than I imagined. He needed me to fight. Leaving the pain for me to hurdle was sucker-punching Satan. This battle went beyond my heart and into the spiritual world. This was bigger than myself.

Sitting still, I lived in the moment of last night, letting it marinate in my heart and soul. Overwhelming joy consumed every part of me. I lifted my hands and praise to God. This was a special gift. This gift is mine to cherish forever.

I could not contain the excitement. I had to tell Christy all about it. After I shared the memory and the verses Jesus spoke to me, she reminded me of the vision she had received during my freedom session. God had shown me to her as a tree, pouring his freshwater in me and reviving me. The written word had joined with Jesus speaking over me and Christy's vision. God was leaving no doubt of his hand wrapped in every aspect of my life.

Any moment I expect Jared to receive the divorce papers. I'm not sure how he will respond, but my hope is that he will finally accept that I'm completely done. His barrage of messages takes no pause. My prayers continue with force, marching toward my freedom. When I receive delivery confirmation, I hold my breath. Is this the end, or the calm before the storm?

Court is set just a few days shy of one month from today. There has been quietness for three days. The stillness before a new storm brews. His messages take on a different tone, and I catch a glimpse of a white flag. Feeling relief eases my rapid heart rate.

He says he is turning it all over to God. He is being still and listening.

"I hope God brings you back to me one day. Thank you for all you have shown me. I want to become the man I should have been all along. I think I will always miss you. Jeremiah 29:11–13."

He chose the very verses I have been standing on, repeating to myself daily. Wow, maybe change is on his horizon. I have spent two years praying over him and will continue.

The next time I visit NLC, the pastor stops to hug me and asks how I'm doing.

"I had a good visit with Jared the other day. He is really doing some soul searching."

"I hope so," I tell him.

Deep inside, I'm skeptical. Jared is all about appearance. When I get to my car to leave, he has left a gift on my hood. He weighs heavy on my thoughts. Why now? It doesn't matter as far as he and I are concerned. I have to stick with what God has shown me. The roller-coaster ride cannot continue.

Day after day, night after night, he tortures me. As soon as this divorce is final, I can block his number and bury the Jared-and-Michelle saga. I'm able to avoid replying until he tells me he and Kent went to the men's conference. He says he rededicated his life and wants to be rebaptized. I tell him I'm very proud of him and to keep it up.

Our court date is quickly approaching, and I still have not received the signed papers from Jared. I send him a message, reminding him to get them to me. He said God keeps telling him not to let me go. That remark is followed by several Bible verses on marriage. He is using my faith against me.

He is set on blowing the storm of bondage my direction.

"Please!" I plead. "Let me go. My heart and soul can take no more. Please let me be free and heal."

As though he never received my cry for freedom, he goes on about studying the Bible and fighting for us.

"God is telling me to be patient. *We* are to be together."

"I understand you feel God is telling you to be patient, but he is clearly telling me to get out."

I arrived home to something completely unexpected. Jared had retained a lawyer and filed to contest my divorce. I slid to the floor in utter weakness. This battle has gained a force beyond anything I imagined. I have been fighting so hard for so long I don't know how to muster a seed of strength. Knowing I don't have it in me, the fight, I pray. God assures me he has my back. I also reach out to my girls for prayer.

I decide to arm myself for the battle. I commit myself to fast and pray. God has 100 percent shown me his plan and led me down this path. I know that more intensely than I know my name.

My devotionals begin a new study as I begin my fast. This series is about Moses leading the Israelites out of captivity. I connect with this ancient story as I look out on my wilderness, struggling for freedom. As empty as the wilderness appears, I long to make the long, weary trek. I crave to be free and wander my wilderness. I see myself like Moses appealing to Pharaoh. "Let me go!" beams as my anthem. I'm so thankful for these stories. I'm able to see that although God has a plan, it doesn't mean the plan will be easy. Stand in faith and fight. Believe.

Each day I await the arrival of signed divorce papers. Each day I'm disappointed and tainted with his tricks. The only arrows I fire back into the battle are my prayers. I don't like the response I'm getting. God keeps showing me that I have to step up to Jared and press him.

"Dear God, please make him sign the papers. I'm afraid to press him. That's not me. But I will obey and do as you lead me."

Six days before the court date, Jared tells me he received a message that my vehicle was requiring a service.

"Let me know when you schedule to bring it in. I'll take you to lunch."

I told him the only way I would see him would be to pick up the signed divorce papers.

"I guess you have no idea what is about to happen."

"I know I miss you and I have to listen to my heart. Extortion is not your thing. Let me know when you're ready to see me. I love you!"

This is where I have to be Moses. God had shown me his plan, but now I have to stand firm, fight, and claim that plan.

"You can't force me to stay married to you. You need to get those papers to me before court on Tuesday."

Early Sunday morning, he is at it again.

"Happy Easter! Can I see you? I have some stuff for you."

His heart must be as hard as Pharaoh's. He really thinks he can treat me like a pawn in his torturous game. He doesn't hear my tears nor see the heartache he consistently causes. This is the moment God has been preparing me for. I channel all of my inner Moses to once again summons my freedom from my captor.

"You need to get the signed papers to me tonight. If you don't, I am scheduled to see the adjutant general on Post tomorrow. I have a piece of evidence that you cannot talk your way out of. Check your email." I then forward him the ninety-minute conversation that includes his confession.

This was a step I did not want to take but could not avoid. I'm literally fighting for my soul. There is no freedom with Jared in my path. I pray for God to move, and I surrender the outcome to him. I receive a calmness and assurance that it is taken care of. I'm able to enjoy Easter with my children.

Late that afternoon, Jared asks when and where we can meet. He asks, if he signs the papers, will I cancel my appointment with the general?

"If I have the signed papers tonight and you drop your contesting the divorce, I don't need to see the general. I just want my divorce."

"Meet me for dinner and I will sign the papers."

One of the last things I want to do is go through the process of turning him in. I agree to meet him and then take him to my cousin's to get the papers notarized.

I have longed for many things the past seven and a half months, mostly to find myself again. That is one thing that is entirely impossible. Who I was will never resurface. Life events have completely altered the me I used to know. Who can I become? Will I have the strength to forge a new path, a new dream?

I thought I needed answers. I thought if he explained why, then I could file the answers into releasing myself into understanding and letting go. The truth is, there are no answers with him. Truth does not exist in the same atmosphere as Jared. He sits across from me with the same lies dripping off his tongue, and for the first time, I let go. I let go of having any sense of what happened. You can't make reason out of nonsense. He is a messed-up soul that inflicts pain and disease on other souls. My eyes release tears as I look at him. All that is left is loss.

He reaches across the table to grab my hand. That electric feeling shoots through me again. He must have seen the spark because he tried to release the words of poison over me like he used to. He was unaware of who I had been altering into these months since he had last seen me. I had gained strength and immunity to his venom.

When we get to the parking lot to leave, he says he has something for me. In the back of his truck, he has a new set of tires for my Pathfinder.

"I noticed your tires were worn. I want you to be safe. This is the service I was saying you needed."

He is seriously demented.

Hours after we part that night, he sends me a long message and several love songs. What is his purpose in this? I now have the signed divorce papers in my hands.

Monday, I check with him to make sure he told his lawyer to withdraw his contest to the divorce.

"It's done," he says.

Morning found me after an endless night of tossing memories with reality. I never saw myself praying for God to guide me through a divorce. My prayer had moved from softening Jared's heart to see God to softening his heart to set me free. Coming to terms with the undeniable fact that letting go had become my new theme left a train wreck of emotions. I had to focus on one step at a time, making sure my steps were on the right path.

*****

Today was a huge, direction-changing step. Court. Divorce. Aiming myself in the direction of freedom. All the paperwork was signed and notarized. Even Jared's waiver to appear was in my hand. Knowing I would not have to face him today gave me relief. My nerves still found a way to shake me up. Knowing Jared the way I have come to, no amount of certainty with him is ever certain. This man had found his way around an iron brigade more than once.

The judge calls me forward and asks for my paperwork.

"Everything looks to be in place, but I have a statement from your husband's lawyer contesting the divorce."

"Your Honor, his lawyer was supposed to send a retraction."

"Mrs. Martin, what is your reason for divorce?"

"Repeated infidelities, Your Honor. On his account."

"I see. Mrs. Martin, your paperwork looks to be in place, but I must set this aside until I receive confirmation from your husband's lawyer. I see he signed the waiver to appear only a few days ago. I will set this for one week from today."

I feel stuck in a washing machine of torment. Will the cycle ever end? Can I ever become clean, washed new, or is my life a turbo cycle of brokenness, unending? I have missed half a day of work and am fuming.

"Breathe. It is difficult dealing with difficult people," I feel God assure me.

I notify Jared of all that took place. "Please get this taken care of."

He assures me it was all sent. "I still feel the electricity of you from the other night. It's all here if you would not walk away from it. I know you felt it too. God's end goal is for us to be together. Our love is magical. I have never felt anything so strongly. I want to talk to you about what God is telling me. I want us to pray together."

I ignore the week of messages he has filled my phone with. The day before court, I ask again if everything has been sent.

"Did you even open the file I emailed? I'm serious about this divorce having to go through."

"Couldn't open it. Unless it is you professing your love to me, it's irrelevant. Can I see you this weekend?"

"We are about to be divorced. We are two people that love each other but cannot make it work. Let me go."

"I'm trying to follow what God is putting in my heart. Divorced or not, that's you! I have trainings that are starting soon for my deployment. Please spend time with me. I think God's message to you will change, if it hasn't already."

His confidence makes me question if I have really heard God at all. Jared seems to be making positive changes. Every time I question myself, the reality of all that happened sinks into my heart. God's told me he has already revealed to me what I need to do. Keep following and do not question. He has led me this far and will not leave me.

*****

Nearly three years after becoming his wife, it's officially undone. This giant step forward, crossing the broken crevices of my bad choices, feels like destruction right now. I look down as I stand on the tightrope, scaling the cliffs. Below me, rivers of my dreams, intimacy, and love rush by, white capping as they gush toward the opposite direction I face. Sorrow washes over me. In the corner of my eye, beyond my full visibility, I see a glimpse of hope. A slight glimmer, but its light is so promising.

I need time to mourn. I need to come to terms with what happened, my part in it all and take the necessary lessons needed to avoid any future mistakes. I have to bury the dreams that will never be, pull close to God, and allow him to replace my fragmented future with his plans.

A text from Jared interrupts my focus.

"What's the verdict?"

"You're divorced. You can legally sleep around," my pain responds. It doesn't faze him.

"Spend the weekend with me. You're my soulmate, my love. I want to hold you, and I have so much to tell you."

"Please stop. I'm working the weekend anyway."

In perfect timing, the freedom conference in Dallas is the next several days. I'm traveling with Rhonda and Jackie. We will be meeting several other ladies from church. I'm in desperate need of concentrated time with Jesus. Healing is pulling me forward.

The brokenness I carry has contaminated more than just my heart. It seeps through every vein; every muscle, bone, and pore of my being. Healing seems so unattainable from the cliff on which I stand. I had come to believe I was so broken, I was unfixable, and maybe parts of me are. I still don't know. God placed something inside me, a desire to fight for more.

*****

Kairos unleashed more of my appetite for God. My brokenness flowed relentlessly. The moment I thought nothing was left, more erupted. It needed it to. I kneeled in the floor of the sanctuary and handed over load after load of unworthiness, pain, hurtful memories, negative words, dreams that were now impossible, unforgiveness, hate.

As I lay there weeping, God took me to my happy place, the beach. He showed me footprints in the sand, but there was only one set. He answered my confusion with a beautiful image. Jesus was walking on the beach. I placed my small, bare feet into his imprints. My hands lay on top of his shoulders as he led me.

The worship sessions were powerful and intense. On the last day of the conference, during the final song, God gave me another image. He showed me Jesus on the cross. He showed me the very stripe he took for me. On his left upper side. It was deep with sweat and blood releasing from its jagged edges. As he hung there bearing the pain, he looked into my eyes. His eyes did not hold sadness though. They gazed at me with love and satisfaction. He wanted to be there in my place. I sealed the encounters into my heart and memory. I knew I would need their comfort again.

The many studies I have done about Freedom Ministry gave me clarity over my misconceptions. Achieving complete emotional healing is proactive and continual. I was sufficiently warned that Satan would target my healing. He would use any means necessary to steal it. I had thought that I would ask God, he would supply, and it was mine to keep. And that is true to an extent, but it's like a gift. Someone can give you a gift; it's yours. But if you don't pick it up and use it, it's useless. I had to pick up, open, and claim my freedom gift every day.

Leaving Dallas, I felt lighter, free, and equipped. Satan noticed. Jared was hounding me, begging to meet him over the weekend. I was covering for one of the hospitals a few hours away. He asked if I would have dinner and talk. He said he wanted to explain how and why everything happened so I could release my anger and make decisions I could live with. He wanted to get a room so we could have plenty of privacy and get our feelings out.

Like I didn't know the dangers that went along with that! Another important thing I was learning was to guard myself. I had wanted answers and reasons in all of this. As badly as I had longed for that, protecting myself was vital, especially in this delicate state in which my heart and soul was currently in.

The weather was perfect for camping, so I threw all my gear into my car. I would work Saturday, camp, then work Sunday. Jared continued his plea for me to spend the night with him. He hit me with paragraphs full of love and emotion. When I told him it was not about love, it was about trust, he guilted me about forgiveness. When I told him I was working on forgiveness but needed healing, he filled me with the inability to heal because our souls were tied together.

I'm not sure why I felt I needed to be gentle after all he had put me through. I suppose that is a fault of my soft heart.

"I would love to sit and talk to you. I miss you like crazy too, and even after seeing those hurtful images, my heart still loves you. But I can't do this. I will never trust you. God is the only one that has never let me down, and I'm following him completely. I need to let him heal me. Please understand that and let me go."

His soft pleas of love turned to anger and blame. "You refuse to let our love into your soul. Last year we had agreed to put everything behind us, but you wouldn't let go. I hid things from you because I was desperate not to lose you. I'm sorry for that, but it was because I love you so much. If you loved me as much, you would see me."

"You obviously do not get it! I could feel your deception, and it crumbled me to my very core. Let me go!" I ignored the rest of the day of his messages. My brain was weary. There is no reasoning with him.

After my day was complete, I drove to the lake. The perfect campsite was waiting for me. It was on the point, water on three sides. I pitched my tent in time to catch the sunset. Off to the right was a rock bluff. I climbed on the edges of the rocks and nestled into the perfect spot. The sunset made its grand exit, with colors reflecting off the water. Pinks, yellows, purples, blues, and oranges filled the canvas before me. The cool breeze collided with the tears that raced down my cheeks. The waves splashed beneath me reminding me that I wasn't completely alone. God sang to my sorrows with the beauty he panted before my eyes. It was just the two of us sitting on the rock bluff. I could feel him near, catching my tears as he had done so many times now.

Following the sunset, I made my way back to my tent. I left off my rain cover so I could gaze at the stars as I drifted off to sleep. I picked up my phone to set my alarm for the morning. Jared had called and text.

"Please let me come hold you. I have been driving around looking for you."

A portion of me wants to tell him where I am. I'm so hungry for affection. The pain of desire torments my flesh with a potency that burns my heart. I curled into a ball trying to hold myself, searching for comfort.

"Please talk to me. At least let me know you're okay."

"I'm fine."

"I'm fine," I repeat to myself. I lay in my bed and looked up to the sky. There must have been a million stars dancing in the darkness. They didn't compare to the last night on the mountain, the last time he held me. I didn't want to ache for that moment, but I couldn't stop myself.

"I'm fine," I repeated. "God, please make me fine again."

Divorce papers were signed, filed, complete. Jared had six months to fulfill the property settlement and restore my savings. A full week following court, I allowed him to interrupt my space with text, photos, and songs he would send. I tried to ignore it, but from time to time, he would manipulate me with a Bible verse, and I would slip into his game. Remembering Dr. White's warnings, I knew what I needed to do. It was time to bolt this door shut.

I sent him a final message: "Please do not contact me anymore. I have realized I have been feeding into your chaos, your pattern. I will not allow it anymore. I'm blocking your number. You have six months to complete the property settlement agreement. You can do that by mail. I'm taking time to heal. I hope you do the same. I wish you the best and will continue to pray for you."

Then just like that, the gigantic, hefty door was bolted shut.

71

There's an emptiness, a sadness closing a door where you never thought there would be one. I have complete faith that God will carry my heart through this, although I have no idea where that leads. My heart will mourn this marriage and the future it lost. It will take time, but I know the path I'm standing on is the Lord's.

God has been sending me specialized blessings. I'm so hungry for knowledge and the spirit. I want to be so full of the Holy Spirit that it overflows into every crack that ever existed in my soul. I want people to feel and see Jesus when they cross my path.

Feeling as a portion of my past had been lifted, I sought hard after God. I wanted to run forward, further from my past. My passion for nature and hiking increased. It was a way for me to step away from the world and closer to heaven. I hiked along a crisp, flowing creek and found my way to a waterfall.

"Please, God, move me forward in the purpose you have for me. I feel like I'm not moving. I'm not doing enough."

"Baby steps," I feel him say. "You are taking small steps to lead to the bigger ones."

I pray for knowledge and wisdom. There is so much to learn. I feel as though I'm missing something.

When I get home, I skim through different verses and resources when I find something that resonates. It is about being obedient with tithing. My tithing has been lacking lately, and it had been weighing on me. It was clear I needed to correct this behavior. Then one of my books fell open to "Hearing God's Voice," which was my purpose for looking for something to read. God needed to address my neglect of tithing, then he allowed me to dive into what I was looking for.

The idea of writing a book and speaking has been a thought for a while, but is it God's will? Don't forget it's me. I'm stubborn, hardheaded.

"God, I feel you are showing me this as my purpose, but what about me not being equipped? The purpose I'm envisioning is not me."

In this chapter I have been led to read, one of the points is "Is what I am hearing beyond me?" The author expressed the same feelings I was holding on to. Now here she is, author of many best-selling books.

The next day at the gym, cardio day, ugh! I take advantage of time and listen to a podcast. The woman speaking was talking about writing her first book as her marriage was falling apart. She also has four kids, two boys, two girls. She is an author of several books and a speaker now too. Confirmation overload!

"Lord, I trust you with every fiber of my being. I'm not capable. I don't see how. I don't have the words. I don't have the confidence. I can't. But I trust you. I have been studying your character and faithfulness. You can. I love that you have called me. I'm under qualified, a misfit, a mess, a failure. But my heart, God, you see my heart. And it is yours. I am becoming less so you can become more. I have put away my desires and have replaced them with your desires. I have no idea how to make this happen. Guide me in every step. Open doors. Send opportunities. I pray my heart and mind to be open to your nudging and your will. Let me recognize your voice and answer in complete obedience."

Remember the three purposes the Holy Spirit revealed to me in my life group study? (1) Mission work, (2) Celebrate Recovery, and (3) through me, Jared would see God. My faith was certain these would all come to pass in some manner. I tried so very hard to show Jared who God really is. I had to believe the future held that event. I know the revelations were not of myself. I had to do my part and surrender the rest.

Celebrate Recovery women's step study meets once a week. We had four workbooks of in-depth healing to dig through. Aside from my cousin, I didn't know any of the women or the issues they were dealing with. I hoped to find some other poor soul struggling with alcohol so we could struggle together. Our first meeting was very emotional. I know God had placed me in this group on purpose. These women were an oasis for me in my wilderness. They were all openly bearing scars and willing to be vulnerable. My heart needed to see brokenness other than my own.

These women were dealing with demons of different categories. One lady, about my age, shared my struggle. I instantly felt connected to her. How many bottles had she hidden in her home? How many mornings did she awaken with no recollection of the previous night? How often did alcohol beckon her to sip its poison and numb her pain? For the first time, I didn't feel completely abnormal. She could walk with me through my canyon. Her footprints were probably already beside mine. My desolate desert did not feel so empty.

The collection of things I did not know far outweighed the things I did know. But I could do nothing about them. I could not waste my energy on the unknown. I had off and on doubts about the book God was calling me to write. I knew I had to focus on inner healing before I could be effective in his kingdom.

I didn't allow myself to date. I actually didn't want to. This wilderness God had lured me to began to give me comfort. Except for work, church, kids' activities, and the gym, I secluded myself. I could feel God sloughing off the broken pieces of my heart. The more he revived me, the more I craved him. I was falling in love with the Lord, and nothing before had ever compared.

All was quiet on the Jared front until Mother's Day. He sent me a dozen red roses. The card read, "We love and miss you." It didn't faze me.

About a week later, Kent text just to see how I was. I told him I was fine and I needed to pick up my jet skis. He said Jared was in Guatemala for training and he could help me hook them up. That was distance I felt safe with. I coordinated a day and time with Kent.

My jet skis were the final pieces of my property I had merged with Jared. I had been afraid to pick them up knowing Jared's skill to climb my walls. I had been invited to a meeting with the Freedom ministry leaders. My plan was to get my skis, then attend the meeting.

Kent and his girlfriend stepped out of the camper as I arrived. Kent began to attempt hooking up my skis. He was having a little trouble. Out of nowhere, Jared walks up. My mouth dropped open, and all the blood drained out of my body. I had been here all of five minutes. Obviously, I was purposefully blindsided. Jared is shaking, breathing hard.

"I thought you were in Guatemala?" I say, puzzled. "Looks like you have been at the gym."

"I got back this morning. Went to the airfield and gym. You look beautiful," he says as he steps in and reaches for me.

I step back. This was the last thing I expected today. Every time I think I'm safe, he pops up. He tells me he's not able to get my lights to work. I had spent the day before having my towing package installed, seems strange.

"Come in, I need to change shirts."

"I don't have much time, I need to get to a meeting."

"Michelle, I'm miserable. I wake up every night crying for you, missing you. I'm afraid I will never find this again."

I pray I never find this again. I pray my heart holds the stitches together as it pounds, beating for life. He touches me. I flinch. The burn rushing through me is a different kind of sting than it used to be. This is the burn of danger, no longer the melting it had been.

"I need to go. I have a meeting at church."

He tries again to get the skis connected, but the lights still don't work.

"I will just drive them to my sister's and park them."

"Michelle, what if I don't make it back from Iraq?"

"So I'm just supposed to be with you because you might not make it back? What if you do? Then I'm stuck living in misery again?"

"What about forgiveness? What if this is your last chance to forgive me?"

"Jared, I've already forgiven you. That doesn't mean I can trust you. Those are two completely separate things. Now I need to go. I'm late."

"Can you come back after the meeting?"

"I'm never coming back, Jared."

I walk into church thirty minutes late for the meeting. Everyone has already eaten, which is fine. My churning stomach couldn't tolerate food anyway. I see so many familiar faces and get hugs. Christy opens the meeting speaking about the effects of the Freedom Ministry they have already seen. Two couples come forward and share their testimony. She asks if anyone else would like to share as she glances at me. I had been crying throughout the meeting. I could relate with the stories that had been shared. Freedom has unquestionably changed my life.

My brokenness is so raw, I know I would not be able to speak effectively. Not now. I'm not ready. After the meeting, Christy said she nearly handed me the mic. I told her God was leading me to share my story but I'm not ready yet. I don't know how. It's such a big story, and he is leading me into sharing, little by little.

"Obey him in the little steps, and he will lead you into the big ones. Who knows, maybe one day you will speak at our very own Kairos."

Getting ready to leave, I had several messages from Kent.

"Please meet Dad and I for dinner. It was so good to see you today, but it wasn't long enough. Dad really wants to see you too."

"I'm sorry, Kent. I can't. It's not a good idea."

Jared knew how to sting my heart. I absolutely could not risk slipping back into his games.

God doesn't want only pieces of us to be whole, but the entirety of us to be whole. The church I attended was offering Financial Peace University. Now that I was truly single, I needed to organize and control my finances. It was time to be responsible. And that scared me to death! Balancing a checkbook, budgeting—the very thought creeped me out. I enjoyed being a free spirit and wasn't sure I could get a grip on any financial mumbo jumbo.

In the six months I have lived with my parents, God's restoration has flowed like the streams of water I enjoyed sitting close by. Breathing in the fresh air and allowing the trickling sound of water to soothe my aching soul. Ashlynn had been staying with me about half the week. I felt more like the mom to her I had been before my undoing. Josie and Brock had school activities that I could now be a part of. I was working through the financial course and getting on my feet.

My studies on healing continued to highlight forgiveness. I had worked so hard to forgive Jared. My understanding of forgiveness shifted. No longer did I see forgiveness as accepting the behavior as okay, rather handing it to God and saying, "This was wrong. This hurt, but I release it to you for you to bring vengeance against my enemy." I prayed out loud for me to continue to forgive Jared.

Forgiveness continued to press on my heart. Not understanding why it was so heavy, I prayed over it. It was then that the Holy Spirit revealed to me that I was harboring hurt, anger, and unforgiveness toward Everett. He had never acknowledged any wrongdoing toward me. Did the night in St. Martin when he forced himself on me ever cross his mind? Had he blotted it out with White Out like that moment and the other times never existed? They remained cut into my soul. Not ever receiving an apology from him gave me justice in my anger.

I was born of the Holy Spirit now. I'm no longer held to the standards of this world. Despite Everett's lack of acknowledging his wrong actions, I have been called to live in righteous indignation. His inadequacy to do the right thing did not excuse me nor make my wrong behaviors right. Forgiveness does not have to be asked for, but given.

After wrestling with this revelation for several days, I knew what I needed to do. This was one of the most difficult steps in my Freedom walk. I cried and prayed, then picked up the phone. I prayed he would not answer, but that would only delay the action I needed to take. My voice trembled even before the words found their way to my lips.

I told him I was sorry for my actions toward the end of our marriage. I didn't put any responsibility on him for my drinking. I asked that he would forgive my poor choices. Memories of him holding me down, squeezing my arms, pushing me toward the ground, hateful words—all cycled through my head. I could not hold them against him any longer. I was called to forgive.

My tears burned as they poured out of my eyes. I never saw this day coming, the day I would apologize to the person I held responsible for destroying the me I had been. The person that created the monster I had become. But that is what God does. He reveals to us what needs to be done, for our good, not what feels good to our flesh. This was soul healing.

A tiny part of me expected him to soften and own up to his actions against me or at least give appreciation for my words. That was a misplaced desire of my forgiveness. This had nothing to do with him. This was my obedience to God. This was like the forgiveness we each receive from him. Not deserved but freely given. I had to release ownership on deserving forgiveness from him in order to give forgiveness to him. The rest is between his heart and the Lord.

Hanging up the phone, I released my disappointments to heaven. In return, I received whispers of the only approval that has any profound eternal effect. God had strengthened me to humble myself to my offender. He allowed me to lessen the importance of my anger on rights declared by the world's standards. The picture was bigger than the confounds of this earth. I gained a portion of heaven's peace as I unloaded another heavy burden.

*****

Another two months of no Jared had come to pass. I grew stronger and freer. God's revelation of writing continued to press on my heart. So did the doubt of my ability to do so. On the last day of June, I sat down to write because I did not want to write. I set out to prove God wrong. I prayed and offered up to the Lord my time.

"If this is your will, Lord, fill me with your Holy Spirit. Guide my thoughts, words, and ability."

SHED

I'm not a writer. Thoughts flowed in and out of my mind. If this was ever going to be, I had to trust. I started putting the thoughts down line by line. I didn't know where to start telling my story, but God did. He started the story in the middle and worked backward. Clever. I never would've thought of that. After hours of applying my focus, there existed a few pages of *Shed*.

On July 2, I received an email from Jared. He would be leaving in a few days for his assignment in Iraq. He asked if we could meet for dinner. He was fearful he may never return. I wanted him to know I had fully forgiven him before he was to leave. I also needed to ask him to completely give me up. No more flowers, gifts, emails. This goodbye was to be sealed in concrete.

I had been immovable in my stance against Jared. I had blocked his number. I didn't reply to his emails. But what I had been doing was reading his emails numerous times. I played the songs repeatedly that he had sent. When he left gifts on my car, my heart thundered with satisfaction. I was holding on to the fact that he was still holding on to me. It took the sting out of being rejected again. I was allowing him to give me the feeling of being wanted, a task that only belonged to God.

This dinner was not for his benefit. I needed to let go of giving him this little inkling of power over me. The spirit had been heavily warning me to stay away from him, but not this time. He knew this was something I needed. Another step into freedom and a reclaiming of the power I had given to him.

The entire way to meet him, I prayed for protection. I also prayed for me to let go of wanting him to hold on to a piece of me. Walking deeper into freedom was stretching the scope of abilities I had limited myself to. I had to relinquish my thirst to be wanted by a man in order to give God full capacity of my longing. I set like stone on that.

My nerves were not vibrating under my skin like the last time I saw him. My steps walking away had increased my strength. When I approached him, he opened his arms for a hug. I responded with a light, quick one, then stepped back. Casual conservation flowed gently between us. My request waiting for the right time.

When we were both finished with our meals, he slipped around the table, sat beside me, and placed his hand on my leg.

"Michelle, please give us another chance. I leave in a few days, and I need to know I have you to come back to."

Obviously, our agendas greatly differed. My intention was complete closure. His was the exact opposite.

I needed to request out loud to him to let me go, for me to free his heart. My ears needed to hear me speak this untying of our souls into the universe. Thinking it was not profound enough, I no longer cared what his intentions were. I had been free of that bondage. This was a call for freedom of the bondage I had carried on his needing me.

Freedom has layers. Looking over the canyon of myself, I could see them clearly. I couldn't see the layers underneath the pain in which I stood. I could only see the layers as I looked back from the path I had traveled. I had to keep God close to guide me in chiseling the surfaces I had built up. He always took me on the path I least expected. He saw crooks and crannies that were invisible to me but produced the most mesmerizing levels. I had no doubt it was him leading me. I was incapable of discovering the views he found.

His plea no longer pulled on my heartstrings.

"Jared, we are not husband and wife. I owe you nothing. I decided to meet you for dinner in order to free myself. I forgive you. The pain will take time and more intense effort on my part. I'm committed to that. I'm not proud of my actions during our marriage, and I ask that you forgive me. I need you to do stop sending me gifts. There will never be anything between us—of that, I'm certain. I release you fully. Please release me."

We walked outside. It was a warm summer night, and the sky held its sparkling stars above us. He walked me to my car. I didn't know if this would be the last time I would breathe the same air as he. I hoped as much. We hugged. He tried to pull me back in as I released him. I was now immune to the toxic poison he had so easily infected within me.

I drove off, windows down, the breeze of freedom blowing in and swirling around me. Eleven months ago I drove away from us with tears so heavy I wasn't sure where I was going. In all aspects. I didn't know if my heart would be able to continue beating, and honestly, I willed it to stop. I wanted the safety of my darkness, whether it was created by the lack of oxygen or the erasing effects of alcohol. I never thought I could bear the strength it took to move toward the light. And trust me, it took strength. The past eleven months were the most difficult I had endured to this date. The most painful and oddly rewarding.

The day the Holy Spirit crumbled me was a moment of beautiful destruction. I imagine that day to be the day he wrapped me in a cocoon. He knew it was necessary to suffocate the me that had been wandering aimlessly upon this earth. He had to squeeze out all my negative beliefs and behaviors. I can just see myself: swaddled, fighting, struggling to be released. Breaking the bad was too painful. But he knew who I was. He knew who I was created to be because he knew the creator. So despite my fighting to be released, he held. He squeezed. He pressed out the bad. He spoke softly and gently to my wounded soul. Then at just the right time, he released a beautiful little butterfly. She had now become a creature that modeled beauty and reflected light. She had to be immersed into the dark cocoon, sheltered and pressed, in order to be reborn. When she came out of that cocoon, she didn't slip out. She didn't roll out. She flew.

Feeling the effects of healing and freedom, I knew it was now time to focus on the project God had revealed to me. I still wasn't fully convinced he had the right girl. I knew my ability was lacking. But my gratitude ran deep. He had led me so greatly that it was difficult to argue with his revelation.

Wouldn't it be great if I told you that it was all smooth sailing from this point on? I would love to. I wish I could, but that was not my reality. You see, Satan had tried to trip me up with Jared, with alcohol, with so many things. This time it was my loneliness, my rejection. When you feel rejected and unwanted, you have the desire to feel special and needed. Satan knew that all too well.

Several men began to approach me, and that felt really satisfying. God had gifted me with discernment though. I was not the old Michelle. I was a new creature with new standards. I was by no means perfect, but I desired God's perfection for my life. That meant holding myself to a higher standard than I had previously devalued myself of holding. I was quick to realize when someone would challenge me being able to hold those standards.

Everett had presented challenge after challenge and didn't let up. My apology and new walk meant nothing to him. He constantly stepped in when it was my scheduled time with the kids. He would make plans with them but tell them they had to ask me. So when I said, "No, it's my time with you," I was made to look selfish.

One particular weekend stands out. I had made plans with the kids to go to church in Cobalt. Brock asked if his girlfriend could come, so I made plans with her dad. She would spend the night, sleep in bed with me, and we'd all get up early to go to church. Everett got wind of our plans, called her dad, and canceled them. When we met that evening to exchange the kids, I pulled up and rolled down my window. He gave me a nasty look and motioned me to get out and talk.

Ohhh, I dreaded it. The same feelings came over me from when we were married. He was not good at talking. He yelled and barked orders. As soon as I stepped out of my car, he started in. I couldn't believe he still thought it was okay to treat me like this. My stomach lurched. So much of the hatred I had for him burned inside me. He attacked my new Christian attitude. I stood there calmly holding my tongue.

He finished off the conversation with something I will never forget.

"You know a few months ago when you called and apologized to me?"

"Yes, I meant every word."

Then at the top of his voice, pointing his finger at me, anger scorching his eyes, he said, "I WILL NEVER FORGIVE YOU!"

I gulped. Then with a restraint and gentle voice, I said, "That's between you and God." I turned to walk to my vehicle.

When I got in and closed the door, I realized my window was still down. Brock was sitting in the passenger seat, crying. Josie in the back, quiet and still. I released a puff of air.

"I'm so sorry you both heard that." I put my hand on Brock's leg. "Is there anything you want to say or ask me?"

"No," he sobbed.

I'm not sure what realizations came to him in those moments. Maybe the picture he carried of his dad was altered in those words. Maybe some repressed memories of the way he treated me were highlighted with truth. I was so very thankful that the Holy Spirit gave me restraint on my tongue. In that moment, a deep understanding settled in. The importance of my character when I thought no one was listening spoke volumes to who I really am. And someone is always listening.

So here I am, declared free, yet still battling loneliness and rejection. I tried to focus on writing. Not convinced it was my purpose, my commitment was lacking. I only dabbled.

The last week of summer, Everett pushed too hard. This time, instead of falling, I stood up for myself. We were supposed to share summers. The kids with me a week; him, a week. Friday to Friday. This particular week, on Monday night, Everett called Brock and told him and Josie to come home.

They were packing up their things to leave when I said, "No. You are here until Friday."

They responded with, "Dad said."

Everett had never given me respect in our marriage, and it was continuing but also being impressed upon my kids. After calming down, I called him. The first thing I asked was that we speak as adults. Many previous phone conversations ended in him yelling and cussing at me. I told him it was in the schedule that the kids are to be with me until Friday and he was not supposed to interfere with that. His response was that they had things they needed to do. Well, the kids and I had plans too. He didn't care. He said they're not coming back and that's that. Then he started yelling at me over things that happened in the past and things that were none of his business. He was attacking the old me and the new me.

It was boldly evident that no matter my words or actions, he would continue to disrespect and manipulate my time. I was tired of it and ready to take stronger action against him. I had already lost enough time with my kids. I hired a lawyer to pursue contempt charges against him. I had plenty of proof to back it all up. A court date was set for December.

Pages on the calendar turned. The September deadline for Jared came and went with no response. Last I heard he was serving in Iraq. I had hoped he would take care of this before leaving. The date was specified in our papers. Because he was serving our country, I didn't pursue anything.

My concentration continued to be directed on freedom. The step study with Celebrate Recovery was helping me shed layers of hurt. I still felt like a baby discovering the power of the Holy Spirit. With thoughts of *Shed* encompassing an ever-present space in my mind, I wanted to run the thought by Rhonda and Christy.

I wanted them to tell me it was way out of my scope and I was far from equipped. I needed them to tell me that they had seen my brokenness spill out all over Christy's living room multiple times and I was a far cry from usable in anything important to God's kingdom. I hoped they would tell me I was better off not wasting my time. Brokenness is ugly, unworthy, and needs to be hidden. I wanted them to tell me what I was telling me.

When I unveiled my revelation of *Shed* to them, their faces lit up. The words they spoke to me were exact opposite to the words I cycled through my mind. They spoke encouragement, belief, and excitement over me.

Then Rhonda had an idea. "Why don't you come share your testimony at life group?" She was leading a Freedom group with another lady from our previous group.

Oh no. How am I supposed to do that? I'm not a speaker.

They both prayed with me, and Rhonda told me to think about coming and speaking.

"There are so many hurting women in this group. They need to hear your story."

I knew she was right. But would my words be right? Would I be able to think, process, and deliver? This had to be prayed up.

By the end of Celebrate Recovery, our group had become an empowered and set free group of ladies. We took the steps very seriously and even stretched the study out over nine months. We hungered to be free. The church that sponsored our study even held a graduation for us. Wanting to continue the experience on an even deeper level, our leader opened up session two to begin after the holidays.

Having become more stable, I found an apartment to rent. Ashlynn decided to move in with me full time. I never expected that opportunity to find me. A few weeks before moving out, on my birthday, I came home to a dozen roses.

"Happy birthday, pretty girl. I love you." No signature. None needed. Question was, how was he able to order roses all the way from Iraq? But then I didn't care. I wouldn't put one single thing past this guy. I knew better.

Following weeks of deep prayer, I told Rhonda I would share my testimony. My daughter, Ashlynn, and Misti from Celebrate Recovery said they would come with me. I invited Jade and her daughter, Kylee, to also meet us there. Jackie would be in town and planned to be there in support. I asked my dad and sister, both former teachers, for some pointers because I was completely clueless on how to approach this. It all starts with an outline.

I prepared for weeks. One evening as I was working on my outline, a wave of absolute inadequacy washed over me.

"Oh God, I don't know how to do this. What if I stumble over the words? What if I lose my train of thought? What if my voice is shaky and not a word is understandable?"

Then as clearly and crisply as my thoughts had bombarded me, he simply said, "This is not about you."

That's all he said. My focus shifted dramatically. *This is not about me. Someone, some hurting soul needs to hear my story. She needs to know she can. She needs to know she is worthy. She needs to know it's not too late.* "She" became my focus.

I was able to share my testimony with full authority of God's grace, love, and mercy. My words were occasionally broken, but understandable. My emotions poured through every syllable, but I was not crying alone. My story was charged with truth so strongly each lady could feel the value of my struggle. And she could see the hope reaching for her. She could recognize that the pain of walking through freedom was worth the cost of unpacking her wounds. She became worthy.

There was not a dry eye left in the room. Many of the women reached out individually to share something that struck them deeply and motivated them to continue their search for freedom.

"If your book is anything like your words tonight, this will be powerful!" Rhonda told me before I left.

Seeing the impact of sharing my story, I returned to my notebook and pen. *Shed* was born the old-fashioned way. When I told God he had the wrong girl, I truly meant it. I didn't know how to type. I didn't even own a computer. This book, being God's idea, I figured would be not simple but not exhausting. I thought I could pray, sit to devote my time, pick up my pen, then hours later, snap out of it and pages of the story God wanted to share would magically exist.

If only! I spent hours holding my pen, staring at blank notebook paper, waiting for words to make their way. The task was daunting. My thoughts scattered in a dozen directions, and I wanted to be doing a list of other preferable activities. So maybe I misunderstood God's purpose for me?

*****

December was upon me now: court with Everett. I knew I had rights to my kids. I knew he had taken those rights many, many times. I had never stood up to him, ever. Anything he had ever wanted from me, I either freely gave him or he took. This was a big deal. On my behalf, my daughter Ashlynn and my ex-sister-in-law were going to testify. I really didn't want it to come to this, but Everett had taken far too much.

I spent hours in my lawyer's office, actually in the office of his paralegal, Kara. My goal was complete honesty. I owned up to my mistakes, no sugarcoating them. It was evident that Everett was not following the custody agreement. I had loads of text messages verifying that, also testimony from Ashlynn, my ex-sister-in-law, and my dad.

Luckily, when the court date approached, our lawyers were able to come to an agreement, and no one was to be put on the stand. Everett and I both wanted to avoid that. The judge reprimanded Everett for not abiding by the custody agreement. He gave him strict orders to follow the papers, and they were to be rewritten with stronger parameters. If he didn't stick to them, he would be charged with contempt.

I could relate to David that day as he watched Goliath fall to the ground with a thud. My earth shook as I witnessed God slingshot justice on my behalf. Years of Everett overpowering me and ignoring what was right came to a sudden halt. I was not used to experiencing victory. It was a humbling encounter.

I guess Satan was watching me walk on air with a smile on my face as he sat, aiming his next choice arrow at me. What am I saying? I guess? Of course, he was! Not even a week after court and right before Christmas, a package with my name on it arrived. Inside was a unique, very beautiful jewelry box. In the jewelry box was a cross necklace made out of lapis lazuli. It is native to Afghanistan and prized for its intense deep-blue color. Jared's note inside the box explained it all. Also, that he had to be sneaky in purchasing it.

His gift did not affect me much. I was not bothered by him until I began to receive his emails. My kids and I were visiting my sister in DC. We went up to NYC for a few days. His emails were reminiscing our Christmases together, and he knew I didn't like to be alone on holidays. I remember driving out of the city when one of the songs he had sent me came over the radio. I sat in the passenger seat, the darkness around me, tears rolling from my eyes. Half a world away, no physical touch, no audible words from him; yet Satan found a way for him to shake me.

My loneliness took root in the memories of my lost dreams. I knew I would never go back to Jared, and I knew he was a door God repeatedly shut, but through the chains of the shut door, I peeked in the cracks. I responded to his emails and tiptoed beside the dangerous dance I had taken with him. I was searching my flesh to console my heartache.

Fully set against allowing myself to go down that wrong road again, I forbid myself to respond to his email on New Year's Eve. I declared my New Year to be void of his presence. Turning my back to that door was a step toward the right path, until I found myself stepping toward a substitute.

Over a year had passed, and I had trudged through mountains of healing, so when the guy I had been talking to for several months asked me to dinner, I thought I was prepared. I made sure he attended church, and we had many of the same interests. Oddly, he too was a pilot. I had defined my boundaries before we met.

After a few dates, he clarified that he doesn't attend church as often as he should but wants to. He was very attractive and affectionate. My deprived flesh longed for more. It wasn't long until I found myself standing outside of God's will. I raked coals of shame over myself. The flames of unworthiness burned my growth and healing nearly to ashes.

The ever-present Holy Spirit whispered truth to my fault, poured love onto my shame. He reminded me of my new identity and put to a smolder the lies that were grasping my loneliness. I remembered all the ways God had fought for me. My flesh ached for satisfaction, but my soul had found something so much deeper. I knew choosing to satisfy my flesh would only be a rotating door of my past.

Knowing it had to be done, I ended the relationship. I confessed my wrong to God and a friend and prayed for forgiveness. My focus needed to shift. Too many times I had sought after my wants. God had spoken his purpose over me, and I wanted to explore his route.

I set a new plan before me. When I wasn't working or going to kid's activities, I would be a writer. Every evening, every kid-free weekend, I would not make plans, no dates. With intention, I offered my time up to the Lord. I listened to worship music, prayed for the Holy Spirit to guide my thoughts and words, and then I wrote.

The very first weekend I did this was exhausting. Mentally, I had to place myself back in time. I relived pain that I had never chosen and certainly did not want to revisit, but this was not about me. I didn't have patients to see that Friday, so I spent three days at home, focused. When I came to the end of Sunday, my heart, brain, and emotions were tattered. I had lived through those heartbreaks in a fog of alcohol. Walking back through them, I had nothing to numb myself. I pressed forward with force.

Some writing sessions offered up pages, some only paragraphs. It was sometimes frustrating, and in those moments, I read over my words. Those words stirred emotions that blew me away. I knew I had sat down at that notebook paper. I knew my pen scribbled those words, but that talent and effect that came through was a gift. The giver of all creation had instilled those abilities inside me. He was creating me in his image; my God-self was emerging.

Ashlynn noticed the change in my behavior and saw me writing a lot. Out of fear of failure, I had not wanted to tell my kids what I was up to, although I had already told Lane. I had planned to keep my God project hidden, but it became all consuming. Before long, all my kids were aware of the book and also supportive. That made it harder to quit or walk away from.

Two months of reliving my worst nightmare took its toll on me in many ways. My brain was exhausted with juggling my work schedule, kids' games, life's general tasks, and constantly bouncing from my life past to life now. My emotions were drained as I literally took myself back, on purpose, to submerge myself into what I felt during those dark moments. I had to in order to capture the vibrancy of the struggle. It was necessary to go back to where I had been. I had to become my lost self again to relate to those lost now.

Having isolated myself, doubt pounded my purpose, making me question again if I was capable. This was more difficult than I assumed it would be. Only two months into dedicated writing, and I wanted out. I'm drained. I'm weary. I don't have the power. I'm a fool for believing I would be called to a purpose that would empower even one soul to stand up to fight Satan and claim God's power.

*****

Spring had arrived. My fever for camping and hiking came in like a lion. With my doubt for purpose pressing my weary self, I had decided that I was being full-on ridiculous. I'm wasting my time. God's message to me must have gotten tied up in the delivery system, and this was meant for some spectacular, Wonder Woman talented writer but fell into my vision. There. Done. Chalk it up to my misunderstanding.

After weeks of the most perfect spring weather, Jill and I planned a weekend camping trip, two nights and three days. I was looking forward to walking away from my book and moving forward. We had everything planned out: campsites, trails, food. We were ready to go. A few days before the trip, the strangest, most unexpected thing happened. A front was moving our direction, and snow accumulations of at least six inches were expected. In Tennessee! In spring!

My heart was set on this trip. I wanted to walk away from this book and the feeling of being an idiot for thinking I was called to this purpose. I told Jill the forecast had to be wrong.

"We'll still be able to go."

The day before we were to leave, it was 100 percent forecasted for sleet and snow. My first free weekend was not to be.

Out of all the winter weekends we could have had snow; it waited. I was so letdown. I had been cooped up with this book, this purpose, this writing, I wanted out from under it. Not understanding much of anything at that point, I bent down in the floor.

"Father God, I don't think I can do this. You must have a more capable person out there. I'm weak from struggling to be free. My voice is soft. My heart is still broken. Please choose someone else."

I cried because it was hard. God had clearly shown me his purpose, his story to be told. I cried because I didn't want it to be me.

I lay in the floor with fresh tears as the snow landed gently on the ground outside my window. As softly as the snow fell, he whispered to my soul.

"This snow is for you. Where you are is where I want you to be."

Inside, I fought, but I sat down to write. The snow lasted two days. I wrote the whole two days the snow glistened on the ground.

The weather forecast promised it was over. Spring and sunshine was ahead.

We had two days of sunshine following that snow. My stubbornness continued to wrestle with God. His purpose for me battled my belief of me. I felt tormented.

"Okay, God. Snow is easy when it's cold. That was in the forecast. It was expected. If you really meant that snow for me, bring it now." I barely had those words out of my mouth before I was apologizing. "That is too much to ask. I'm sorry, I shouldn't try you like that."

Forgetting about my silly request, I went into work with my patient. It seemed to get darker outside as the sun was not shining through the windows anymore. As I left her house and headed toward my car, I caught a glimpse of a tiny white flake. Trying to shake the crazy out of my head, I dismissed the thought of snow. Before I could back out of the driveway, my windshield was covered. I put my car in Park, opened the door, and stepped out to catch the snow. My snow.

God spoke to my heart, "This is for you."

I had wrestled. I had fought. I had challenged his purpose for me. He spoke. He showed me. He confirmed. I never again questioned if I was his chosen author of *Shed*.

Brushing aside my attempt to escape God's purpose, I went back to writing. The only time Jared interfered in my life was in the memories as I wrote. Our mutual friend Rex messaged me one day asking if I had heard from him. He told me there was a big party celebrating his last flight and return from Afghanistan. He would be retiring soon.

Wanting the complete end to all things us, I sent Jared an email reminding him he was seven months past the deadline of our property settlement. If he did not complete his part, I would file contempt. A few weeks following that email, I received a phone call. A process server requested to meet with me to overlook papers. Papers? I asked what this was concerning, but he couldn't tell me. He said he could only tell me who they were from.

"Looks like they're from your ex-husband."

Oh dear. Which one? Had Everett found some minute thing I'm not aware of and is challenging my rights to the kids? Mine and Jared's divorce has been complete and filed over a year now. What in heaven's name could he be up to? I had absolutely no idea what battle was laid out in front of me.

In pure confusion and curiosity, I met with the process server. As soon as I signed and he drove away, I demolished the envelope to get the papers containing the answers. A stunned effect jolted over my body. Once again, Jared's poison halted my abilities. I was unable to move as I stared at the papers. My lungs held their position, refusing to breathe. My only organ able to function was my brain, and it was washed with fear.

Jared has filed for relief from our property settlement agreement, charging me with extortion. And just like that, with one thin sheet of paper, one of my slain giants rises up and towers over me. How is this even possible? I fought him and believed with 100 percent conviction that God had led me to freedom of him. How could he now rise up to again threaten all my stability and freedom I fought to have?

A whirlwind of doubt, fear, and instability shook all my believing in myself and God. Am I guilty of extortion? Trying so hard to do the right thing, did I neglect, not see, or misconstrue what I should have done? What will happen if I'm charged with extortion? That is a serious crime.

All my steps heading in the right direction started kicking the validity of God's words to me. I don't remember how, but I made it home. I sat. My head pounded as scenarios of what-ifs struck me sucker punch after sucker punch. I gave serious thought to what brought me to this point. I had told Jared I would not turn him into his superior if he restored my savings. Was I taking the easy way out? Was it my responsibility to report this?

This situation was nowhere on my radar. A new cloud of torment moved over me. With two giants down, my freedom was looking clear with hope and excitement on the horizon. A slain giant is not supposed to rise, especially this giant. The one God so clearly and mightily led me away from.

To revisit the events, I pulled my phone out to make myself look at the photos again. It had been awhile since I had because I wanted to heal and blur the images in my memory. I had over a year of healing since I left Jared. His poison no longer cycled through my blood. For the first time, seeing the photos, I did not see my husband's infidelity. I saw women that were being taken advantage of. They were placed in demeaning positions and photographed. I reread Jared's texts to them, especially the young colored woman. His words were racial, forceful, shameful, devaluing words. My stomach wanted to lurch with vomit. I felt agony for these women.

I sat in my floor and cried tears of afflictions for what they must have felt. I emulated their pain as if it were my own. How many others has he done this to? How many more will be in his sights? The responsibility of standing up to defend them all rested on my shoulders like an anchor pulling me underwater.

Maybe God wanted me to stand up now? My heart was way too fragile when I first discovered these photos. I wasn't able to see clearly then. All I saw were women having sex with my husband. I am now the only voice they may ever have.

My lawyer wasn't able to see me for a few weeks. I prayed over turning Jared in. Again, I found myself faced with a task I wish would be given to anyone other than me. Rex told me Jared would be retiring soon. I was sure his gifts and delayed response was his attempt to stall me until he was free with full retirement. Feeling pressed against time, and with the opportunity and strength, I decided I had to turn him in. If for the second time, I did not, I would wrestle the guilt forever.

After Googling and a few calls, I was instructed to contact the inspector general. He worked in conjunction with the adjutant general. An investigation would only be launched if the inspector deemed it to be worthy. The man assigned to work with me was very professional and concerned. I felt he was seeking true justice in this issue. That gave me relief. He took down tons of information from me and said he would be in touch.

The day of my appointment with my lawyer, I walked into the office with panic screaming on my insides. I sat down at Kara's desk.

"I pulled all the files we have on your court case with Everett." She was stunned as I told her this had nothing to do with Everett.

Then I handed her the complaint filed against me.

"I have never seen a situation like this." She sighed.

My eyes looked at her begging for answers, for an escape. "How can he do this when he had signed the property settlement agreement and then failed to respond by the deadline?"

Accessing court files, she discovered that Jared had filed for relief from the property settlement the day before the deadline. However, he failed to serve me until over seven months later. His filed action was technically void due to it being older than six months. We both hoped it would all be thrown out due to his failure to serve me. We then filed contempt charges against him.

Along with this mental stress, my longtime neck issues increased. Whiplash from a car accident over twenty years ago left me in constant pain. It had reached an unbelievable point. I was experiencing numbness and tingling in my left arm. I have a high pain tolerance, but I was reaching the end of my ability to withstand it. My doctor referred me to therapy.

The assistant inspector general I had been speaking with requested that I send him all the evidence in my possession against Jared. I had transferred the audio recording to a file so I could email it. The photos, due to content, were blocked from being able to be accepted on their end. He told me I would have to print them and mail them to him directly. He emailed me a form in case I had trouble with the photo shop printing such explicit photos.

Several weeks ago, Jill had invited me to join her and her husband on their annual beach trip. Before I was to leave, I had X-rays scheduled for my neck, and I needed to get all evidence in the mail to the inspector. Keeping in alignment with the irony that seemed to grab hold of my life, my daily devotionals were on Job. Reading about everything he went through, knowing it was all a test, actually gave me comfort. Maybe Satan, seeing my strength emerge, had asked God if he could test me?

Why did my tests have to be so extraordinary? One or two of the extreme situations I have dealt with was more than most see in a lifetime. Job dealt with loss in all fields of his life. He was in torment. He questioned God and desired to be vindicated for his righteousness. He even asked for death. More than all he hungered for was an encounter with God. After all his silence, Job wanted to know if he still mattered.

Job's desires transformed in the presence of God. God came near. The atmosphere of Job shifted in mere seconds. I believe the glory of God was so brilliant upon Job's face that it melted away all concerns of physical, financial, and mental instability. Job realized God's force of power only by proximity. He came to full surrender, knowing no concentration of calamity on earth could ever out scale the magnificence of God, even in the tiniest increment.

My faith transformation had to continue in full confidence of who God is. The day before my beach trip, I went to the photo shop. The images never left my mind, but now I had to request them to be printed. I had to hold in my hands the pictures that seeped the life out of me. I dreaded this. How do I go about this? Knowing I could not pull the photos up on a kiosk, I requested to speak to a manager. When I explained my situation to him, he glanced at me with sympathy. I'm sure he could see the tears sitting in my eyes. He probably noticed my trembling as well.

He stepped me behind the counter, so privately the photos could be printed. I wasn't able to send them all at once. I had to open each individual photo in order to send them to their machine. Each one of the thirty-eight images flashed in front of me, and then the photo was placed in my hand. Photos typically represent treasured memories. I held in my hands filth, disgust, heartache, betrayal. The bullet that had been lodged in my heart, the death of my marriage.

I walked out of there sloshing in shame. Seeing those images, holding them, broke my stitched-together heart wide open. I sat in my car as I met tear after tear. Is this really happening?

"Dear God, give me the strength to survive this fight."

I went straight to the post office to rid myself of the images.

Feeling emotionally drained but ready for my beach escape, I went home and grabbed my things. This was a camping beach trip. I decided I would drive a little, then pick out a spot somewhere mid-route and camp. I put on a ball cap, rolled my windows down, turned the radio up and drove.

*****

Nearly two months following the time I had sent my evidence to the military, I was asked to come speak to an investigator. The adjutant general wanted to launch an investigation. The inspector general's office returned the photos so I could present them. The offices were separate but also worked together.

I finally felt safe. Although delayed, justice was going to prevail. Jared would not be able to manipulate his way against the military. Against his own words of admission and photos of proof, I had both with me. The actual recorder I had used to tape our conservation and once again those disgusting pictures.

This entire process felt like a walk I was taking out of someone else's life. Leaving Jared was hard enough. Exposing his misconduct to the military, that was an act for a woman of intense strength, not me. Looking beside me, to the left and to the right, behind me, no other woman was standing. For whatever reason, I had to be that woman. It was time to dig deep. To develop and call upon the power that God had placed within me.

Before going in to meet the investigator, I prayed. I asked God to give me the strength to be honest, no matter what. I stepped out of my car with those trembly little giraffe legs, clumsy and awkward. These were new steps to me. Being caught in the middle of a military misconduct investigation was never near the scope of the future I envisioned for myself. I looked up to God to regain my twenty-foot, born-to-run potential. I held my head up and opened the door to the office of the adjutant general.

I was led to a small room. One table, two chairs, the investigator and I. He had me sign several forms, and then the questions began. I attempted to remove myself from being the wife in this saga, to simply being the person asked to provide the designated information being requested. I was able to assume that character until he took me through the photos, one by one. The deception quivered in my lips and released through my tears. This was hard. My heart felt like leaping out of my chest; but it was too wounded, weak, and weary.

We then moved to the recorded confession. He asked me to play the portion where Jared admitted to being unfaithful. I could have recited it word for word for him. It stays paused in my mind. Hearing those words from his lips crashed my world. They annihilated my heart. The investigator wanted to make sure it was Jared on the tape.

"That's him," he said. "I've known him my whole career. We joined at the same time. I'm not sure we can use this since you recorded it without his knowledge."

He left to confer with the general on the matter. I prayed so hard when he left.

"Please, God! Tell me I have not suffered through all this for nothing."

I held my breath when he returned. He said the recording is immiscible as long as one of the parties of the conversation consented. Me. I consented. I consented to finding the truth.

The actual recorder had not left my possession since the night I recorded the conversation. Part of me was afraid to let go of the hardcore evidence. I had digitally downloaded the conversation, and on my way that morning had taken photos of the recorder. Knowing Jared as I had come to, I knew to not be too trustworthy in giving all I had away. I made sure to have proof that the recorder existed. The investigator wrote out a receipt for the recorder, along with its serial number (which I had in my photos) and stated it would all be returned at the close of the investigation.

As he reviewed all the evidence I had handed over, he said, "Hmmmm. Looks like I need to requestion some people."

"Excuse me?" I asked. "Sounds like you have not been getting the whole truth."

He simply shook his head and replied with a, "Never mind." He walked me to the door, shook my hand, and assured me he would perform a thorough investigation.

Driving off the military base, an uncomfortable feeling settled over me. The investigator let two things slip: He has known Jared for over twenty years and had already questioned several witnesses. But it was not lining up with the facts now in his possession. I phoned the assistant inspector general with my concerns.

"Look, Jared is a very manipulative and deceptive person. He obviously had the women lie for him. I fear he will bend the system to cover up his actions. Justice needs to be served here."

He assured me that the highest-quality investigation would be done.

I could not trust anything connected in the slightest manner with Jared. I felt pressed on every side. It felt like I was sliding back down the canyon I had perilously been climbing out of. He had even been able to delay the civil suit another five months. I knew what he was trying to do. He wanted to be able to hide his misconduct in the military, receive full retirement, and slither his way out of the property settlement, unscathed and shining.

Two and a half months after the AG opened the investigation, I received a letter from the IG. Holding the envelope in my hands, I held my breath, terrified to read the words inside. I had been praying deeply for justice. I reopened wounds that had been repairing. Their fresh blood seeped daily once again throughout every heartbeat and thought. The shadow of the giant hovered over me no matter which direction I turned.

No matter what was on the other side of the envelope, I had to trust God. I ripped the flap in my usual unorganized, tattered way. My breath stopped as I read, "We conducted a modified investigation inquiry using a command product and determined that the allegations against Chief Warrant Officer Martin were not substantiated." Signed by the colonel, US Army, state inspector general.

Immediately my head pounded. The tears found their exit, but my breath was nowhere to be found. I sunk to the ground. Maybe I misread those words. I sat in the parking lot of my apartment, numb to the black, hot pavement, trying through blurry eyes to read the truth. It still said the same thing: "Not substantiated."

"Wait. What? How? God, where are you? I thought you were the God of justice? I know you are the God of justice. I don't understand."

I melted with disbelief. God had led me to find those photos. He gave me the strength to fight for the truth and record the truth so Jared could no longer deceive me. He held me up as I walked into the AG's office to demand justice. How, being fully powered by God, could I be blindsided with this injustice?

Feeling as though this giant was pressing my chest, squeezing my faith out of me, I battled to regain my stability. There must be some mistake. I phoned the IG's office and requested to speak to the general. I asked him to explain how the evidence could be wrong. He said he only had the report from the investigator, that he had not personally done any investigating. He said it was inconclusive as to who the women are.

"Their faces are in the photos, and Jared says their names on the recording, sir."

"He doesn't say he had sex with them," he responded.

My ears burned with frustration. "He mentions it several times in the recording. I even asked him how he lured them to his camper. He had them sprawled out in demeaning positions with photos of his privates too. That is proof over proof."

"The investigation is complete," was his final answer.

There was a loss of space and time as I sat bewildered. I couldn't think. My head hurt as shock penetrated flashes of the moments I lived through the past two years. The broken pieces I had begun to place back together started ripping. Not only was I standing in the middle of my canyon again, but the giant was throwing boulders at me, his target. The shadow he cast darkened and swallowed me. If he was able to manipulate and win this battle, what were my chances with the next one?

Walking around with anger was draining. I had to reset my foundation. I had absolutely no doubt that God had been leading me. The miracles and encounters he sent my way were undeniable. This was testing my faith muscles. Knowing God intimately, I knew there was reason although unknown to me. He had led me through the dark before; he would do it again.

Depositions for the civil suit were only a little over two months away. The trial just over three. I glared at my raggedy armor and unleashed the warrior within me. Time had come to rise and prepare for battle.

I picked up my girdle of truth, holding it tightly to my center. God's truth would be victorious over Satan's lies. I polished my breastplate of righteousness to guard my heart, protecting me under the blood of Jesus Christ. My sandals of peace had been worn thin, but as I placed them on my feet, they renewed, and I stood firm on the Gospel, with a fresh light of peace washing over me. The shield of faith was pegged with countless fiery darts from Satan. I buffed it fresh and strong, prepared for Satan's darts of doubt, denial, and deceit. My helmet of salvation set my focus on God and shielded my mind from strongholds. With both hands clasped, I lifted my sword of the Spirit. Its two-edged power would slay any demonic presence pressing toward me, and it would unleash God's power in, over, and through me.

This warrior daughter had fought to become free. I declared victory over Jared. This was about more than a civil suit; this was a fight for the woman I had become. I surrendered the outcome to God.

"No matter what happens, I will walk in truth, faith, and complete trust. If it's not your will for me to win this suit, protect me against anger. Reveal to me the lesson you are teaching me."

*****

My neck pain had intensified to the point where I could hardly function. I visited my doctor in fear of what outcomes I could be facing. The therapy was not helping. My pain tolerance is high, but I would be in tears at the end of my work day. I held my tears as she examined my muscles and reflexes. She ordered an MRI and gave me pain medicine and a nerve blocker to be able to sustain until we could find answers.

She called a few days later telling me I needed to see a neurosurgeon. There were herniated discs, bone spurs, signs of arthritis, and degenerative disk disease. All these were causing nerve compression and extreme pain, numbness, decreased function. It's difficult hearing a diagnosis like that. I gave it to God and declared there to be victory and purpose in dealing with this.

I worked closely with Kara, my lawyer's paralegal. I made out a timeline of events, gathered important text and emails, and, of course, handed over the photos and emailed the taped conversation. The evidence I submitted to the military was never returned. I spoke to the investigator three times, and three times he told me it was in the mail. He never answered another call after that. My voicemails were ignored.

Luckily, the neurosurgeon was able to get me in quickly. He sat me down, pulled up my X-rays on one screen, MRI on another. He said my neck was a mess, and I definitely needed surgery. I had expected as much. My fear was that I would have one issue after another, but I have learned not to look too far ahead.

Digging the good out of an unwanted diagnosis can be challenging. I would need to be off work at least two months because of all the driving and physical nature of my job, even that might not suffice. I chose to be thankful for the time I would be off. I would set my alarm, get up, and write all day. Having a job interfered with ample time to write. Maybe God would help me finish in this time so that I could move forward. I was also thankful he had provided savings to supply the funds for surgery and living cost. My jet skis had sold a month ago.

For several days after surgery, I had to be immobile. My neck muscles, trachea, and esophagus were pinned over in order to reach my disc. Eating and drinking were not easy. Three days of recovery, then I got busy. I wrote all day, every day. I had to keep myself in an upright position and was limited on neck movement. I found a way to make it work. I was dedicated to finishing. I couldn't wait to see the end of this wearisome work.

A week before depositions, I spent a lot of time in my lawyer's office prepping. I made it clear to him that my main objective was complete honesty. Very raw and true, even the bad parts. I continually prepared myself to trust God 100 percent. Even if the trial did not end in my favor, I knew I had been obedient. I prayed to keep my heart pure and surrender the future, my way or not, to God's perfect plan.

*****

My nerves fired up the day before the deposition. By morning of, they were fully inflamed. I spoke several scriptures out loud to release my anxiety and replace it with comfort, peace, and trust. After seeing a few patients, it was time. It had been over a year since that final dinner with Jared. I did not want to have to look at him, especially being caught again in the middle of his manipulation and deceit. I called Kara and asked if she would let me in the back door. Sitting in the waiting room with him could not happen.

She let me in and led me into her office.

"Are you making it okay?" she asked.

"It's been over a year since I've seen him, and I'm dreading this. Will you do me a favor?"

She responded with a sincere, "Anything."

"Will you pray with me?" I grabbed her hands and led us in prayer. My biggest plea was that God would only allow me to speak the absolute truth.

When time came, my lawyer, Tom, came in to get me. He had already explained the process. He would question Jared first, then Jared's lawyer would question me. He escorted me into the conference room where I had spent hours the week before. The walls were lined with bookshelves. I wondered how many of the hundreds of books he had read. He was a very intelligent man.

Not wanting to look at Jared but wanting to see him, I tried to get a glimpse of him in my peripheral vision. How did I ever love this man? What lengths did he go to in order to foul the investigation with the JAG's office? How did he persuade the women to lie or manage to get the evidence destroyed? I remembered his thoughts that were revealed to me while in Haiti. The visions of him with other women encompassed my mind. It all hurt so very deeply. But now I stood at a different point in the circumference of his madness. Grasping closure ebbed increasingly closer.

Mr. Kenton's first questions were basic: name, address, job, etc. Then he questioned Jared about me moving out and him filing for divorce. Jared claimed it was due to my alcohol issues and me having adulterous affairs. My face must have exhibited the definition of shock. You would think at this point I would be desensitized to anything the man said, but this got me.

Anger inflamed all inside me. I had to pray to keep calm. As Tom pursued truth, Jared was unable to give any names or reliable information about the subject.

Mr. Kenton then proceeded to question Jared about his adulterous affairs. Photos and the recording had been sent to Jared's lawyer. He could not cloud evidence in this situation. Jared gave first and last names. He verified that two of the ladies were military. One was African American and was under his command at one point. He also verified two to be his ex-wives.

Questioning then moved to the subject of my savings that we used to purchase our house and what became of it. Jared admitted that we discussed terms of the property settlement, that I wanted to identify his infidelities as my grounds for divorce and I wanted a portion of my savings returned. He also admitted that he asked me not to site infidelity as my cause because it could jeopardize his military career. He stated that, as a military officer, under the Uniform Code of Military Justice, that his behavior was not condoned. He was concerned they would demote him, court-martial him, or could put him out.

Tom mentioned that I did turn Jared in after he filed to be relieved from the agreement citing extortion and duress. Tom asked if Jared, in his sworn statement, acknowledged his adulterous affairs to the military. Jared declined answering, stating he could not discuss anything he told the military. Jared then stated that nothing became of the investigation. The letter from the inspector general declared the charges to be unfounded.

TOM: But we know from your testimony today that if the gravemen of the complaint against you was that you had engaged in adulterous relationships during the term of your marriage to Michelle, you had, in fact, engaged in those relationships?

JARED: I had.

TOM: All right. And if the charge was that you did that and they came back with a ruling that it was unfounded, you cannot provide me any information today as to why they so ruled?

JARED: I can't.

TOM: But you did not lose anything. You were not demoted in any way?

JARED: Correct.

TOM: You were not discharged with a less than honorable discharge from the armed services?

JARED: I was not.

TOM: You took your ordinary and usual, customary retirement.

JARED: Uh-huh.

TOM: You are receiving your full retirement benefits?

JARED: I am.

Tom then highlighted the fact that Jared filed his action of extortion against me the day before the deadline he was supposed to fulfill the settlement. When asked why he didn't serve me, he blatantly stated he was stalling. He flat out said he never had any intention of paying the money. Once he deployed, he fell under federal military, as opposed to state.

"Once deployed, it's very hard for them to get you."

Tom asked again about Jared's intent to stall. He stated he was trying to protect his career and from losing his retirement. Jared stated again he never had any intent to pay the money. Jared admitted when he signed the agreement, that he had asked me not to disclose his infidelities to the military, that he would agree to the terms and signed before a notary.

The photos I had found came into question. Jared admitted they had been on his phone. He also admitted the JAG office had copies of the photos. When asked again if he acknowledged his relationship with these ladies to the military, he deflected.

"I am not supposed to discuss anything from those meetings."

"And the investigation never went anywhere?"
"Correct."
"And that cost you nothing?"
"Correct."

I released prayer after prayer as I listened to Jared's sworn statements. Lies and deceit oozed from his mouth continually. Several times I simply closed my eyes. Sitting still was against everything my body desired to do. I was close to chewing my lip off in order to stop myself from bursting out in anger at the many ways he twisted truth. Every particle of my flesh was provoked in anger. Fighting self-control, I called upon the Holy Spirit to deliver the fruit my flesh could not.

Questioning turned from Jared to myself. Jared's lawyer, Mr. Adams, began with all the typical routine questions. He hounded me about being the one to talk Jared into buying our big house and that I had no credit. Neither of which was true. He asked questions about finances, credit-card debt and the fact we lived paycheck to paycheck. I kept my answers honest. I did not have credit cards in my name. Jared handled all the finances, and he had several different bank accounts and credit cards in his name. I trusted him 100 percent to handle our money.

Mr. Adams questioned why I gifted $88,000 to Jared. I made it clear that I trusted him completely. When he told me he would buy us a house and take care of me, I believed him.

He said, "He could have simply ran off with that money."

His question only highlighted the facts in my direction.

"Yes, he could have. That is how much I trusted him. I trusted him with everything I had."

Mr. Adams pulled out copies of texts between Jared and me, the same set I had submitted to my lawyer.

"You used the word *extortion*. Would you read the text and tell me how many times you used the word in that?"

Reading the text, I responded, "I said, no, extortion is not my thing. So there is one. I also said, for the second time, I'm not extorting anything from you. There's two. I said twice in this conversation that extortion is not my thing."

"So why are you using the word *extortion*?"

"Because he used the word *extortion*. He also said he knows extortion is not my thing. I was only trying to get back what he took."

"If you would not have threatened, he would not have signed this, correct?"

"I wanted to file that he had been unfaithful. He asked that I not do that. I told him if he would repay my savings, I would not file like that. That is why when I filed, it says indifferences. That is why it does not say infidelity, because he asked me not to say that."

"Do you really think the military looks at divorce complaints?"

"He was afraid of it because he told me. He said, 'Please do not put that.'"

Mr. Adam's next question was for me to clarify how I came up with the amount of $65,000 to be returned to me.

"I'm going to give you a very honest answer, and it may not make sense to you, and that's fine. But I had started praying about it around November. I had just started praying whether I should just let it all go and walk away, and that is even in my text messages to him, that my first gut reaction was just to walk away. And I prayed. I prayed about it. I fasted and prayed some more. And God kept revealing to me to ask for some of my money back, and it was 65,000. I continued to pray, I didn't know why it was 65,000. Then whenever I did file for divorce, I had 25,000 to my name, and then it made sense to me why that is what I was receiving as an answer, and that is my honest answer."

Questioning continued on and on about my threatening to turn Jared in. I admitted to doing so. Jared repeatedly said he would not let me go. He would not divorce me. I felt I had no options. Staying with him was destroying me. He was nothing but toxic.

Following the depositions, Tom and I went into his office to discuss what had taken places. He said he was very impressed with my bold honesty. I told him that I could not believe Jared gave the answers he did. They proved how deceitful he is. He agreed.

"I believe you have a very good chance here."

The trial was a month away. Either way it was ruled, I would ultimately be freed of Jared.

Not long after the deposition, I received a phone call from Kara. I assumed we would begin trial prep.

"Michelle, I am so, so sorry to tell you this. Jared has had the trial set aside for nearly another year."

Thinking I must have heard incorrectly I stuttered, "W-what? This can't be. I'm tired of being trapped in connection with him. No. No! This has to happen!"

"I tried to get it moved to January. Jared reports that he will be out of the country flying for his new job. It is now set for August. There's nothing we can do."

Held down by the force of Jared another year? I can't take this anymore. This man continues to plague my life. I get up, fight, get knocked down. What are you doing, God? Where are you? I held defeat for a week. I went to sleep defeated. I woke up defeated. I walked around with chains clinking, keeping me tied to the one person I have fought diligently to be freed of. The one person I knew without a glimpse of a doubt God had persisted until I listened to remove me from his clutches.

Defeated, I lay in my floor. Defeated, I prayed. God reminded me how faithful his leading has been the two years since my leaving Jared. I gushed out honesty to heaven.

"God, I'm frustrated. I'm mad. I'm so exhausted from fighting this giant. This makes no sense. I don't understand. But I trust you. Please increase my faith. Please give me strength to lean only on you and teach me, build me, grow me during this battle."

My fatigue followed me into the morning. Disheartened, I open my devotional. A new one had begun. The current study was 1 and 2 Samuel. I was immediately immersed into the story. David had been a recurring character during my fight. Anointed king as a young boy after being overlooked, he was repeatedly sought after by his enemies to be killed. His main adversary King Saul could not thwart God's plan.

I rekindled the moments I agonized over filing for divorce. I had prayerfully sought answers. God filled me with assurance that he was guiding me in each step I had taken. Deep inside I set at ease in believing I was on course, although the path cut undesired curves.

My study led me to 2 Samuel 22. The words entranced me. My heart fluttered. God was giving me a song of praise to sing now, midbattle. I felt it in my spirit as my joy declared victory.

I decided at that moment I would sing David's song of praise as my own. Out loud, every day I would declare God's faithfulness. Tucked in the middle of the chapter God told me why he chose me. Verse 20: "He led me to a place of safety; he rescued me because he delighted in me." I clung so tightly to that specific verse. I surrendered the trial to my God. I did not focus on it anymore.

*****

Four to six weeks still remained for recovery from my neck surgery. With the trial in God's hands, I returned to writing. I desperately wanted to finish the book. I felt the completion of my story was God's doorway into my destiny. I longed to be Jesus's disciple, as he had called me the day he sat beside me by the ocean. He had replaced my old dreams with new dreams to do ministry and mission work. My life of utter despair turned into complete restoration would bring so many into hope. I wanted the lost and hurting to understand the fight for freedom so they would also be empowered to do so.

Intense pain and fatigue struck me daily, but I proceeded to write. I didn't want to continue wandering the wilderness. Writing was strenuous emotionally, physically, and mentally. I wanted the promised land portion of my journey.

Weeks flew, pages filled and turned. Time had come for me to return to work. *Shed* remained incomplete. So maybe it will only take a little longer than I expected? I could not abandon the project. So many words were breathed of the Holy Spirit, and I knew God commissioned this task to me.

Returning to work was a painful endeavor. Driving and bouncing through the hills, carrying my bag of supplies—all of it was very agonizing. It had been an entire year since I fully dedicated myself to writing. I found myself disenchanted with this stage of my life. My heart was fiercely lonely.

One of the men I had previously dated reentered the picture. Because of the state of my fatigued heart, slipping was easy. I found myself outside of God's will again. I knew I had to end my disobedient behavior. The very next day, another guy I had dated invited me to a New Year's Eve party. Not wanting another holiday alone, I went. I took part in the traditional NYE festivities and got trashed.

Destructive thoughts and feelings pelted me. Would I ever be worthy of true, complete freedom? Only two things I could not waiver from: God led me away from Jared and God confirmed writing *Shed* was my call. How could I meet his standards if my lonely heart was so easily quenched with a man's touch and the pain of disappointment simply numbed by alcohol? That is not the characteristics of a women called.

Condemnation wrapped around me like a warm scarf. I didn't know if I could be her. The woman called to preach the wonderment of freedom as I tightened my chains to bondage. I had thought I could occasionally be normal and enjoy a drink like everyone else, now that I was free.

Three straight days I did not fight alcohol. I bowed down to its poison gulp after gulp. What is freedom? Does it really exist? If it really existed, why do I find myself defeated again? Lying in the floor, covered in shame and disappointment, I wept.

"God, I can't be the freedom fighter you need me to be with this continual affliction. Please! Remove this from me."

God spoke by releasing scripture to me. Second Corinthians 12:7–9, "So to keep me from becoming conceited because of the surpassing greatness of the revelations, a thorn was given me in the flesh, a messenger of Satan to harass me, to keep me from becoming conceited. Three times I pleaded with the Lord about this, that it should leave me. But he said to me, 'My grace is sufficient for you, for my power is made perfect in weakness.' Therefore I will boast all the more gladly of my weaknesses, so that the power of Christ may rest upon me."

I cried even harder after receiving this passage. God would not remove my affliction. I wrestled with understanding. I have been called. I carry an irremovable thorn in my side. Isn't my ailment counterproductive to my destiny?

I believed all God has spoken to me. I did not know how to proceed toward my destiny while the thorn remained. Prayers that God would give me understanding and show me how to still be effective continued.

My devotional brought me to the life of King Uzziah. I don't recall ever studying about this king, but his story was brought before me with purpose. The king was very successful politically, militarily, and personally. He was influenced to follow God's will, until he took his eyes off God and placed them on himself. His pride blinded his need for humility. He was disciplined by being afflicted with leprosy.

It doesn't sound loving, but it was out of protection. God's correction showed his affection for King Uzziah and his involvement in his life. In my study, God revealed to me why he was not removing the pull of alcohol from me. He is using the affliction to protect me from the wrong people and disobedient behaviors/atmospheres. He is also keeping me humbled to the realization that I continually need his strength to serve as I carry my thorn.

This theme was confirmed during the sermon at church that day. The pastor was speaking about what is right and what is wrong behavior as Christians. He said each person has to come before God for their personal clarification. As for him, being a pastor, he is held to a higher standard. The quickest way he could destroy the congregation would be to go to lunch after service and slug down a few beers. Photos would swarm social media, and the church doors would be closed.

Looking into the destiny spoken over my life, I had to choose behaviors worthy of the call. My choices now, set the path to come. If I could not step daily in humility with the thorn in my flesh, I could never carry the responsibility of God's will for my future. Once again, it did not come down to what felt right, was easy, or what I wanted. It came down to choosing my way or God's way.

A break from *Shed* was needed. It was necessary to reformulate the concept of obedience in my life. What actions previously caused me to stumble? How could I guard myself to prevent a repeat situation? Alcohol was banned from touching my lips. The only control I had was abstinence. To be an effective example in the future, I had to be an example now.

72

Men. I thought asking if they attended church was a safeguard. I needed more than that. He had to be a man that attended regularly and was spoke of well by others. Making my sexual boundaries clear prior to dating was a must. He had to agree to respect those boundaries. I was not looking to date anyone, although the desire was still alive. My focus was on building the character needed to walk in my destiny.

My studies about character brought me to an impactful series by Robert Morris, "Dream to Destiny." He followed the life of Joseph and pointed out nine character traits that had to be strengthened and tested. The one point he made very clear, and I am so thankful for: if you fail a test, God lets you take it again. I lost count on the number of second chances I had been given. I was learning that it is impossible to be perfect, but most important is to be repentant. Getting down on myself for mistakes prevented me from moving forward. There is only one Jesus, and I'm not him. Continuing to keep myself secluded, learning about the character I needed strengthened, and writing kept me busy.

One evening Jill messaged me about a guy that had been asking about me. My defenses were high again because I did not want to stumble. She said he was a really good man, attended church, is big on family, and well liked in the community. He was a widower. His wife had drowned in their pool and was found by their daughter. I remembered hearing about the situation and the little girl that had found her. My heart had been broken for them. I spent nights in my floor crying and praying for that family, especially the little girl. I didn't even know her name.

I waited for him to approach me. After about a month, I learned that his wife was an alcoholic and that had contributed to her death. Knowing that made me realize I may not be a good fit for his family. I prayed over him, his children, and the situation. I prayed they could find healing. Then unexpectedly, God whispered, "Through you, he will find healing."

Not wanting to enter the picture and reignite his past, I prayed, "If it's meant to be, bring it together, Lord. Show me my part."

It was another month before he approached me. We had a week of great conversation before our first date. I told him my boundaries, and he said he would respect them. He had not dated since his wife passed. We had plenty of stares at dinner, but conversation flowed smoothly. There was that instant click, spark, the thing that is difficult to put your finger on but is there.

We saw each other daily, and not long after that first date, I stopped in his office and even met his family. We all hit it off. He was concerned about his daughter's reaction to me; they were very close. Feelings progressed quickly. I remember walking into his office, our eyes connecting, and my heart was bursting to tell him I loved him. That feeling did not find me often. It took me by surprise.

He soon decided he wanted me to meet his kids. That was an honor I did not take lightly. Honesty being my new standard, I had to open up to him about my past. If he then decided he didn't want me to meet his kids, I could understand. I was terrified he would deem me unworthy, but I was more terrified of disrespecting him or causing any pain to his family.

It was late one Wednesday night. I had been driving an hour and a half to Cobalt for life group. When I got back, he met me outside his house, and we sat in his truck. I had prayed my entire way to meet him. I prayed he would see my heart and the woman I was now, not my past mistakes. The tears arrived before any of my words did. My life had been a pathway of rejection; I was prepared for it again.

He looked into my eyes as I told him my story. He held my hand and stroked my arm. I was so afraid my truth would tarnish who he saw me as. His eyes were soft and tender.

"I respect you more now than ever. I know that wasn't easy. You are not defined by your past."

Was it possible? Had I finally found the man I had prayed for? The one to see my heart, not my past?

We decided Easter Sunday would be a good time for me to meet his kids. Church, then lunch. I was impressed. They were great. I went to their house and hung out for the afternoon. As I went to leave, his daughter stood there, telling me goodbye.

"It was so nice to meet you," I told her sincerely.

A few days later, she told her grandma, "I don't feel like that was the first time I have met her."

I truly believe the nights I poured my heart out praying for her bonded us. She knew me because my soul cried out for her healing. Our souls had been acquainted in another realm.

The following weekend a group of us rented a cabin and had a big hike planned. He rarely left his kids, and this would be the most alone time we had since we started dating. The cabin was warm and cozy. Snuggling him felt safe and thrilling at the same time. I felt accepted for the very first time, all of me. He said the words our hearts and minds had been telling each other, "I love you." I explained to him how I had been looking for the man worthy of doing things God's way, waiting until marriage for sex. I wanted God's blessings, and I saw him worthy to be the one.

"You're worth waiting for," he told me.

My entire family adored him, and his adored me. Only God could bring two people together like this. Histories of alcohol abuse, although perpendicular to one another. My strength in being honest with him allowed him to open up to me about issues he had been carrying. Even prior to our first date, he told me he didn't think he'd ever want to marry again but said that could change. He brought up marriage on several occasions. He asked me my favorite diamond cut, where I wanted to get married, and if I could see myself living in their home.

SHED

I could, I could see it all. I never saw myself staying in Balston until then. We were together every day, and sexual temptation was heavily present. I reminded him why it was so important to me to wait for marriage. I could not choose disobedience and remain close to God. He pushed what he had told me that he would respect.

73

One afternoon, after a long day of work, I got a call from my dad. He said there was a white vehicle in his driveway when he got home. A man was sitting inside with his window down, waiting. When Dad approached him, he asked if he knew me and where I was. Dad questioned who he was. He said he was a private investigator hired by my ex-husband. Dad told him he had no idea where I was living.

The breath of my giant blew across my neck causing fear to rise up and overshadow my freedom. His hunt for me was warping the new, clean present I had been creating. I looked 360 degrees around me, searching for a man with binoculars peering at me through the window of a white vehicle. I went to my boyfriend's to share my newfound threat.

He wanted me to drop the property settlement agreement that Jared was forcing to be relieved from. He said if I would do that, Jared would have no reason to continually seek me out. All ties would be fully broken. He even said he would give me the $65,000. He was well-off, and that was only change to him. He was afraid Jared would erupt our relationship.

I considered it for a mere few minutes. This was an instant out to the war of Jared. This would be easy. But it wasn't about the money; it was about the battle. One of the deepest truths I knew was that God was creating a warrior out of my tattered soul. He had to be my source no matter how long, difficult the battle and no matter how gruesome the giant. I was a warrior that didn't require an easy out.

*****

My heart was torn, holding so much of what I wanted in one hand and seeing my connection to God's will slip through the other as I was living in disobedient behavior. Praying became difficult for me. Sitting in church, I felt like a hypocrite. I saw God holding an umbrella and I stood just outside of its covering. My heart, flesh, mind, and soul battled intensely. I knew what I needed to do, but it was the last thing I wanted. I could lose it all.

Days of conflict surrounded me. I could no longer walk in disobedience. My heart sank, thinking of him leaving me because of this. One morning as I was getting ready and thinking about how to tell him, God paused me as he spoke.

"How much do you trust me?"

The song "Just Look Up and Know You Are Loved" came over my Pandora. The same song used in confirming God's purpose to me. That song had never played on my Pandora and has not played since. I knew I had to do what I did not want to do.

The house was still and quiet. The moment had come for me to tell him. I told him how badly our behavior was stalling my relationship with God. I could not continue doing something I knew was wrong and at the same time pray for blessings.

He saw it differently. He said, "God knows our hearts. He knows we love each other. We will just ask for forgiveness."

True repenting means to stop the behavior. His method would not work for me. I told him I could not keep doing what was created for marriage.

He replied, "I don't know if I will ever be ready for marriage."

The anniversary date of his wife's death was approaching, and I felt him distancing himself. I prayed for him and his children to receive peace and comfort during this time. On the date of her passing, he, his son and daughter, and I spent the day together. God was pressing on my heart to tell him something. It was bold, deep, and I was afraid to say it. I knew it would stir emotions, and I was terrified of pushing too hard. My heart raced all day knowing I was supposed to deliver this message to him. At night, after both kids had gone to bed, I sat in his lap with my heart weighing a ton. I could see pain in his eyes, and my tears flowed in pain for him.

Taking his hands, I nearly choked with fear and emotion. "Losing her was not your fault. It was never your place or capability to save her. You did all you could do. She was the only one that could save herself."

I knew because I had been there in her place. I could feel the guilt he had been carrying. He was not allowing himself to accept God's forgiveness, nor forgive himself. There were many choices he had made that were holding him captive. I knew the feeling of freedom and wanted for him to know it too.

The following day, he and I went to her graveside. As we cleaned up the old arrangements, waves of his pain penetrated into my heart. God had given me strength to lay down my brokenness to be replaced with healing. I so desperately wanted to lift his and lay it at the cross. Just as he could not save her, I could not save him. As we began to drive away, he had the most solemn, sunken look.

My heart breaking for him, I said, "Stop the truck." Taking his hand, I asked, "Please open up to me."

Tears streamed from his eyes as he responded, "I can't do this right now."

Four days later, following a successful get-together we had planned with a lot of people over, I made a simple request.

"Can we have a date night? Just us?"

We had only had two dates alone since our very first. That set off something unintended within him. He became angry and even asked me to leave. I tried to talk to him about it, but he refused. Before bed I sent him a message telling how much I loved him and that I only wanted some alone time. He did not respond.

The next morning, no response. My heart was bleeding in fear that my fairy-tale romance had ended. That afternoon I sent him a message, "Please talk to me."

As though I had not meant much to him, he sent a simple text. "This is not going to work. We have different priorities right now. Plus, I don't think I will ever want to marry again."

In mere seconds, with words coming from a text message, my heart was knocked over and shattered into tiny minuscule crumbs. It would seem that my heart would come to expect brokenness, it had taken it so many times, but this time stabbed to the core of my core. I had not presented him with the broken version of Michelle. I gifted him with the best version of me. I gave him a me that even I had fallen in love with. I had been open, honest, accommodating, accepting, supportive, and compassionate. I sunk into my bathroom floor; my legs were even unaware of their function. All I could do was sob.

Every time I told him "I love you," he would say, "I love you more." This was not more. This made no sense. I asked for explanation, to talk, to sit down with me. He would not. All he said was that he really does love me but he could not give me the time and attention I wanted and deserved. I knew he was walking through hard things, and I wanted to walk through them with him, but he didn't want me to.

How under heaven's covering do I resolve the entire situation? I absolutely could not imagine the burden he bore to be the only parent to his children. The hard part was I could see them in the mix of my children and love them as much. I had prayed before ever meeting him. If it was not meant to be, that God would protect me from the situation. But God had revealed that he would find healing through me. Things had clicked on so many levels. Deciphering my path in the middle of this storm would be another heart-wrenching work.

Broken. Again. I'm so tired of being broken. And why? Was this another test? I know I had stumbled into disobedience, but I took control and repented. Was my heart sacrificed to show him forgiveness and freedom is possible? God had strengthened me to stand and heal. Maybe because he was the glue that pieced my heart together again, he knew that I would survive this. I loved him and his kids very deeply. If it took my heart another breaking so healing could come to him, so be it. It's not always about me.

Having done this before, I knew how to heal. I also knew it would be painful. Again, I had to let dreams die and, with them, a part of myself. I mourned greatly. This rejection was savage. The best of me was not good enough? My attempts to surrender the future to God was lacking. The pain was so heavy it was grueling to drag my load to the cross.

Daily, I prayed for his healing, that the Holy Spirit would soften his heart to accept forgiveness from God and from himself. I prayed that God would lead us back together, if it was his will. And again, I prayed fervently for my broken heart to be healed.

Moving on seemed impossible, and I felt part of it was because he did not give me closure. I reached out and pleaded with him to speak to me. He wouldn't. I knew coming against this pain and rejection would take great force. I set out to do a ninety-day prayer and fast. I needed heaven to recognize my fortitude and grace me with answers. My request was for his healing, the mending of my heart, and a new fire for *Shed*.

My heart and mind had been so derailed I was not expecting a call from Kara, my paralegal.

When I answered, she said, "Girl, we have got to get you in here next week!"

I'm sure she thought I was crazy because I had to ask why.

"Trial is in less than two weeks! We have to get you ready!"

Holy cow! That totally snuck up on me! I had been reading 2 Samuel 22 and praying for God to line up and prepare the events before me, but I had so surrendered the outcome I had not focused on the time frame.

Thankfully, I had given God control over this trial. Honestly, I was struggling to breathe with this broken heart. I thought I had given him so much of what was missing in his marriage; I expected him to come back. Each day that passed took me further away from him, deepening my rejection. I had to block my heart in order to focus in this moment. This trial was three years coming. Three years since I had left Jared, two years past the agreement deadline.

It was unbelievable the ease I had going into trial. I had no doubt that the perfect outcome was before me. God had developed such pure trust in my heart, no matter what verdict the judge ordered, his hand would carry me through.

Entering Kara's office that morning was a different me than the terrified woman a year ago at the depositions. My fear, through David's song of praise, sounded the anthem of deliverance from my enemy. He rescued me because he delighted in me.

It was time to face my risen giant. He had wielded weapons of lies, manipulation, deceit. My weapons of choice were the armor of God. Jared had no idea the greatness he was fighting. It all came down to this moment. Those four and half years ago, when the Holy Spirit revealed that, through me, Jared would see God, this was not what I had hoped; but his heart remained hardened. The army of angels prepared the way.

Rising and falling multiple times could no longer keep me down. I walked into the courtroom unrecognizable to the woman Jared had found me last. The broken woman that crumbled outside his camper that day had blown away with the wind. The girl sobbing in the floor, staring at her husband's photos of infidelity, she stood back up. The Michelle he bailed out of jail had found her strength from the only life-giving source.

God had worked a masterful mosaic from my broken pieces. His light had become so intense inside me everything the rays struck beamed a new creation. No price could be adequate for the peace he so freely filled me with. This last battle was a technicality. I already stood as victor in this war.

Sitting at the table with my lawyer, I swiveled my chair to avoid focusing on Jared. As the judge was being announced and entered the courtroom, my prayers flowed, requesting justice at last. The format was similar to the depositions but with much more intensity. Tom asked even more questions about the military scandal. Frustrated with Jared's ambivalence on truth, the judge directly asked him questions. He continued to skew honesty, making his deceit more apparent.

My intent on the stand was the same as it had been during depositions: honesty. Jared had gotten away with so much his entire life. I had been the only person to ever find proof against him. Shockingly, he snaked events his direction with the military. He was no longer shielded by his standing as an officer, not in this court.

In the manner of an instant, all questioning ceased. My breath stilled as the moment of truth floated into the room. I kept my chair swiveled away from Jared. Emotions hung in my throat as I recalled all the broken moments of suspicion I had lived in. It was years of looking for proof of what my gut could not deny, years of feeling insane for "knowing" but not knowing, years of feeling like a failure because I was not able to trust him. Leaving expression off my face, I closed my eyes and listened.

THE COURT: The Court finds specifically that the Defendant, Jared Martin's credibility is lacking. His answers were not forthcoming by his attorney. Their conversations, the advice, meetings, that was not objected to and he testified as to those matters, and his memory suddenly became very vague when there were questions asked about the advice that he had gotten prior to the entry—his entering into this particular agreement. His general demeanor suggests to the Court his untruthfulness. He even admitted, while he was on the stand, that he has been dishonest previously in proceedings concerning some of the same issues, or at least some of the facts that were in contention here today, or were being testified as to today. He's told us that it was his intention to never abide by the agreement even though it was submitted to this Court previously. And he readily admitted that he was trying to get back into this relationship with the Defendant, and it appears that after the Plaintiff had rejected his attempts to get back into the relationship, only then did he have the Plaintiff served with his complaint. The Court is aware that people often use terminology that is not correct. After being a prosecutor for twenty-four years I'm pretty sick of the term, robbery, when someone gets burglarized. And the Court finds that, or at least understands that the Plaintiff, when she used the term extort or extortion in one of her emails was probably not reading from a Black's Law Dictionary, at least there's no testimony to that affect. There's never been any threats that the Plaintiff made that she could not legally do, or she had a right to do, under the law. The Court finds that the Defendant has intentionally stalled either to give himself time to see whether or not he can get back into the relationship and then sought revenge, or to get some type of advantage over the Plaintiff. This was calculated conduct as far as waiting on this lawsuit, the service in this lawsuit, and the Court finds that latches does apply and it's stopped by latches. The Court further finds that there has been no theft, by definition, based on the facts that's been introduced in this case that there has been no duress, that the Defendant allowed the Court to enter the decree knowing full well that he was not going to abide by that decree. The Court would point out that the Defendant was represented by an attorney, and that the Plaintiff was self represented during the previous negotiations and hearings, and this was all during that time that an agreement was executed and being considered by the parties. The Court further finds that the Plaintiff's claim in the initial action is a marital claim based on what she believes she was—what she deserved, what she'd earned, and for her contributions in the marriage, what she perceived to be hers, that she had an intention of getting back what was hers. The Court can see how she understood or came to the calculations she did. There were reasons why the Defendant would have entered into this agreement. And, again, this is evidenced by his gifts to the Plaintiff later, and then finally having her served a summons after his attempts had failed. The Court finds that the text that were sent that used the phrase, forcible sex, could be understood based on the text of the Defendant where he's talking about force or using force, slapping ass, a bit sore, indicates at least some type of roughness where she could very well have used the terminology that she did. The Court finds that her threats do not constitute duress, nor do they constitute extortion by definition. And the decree is going to remain in effect. Can you get an order on that, Mr. Kenton?

MR. KENTON: I will, Your Honor. Are you going to make any finding with respect to contempt?

THE COURT: I think I have to. The Court is going to find Mr. Martin in contempt.

MR. ADAMS: Your Honor, I mean, the Court can find a judgment without finding he purposefully and willfully, maliciously thwarted his word.

THE COURT: His testimony was that I never intended to do this. Even though his credibility is zilch, I'm going to believe him on that part when he says, I never. "I let this Court enter that agreement, but I never, ever intended to comply with that." He is in contempt. Now, I'll let him purge himself of contempt.

Mr. Adams: I understand. I just thought he was being honest with the Court because he thought he was being extorted.

The court: No, he never thought he was being extorted. You know, he admits that he was represented by an attorney when he entered into this. I think I would probably leave it where it is, Mr. Adams, because you were the attorney during that period of time and I would hope that you did not allow this Court to enter into that agreement, or enter that judgment knowing that your client was not going to abide by it.

Mr. Adams: I got fired, Judge.

the court: Huh?

Mr. Adams: I got fired.

The court: At a convenient time.

Mr. Adams: I agree.

The court: But, at any event, if he complies with the agreement I'll let him purge himself of the contempt, otherwise he's going to spend the next ninety days in jail, and I'll give him thirty days to purge himself of the contempt.

I remained frozen, all of me except the tears that streamed my cheeks. Part of me wondered if I had heard the judge's words correctly. Somebody finally believed me. Validity coursed through my turmoil and released the knots in my stomach. Jared could no longer cast stones at me. All ties to him were now frayed, diminished to ashes that no longer recognized the intertwining we had been in what seemed like another life. Tapping my arm, my lawyer awakened me to the moment.

"Let's get out of here."

Kara had slipped in just in time to hear the verdict. Still in a daze, I walked out of the courtroom, into the sunshine.

Once at the office, Kara asked me, "You were so calm as the verdict was being read. What was going through your mind?"

Softly, I replied, "Relief. Complete freedom."

This was more than a courtroom victory. This was a confirmation of the woman I had become. It was not the ruling that defined my strength. It was the multiple times of surrender, putting on humility, bowing myself down to a power so much greater and beyond myself. It took lying down in order to stand strong.

One week after the judge's ruling, Jared's lawyer contacted Mr. Kenton's office, notifying him that the check was in the mail. When it was received, Kara invited me to lunch. As she handed it to me, her smile beamed with satisfaction. She had seen me battle both Everett and Jared.

"It's been an honor taking this journey with you." She had become a friend.

As I looked at the check, I was not seeing numbers. I was standing firm on the other side of the canyon with my sword lifted in victory. Turning to see all the treacherous landscape behind me, at times I saw two sets of footprints. Other areas, the most dangerous areas, only one set of prints. Looking closely, I could see tiny prints in those bigger steps. I knew those had been my most fearful, weakest moments. Those were the moments I walked behind Jesus, my hands on his shoulders while he led me. I had no view of how perilous the terrain had been. My eyes were on him as he protected me from seeing the steep grades we were scaling. He was there just as he had shown me.

Looking at that check, I also knew revelation had come to pass. When Jared wrote out that check, he saw God. He had seen me walk with a strength he knew I did not possess. The actions I successfully accomplished were not of myself. The turn of events was the processing of God's favor. Through me, Jared saw God.

God had shown himself faithful to me. My heart cried in awe of his power and glory. My thankfulness broke into worship and praise, gratitude so deeply striking it melted every imprint my scarlet *R* had ever branded me with. All those scars disappeared. God had marked me as his in every way, internally and externally. He presented my life to me as a clean slate, and with a new heart, beating with purpose. Wanted. Chosen.

MICHELLE MARTIN

Wrapped in the middle of God executing his faithfulness after such a long, intense war, my trust had been magnified to new levels. I carried my broken-again heart to the cross, kneeling, but then completely crumbling before him. I didn't know how long healing would take. I prayed he would snap his fingers and release the glue to hold the shards of brokenness together again. Regardless of his time frame, I knew he was the source, not alcohol and not another man.

74

The prayer and fast I had started continued. I added another request: for God to show me how to properly steward the money I received from the trial. As I leaned in closely to him, he came nearer and nearer. He pulled me into him in a way I was not expecting. He was calling me to make a pilgrimage journey. He had met me on my ground; now he was summoning me to his land.

My research led me to this one particular trip that included Greece. I had always wanted to see Greece, but when I checked the availability, it was booked quite some time out. As I was beginning to think this trip may not be a good idea, something caught my attention: the Exodus tour.

Thousands of years before my time, Moses had led the Israelites out of bondage. His strength ran through me many times when I pleaded for Jared to let me go. I had envisioned standing in a desolate area with Jared sitting high in his grandeur, steps above me, towering in power. I softly and humbly made my requests for freedom. Just as Moses's words gained weight with the plagues, my voice became mightier with heaven's breath. This trip was destined for me.

Everything lined up in a matter of moments. I asked my boss if I could be off for three weeks. No problem. I contacted the tour company to solidify a spot. They had one for me. I made the payment and received confirmation. In less than six weeks, I would make my Exodus journey.

Immediately, I began preparations. I reread Moses's story and the Gospels. I wrote down every place we would visit, then did a historical and biblical study. Not watching TV was part of my fast, which lined up perfectly in removing distractions. Closer to time for the trip, I started getting up at 3:00 a.m. to prepare for the seven-hour time difference. The extra prayer and study time was phenomenal! God had prepared the way for me, and I needed to do my part as well.

Stepping out of the airport, I entered a new world, the ancient world. The presence of biblical characters came alive as I breathed in the Egyptian mystique. This land of intrigue had become a place of bondage for God's people. Signs of old lingered among the new. Time could change, but history could never be erased.

After a short overnight in Cairo, we took a small flight deeper into Egypt. The next four nights, I would sleep on *The Moon Goddess* as we cruised the Nile River. My journey in Egypt began similar to Moses's, being surrounded by the Nile waters. At sunset, I sat on my balcony watching the beams dance across the water. In the distance, hills of sand rose and fell across the horizon. In utter awe, I lifted prayers of thanks that God had brought me here.

At 3:00 a.m. the next morning, I strapped on my hiking boots, grabbed my fedora, and disembarked the ship. We took an excursion across the Sahara desert to the Abu Simbel temples built by Ramesses II. From the window of the bus, I watched the sun rise over the desert. The rays brought into view landscape untouched by time or human influence. The scene cast in front of me was the same of thousands of years in time.

Walking toward the temples, their splendor increased as I shrunk in size. The artistic impressions were flawlessly executed. Great planning and effort merged to build these temples. Ramesses had commissioned the structures as monuments to himself and his queen to commemorate his victories.

Driving back to the ship through the Sahara, our bus made a stop on the side of the road. The sunlight and heat mixed together to create an unbelievable mirage. I thought they were only a myth! It was stunning, looking so real. In my imagination, I could see a caravan of camels and people making a long trek in the scorching sunlight.

Over the next several days, we visited numerous temples. The pagan culture worshiped men and animals, setting them high as deities. In the Valley of the Kings, tombs had been discovered containing mounds of treasures; their belief being that their riches followed them into the next life.

My last night on the cruise, following dinner, I went alone to the upper deck. Sun had set bringing a cool breeze along with a soft calmness. I stood on the forward deck watching the waters of the Nile part in the ripples created by *The Moon Goddess*. The moonlight glimmered across the date palms growing on the banks. Just beyond them, the hills of sand continued as far as I could see. Looking down into the waters, I pictured baby Moses floating among the reeds. So innocent, pure, unaware he had been chosen. He had no idea his choices, words, obedience, and example would carry forward thousands of years to a woman now standing in the same waters that birthed his story.

Luxor was the final temple to visit before going back north to Cairo. Approaching the legendary fortress as a tourist was magically intimidating. Enormous statues of powerful Pharaohs perched high on solid granite thrones. My mind drifted to Moses.

His encounter with God at the burning bush could not be denied. As he came near to Pharaoh, to request freedom for the Israelites, I wondered if he felt like a small speck of dust as I did standing beside this throne now.

God called his name from the bush, "Moses!"

"Here I am," he replied. Feeling the potency of God's power then, was he afraid now? Did he want to run? But with the force of a magnet, he was drawn closer. Standing now looking at the power of Pharaoh, having been warned this would be hard, did quitting cross his mind? He had questioned God, "Who am I to bring the Israelites out of Egypt?"

I wonder if he travelled back in his memory to removing his scandals due to the magnitude of God's glory. He could only proceed with his task by drawing on the power established over him at the burning bush.

Unlocking Egyptian history unearthed mesmerizing treasures of an ancient people. Their beliefs were intriguing, yet lonely. They labored to build temples and lay up treasures for themselves that amounted to nothing more than loot for tomb raiders. The pyramids stood impressively bold in the Egyptian sun, built to endure an eternity. As captivating as they were, I was eager to continue in Moses's Exodus.

Leaving Cairo symbolized Moses and the Israelites fleeing captivity, in perspective to my trip. I was eager to reach Mt. Sinai. It was one of the places I looked forward to most. The scenery lost all evidence of progress as we entered the wilderness. I was reminded of a verse God stamped on my heart as I left my marriage and everything behind me: "Therefore I am now going to allure her; I will lead her into the wilderness and speak tenderly to her. There I will give her back her vineyards; and will make the Valley of Achor a door of hope. There she will respond as in the days of her youth, as in the day she came up out of Egypt" (Hosea 2:14–15).

Three years ago, the wilderness God was leading me to was the safety and quietness of my parents' home. He spoke so tenderly to me in those broken, still moments. In the valleys of my despair, he created doors of hope that I thought had no longer existed due to my repeated mistakes.

Looking out my window, scenes of the wilderness scrolled by. It lay in front of me, behind and beside me. All around me, nothing but wilderness. I never dreamed God would encompass me with the same wilderness as the Israelites. Just as he had delivered them, he delivered me. He brought me up out of Egypt. He rescued me because he delighted in me.

Before reaching Mt. Sinai, we stopped for lunch in Dehab. It was an oasis in the middle of the wilderness, located in the Gulf of Aqaba of the Red Sea. Looking across the waters was the country of Saudi Arabia. On this day, the Egyptian land boasted beauty and serenity.

Sitting on the pebbled beach, I took off my socks and shoes. Countless messages and Bible verses ran though my memory of the miraculous parting of the Sea. Tiptoeing across the bank, I stepped into the Red Sea. Closing my eyes, I felt the terror of the Israelites as their promised land escapade stopped at the water's edge. Sounds of chariots thundered louder and louder as their newfound freedom was being threatened.

The Israelites cried out in intense fear, "Why did you make us leave Egypt? It is better to be a slave in Egypt than a corpse in the wilderness!"

Moses picked up his staff and raised his hand over the Sea. The Lord opened up a path through the water with a strong wind. He crushed their enemy and had the Israelites cling tightly to their freedom.

Oh, how I related to their fear. The day I was served papers, Jared claiming extortion against me, an entire year after our divorce, he interrupted my wilderness of freedom. I felt hunted down and trapped, like a Red Sea of complications flooded my promised-land path. My conquered enemy seemed relentless to chain me to my past. Lying hopeless like a corpse in the wilderness seemed easier.

But oh the wind of God stirred up a mighty fight in my soul. He lifted me up from the floor the many times I was drowning in my tears. He strengthened me in the small battles in order to arm me for war. In the humility of surrender, he made my path clear, crushing my enemy in the wake.

Standing in the greatness of the very Red Sea God had parted with only a breath made my heart erupt with praise. The God with such mighty power in a simple breath had brought me to this moment. The clear waters ran soothingly over my feet. I knew nothing he did was without purpose. His every breath was driven with intent.

Our Mt. Sinai hike was set for sunset. The atmosphere altered from a quaint seaside oasis to a rocky, desolate mountainous wonderland. I was so anxious to scale this mountain. God met Moses here many times. I wanted to intervene on their space, to absorb the moment God made his covenant to the Israelites and marked them as his treasure. This was ground where promises and fulfillment collided.

There was a vibe among the space of Mt. Sinai. A presence existed here that I could feel deeply in my soul. That presence was calling me upward. The air gained a coolness and carried a majestic silence that piqued my curiosity. Our ascension up the mountain would be on camel for about 2.5 hours, followed by a steep trek up 750 rock steps.

I was immediately captivated by the camels. They represented an ancient time. Quiet but smiling, what secrets had they carried forward? Climbing onto the back of my chosen one-hump camel, again I entered into another time.

Our camel caravan began the long assent up Mt. Sinai. Every click of the camel's steps, the beauty and stillness unearthed mysteries that invited me deeper into Moses's Exodus. My story was erased as I melded into a time thousands of years before me.

Moses must have felt lonely and doubtful. No one was standing beside him at the burning bush. No one could corroborate the insanity of what he experienced and heard God speak over him. I felt the same way. God spoke a purpose over me needing capabilities to complete that I did not possess. Here I was climbing a mountain that neither Moses nor I had seen in our futures.

Just as Moses had questioned God, "Who am I that you would choose me?" I wrestled with disbelief until I could no longer fight God's destiny. God unquestionably called Moses to lead his people to freedom, release their bondage of slavery. How ironic thousands of years later, his call to me would echo the exact instruction?

My eyes had never taken in this kind of beauty unique to Mt Sinai. The higher we went, more and more rocky peaks came into view. When we left the base of the mountain, the rocks were different shades of brown. Now the sun was beginning to set and cast colorful hues of yellows, pinks, blues, and purples. The winds blew a soft howl of isolation. Reaching the camel station, the final leg of our climb would be on foot. Sunset was approaching quicker than we had anticipated. I was dying to reach the summit before the sun's light took away its view. I wanted to run ahead; I could not miss it.

The group I was with was not used to hiking, and our pace was slow. My heart was beating with anticipation to get to the top. Not able to wait any longer, I asked the guide if I could go ahead.

"Please stay away from the edge and be careful."

One of the younger guys in the group took off with me. He kept a good pace at first, then started lagging behind.

"I'm sorry, but I have to reach the top. Are you okay with me going on?"

Once he gave me a nod, I darted off.

The climb was rocky and steep, but I was determined to see the top of Sinai before the sun went down. The higher I climbed, the more I left the world behind me. Stopping to catch my breath, I took in the 360-degree view. Nothing but God's creation lay before me. Neither time nor man had a fingerprint on this space.

Hiking on to the summit, the church I was told about came into view. I knew I was nearing the top. Looking at the trail behind me, I could not see anyone coming. God was giving me exactly what I had hoped for: time alone on his mountain. Knowing my love of sunsets, he polished off my request.

I walked around the summit of Mt. Sinai in absolute astonishment. Peace settled in my heart like the blanket of stillness covering this mountain. I made a couple walks around the top, drinking in the beauty of the moment. The sunset began touching all the mountain peaks I could see, releasing even more beauty each passing second. As lonely as Moses must have felt walking out his calling, I imagine he treasured the solitude this summit restored to him. The Lord called him here and fulfilled promises he set in motion even before Moses's time.

Finding the perfect slab of rock, I sat as the sun sank deeper into the mountain peaks. Tears of gratitude rolled from my eyes. Looking over the landscape reminded me of the canyon I had scaled in my freedom journey. It had been such a lonely, dry, desolate hike out of my brokenness. All I could do was cling to God. I was in unmapped territory. Sometimes it didn't seem like my steps were taking me anywhere. Then, just like that, God has me here on top of Mt. Sinai!

My presence here, just like Moses's represented fulfillment of promises. God had declared many things to me. Some had already come to pass. The things yet to be, I stood believing on. Nobody could take them from me. They were breathed of God, owned by me. No heartbreak on earth would ever steal my freedom.

As the sunset descended on Sinai, I lifted prayers up to heaven. God released to me his purpose for my journey here. He wanted to pull me closer to him. My heart smiled as he told me, "I am fully washing you. This is a complete rebirth." While his words were settling in my ear, distant footsteps became louder. One of the guides walked up to me.

"Do you know where you're sitting? The stone you're on is the top of the cave where Moses stayed while he was here."

He walked me down and around to the entrance of the stone cave. This cave, among other findings, has led scholars to believe this is the actual Mt. Sinai. Regardless of specifics, I had collided with God and Moses on this mountain. Gradually, the others in my group reached the top. I was the only one that arrived before sunset, thankful for my alone time here.

75

With no more sunlight it became very cold on the mountain. We descended in complete darkness with only the light from our flashlights. I started walking and talking with one of the two guides that had taken us up. I was curious about his life and beliefs.

He was born and raised in the Mt. Sinai region. He has a small hut at the base of the mountain where he lives with his wife and children. They have a small community there. He has learned to speak five languages just from guiding people up and down the mountain. He has dreamed of traveling the world but would never want to call any other place home.

Not being very familiar with Muslim faith, I asked him to share with me. I told him how incredible I thought it was that they dedicate to the call of prayer five times a day. He was open and shared freely with me. He said he had made so many trips up and down the mountain he could do it with his eyes closed. His life was so fascinating to me. We spoke all the way down the mountain. When we reached the bottom, I realized I had not introduced myself.

"It has been an incredible adventure. I'm Michelle."

"For me as well. My name is Moses."

Oh, the irony of God! I could not help but chuckle. I had just been led up and down Mt. Sinai by Moses. What a day! Only God could weave such a wonderful twist of events.

The following day before leaving Sinai, we visited St. Catherine's monastery and the site of the believed "burning bush." Despite any debate of authenticity, I believe what matters is paying homage in your heart to the miracles of God. The monastery was built around the bush, giving it protection. It is a rare species that stays green year round. Areas around the bush, special rocks can be found. Any place in which they are broken reveals an imprint of the burning bush.

Stepping aside from the group, I had to let this resonate. A huge boulder recovered from the area set out for display. It had been broken to reveal the beauty of the imprints inside. Sitting beside it, I rubbed my hand over the unique imprints. Glancing to look at the burning bush, the impressions in the stone were identical.

My mind gulped as I related this to the words God spoke to me on the summit yesterday.

"This is a complete rebirth," he said to me.

He was imprinting himself in my heart. My broken spaces now revealed his beauty. I placed my hand over my heart, realizing the impressions were identical to the maker.

Continuing in the Exodus journey, leaving Sinai was bittersweet. The imprint God marked in my heart on the summit would go with me forever. Watching the sunset over the mountain peaks, in complete silence, alone with God, was a pure gift.

We were traveling to Jordan, but had to cross the tip of Israel in order to enter the country. This had to be done on foot. Our guide dropped us off at the edge of the Egyptian border. We each had to drag our luggage and go through each countries' checkpoints to leave and enter each area. The pathway we walked was guarded with barbed-wire fences and military soldiers holding machine guns. It felt like a scene out of a movie.

The entire next day was spent exploring Petra, my second Seven Wonders of the World within a few days, the pyramids being the first. Petra was its own world of mystique. Centuries ago settlers carved this Rose City out of stone. It's an archaeological gem and an adventurers dream. It's said to be the location of the Tomb of Aaron, the burial place of Moses's brother.

The entrance leads steeply down through a dark, slim gorge called the Siq, formed from a split in the sandstone. It appears as though the adventure is ending as you walk through the narrowing of the Siq, but rounding a curve of the rock, the Treasury is revealed. It's an entryway into even more mysteries held in Petra.

It would be impossible not to stand in awe of the beauty preserved in time. Donkeys, camels, and locals meander as if time had stood still at the birth of this hidden city. Even the feeling in the atmosphere breathes another time. This was a place I could explore for days, but with sunset nearing, our time here was ending.

The following day's main point of interest was Mt. Nebo. I had not given much thought to the mountain until my studies last night. After connecting so deeply to Moses on Sinai, I realized today our journey together would end. I could not help but carry my sadness to the mountain.

Approaching Mt. Nebo, I already felt like a piece of me was being left behind. The journey from the Nile to Nebo had taken me eleven days. For Moses, it was a lifetime, 120 years. Moses was the only man to ever come face-to-face with God. The very moment God's fire from the bush shined on Moses's face, he became a new creature. He entered the life of a prophet, chosen to set God's people free. I wonder what emotions Moses carried with him up Mt. Nebo. His journey had been long and strenuous.

Walking up the mountain, the sun shone on my face and a mild breeze blew. Close to the top was a memorial to Moses carved in stone, resembling a tablet. I stepped over to the side viewing the Jordan Valley from which we had just come.

Upon reaching the top, our group gathered for prayer and a spontaneous lesson. Our guide opened his Bible and read Deuteronomy 34:1–4. I cried for Moses. I too could see all the land the Lord had just spoke of. Looking to my right was the ground Moses and I had traveled together. To my left was the Dead Sea and beyond was the promised land. Moses stood with me in this very place; our eyes shared the same view. Sadly, his feet would not take the steps ahead with me.

Moses was instrumental in leading the Israelites into freedom. Unknown to him, he led me as well. Drawing from his story empowered me in creating mine. Moses represented promise, law, obedience, and unfortunately disobedience. Mostly, he exemplified relationship to God. He was only able to display miracles because he let God work through him. He must have gotten so frustrated at the

Israelites' repeated grumbling and disobedience. In the act of misuse of God's power through him, striking the rock instead of speaking to it as commanded, he turned loose of his entrance into the promised land. He chose an act of disobedience.

Oh, how it must have broken God's heart. God had to enact punishment to highlight the importance of obedience. So sweetly, God kept Moses for himself. Upon his death, he carried Moses to his grave and buried him, leaving his grave unmarked so no one could defile his memory.

Leaving Moses on Nebo was difficult. He had been such a leader and companion in my wilderness. Walking down the mountain, I turned to look over the promised land. I whispered a soft farewell, clinging tightly to the lessons he taught me. I promised to continue my Exodus journey and finish well.

As a goodbye to Jordan, our guide treated us to a traditional Jordanian lunch, maqluba. It was a delicious way to say goodbye and great fuel for our passage into Israel. So many phenomenal moments had occurred in Egypt and Jordan. I knew Israel was holding even more.

The drive was long to Israel and very tiresome. I decided to skip dinner in order to shift my focus and prepare to walk in the steps of Jesus. Stepping out on my balcony, I had a view of the Mediterranean Sea. The rush was so overwhelming. This seemed like a clip out of someone else's life. Three years ago I was wallowing in the floor, gasping for air. Now, God has me drinking in his Mediterranean Sea.

Standing in spell-bounding wonderment, I blared my worship music and fell to my knees. I erupted in tears. God had exchanged my tears of pain for tears of joy. Those three years ago, I had no direction. The broken woman of that day now stood half a map away and a world of distance from who she had been.

Raindrops began to fall obscuring my view of the sea. Nothing could damper my joy of being right here, right now. I would trudge through snow for the chance of following in Jesus's steps. Our guide had told us that rain is rare in this land, so it was a wonderful gift from heaven.

The rain continued into the following day. Although it made touring difficult, not a single person complained. We traveled along the coast of the Mediterranean Sea to Caesarea where Peter shared the Gospel with the Gentiles. We saw Mt. Carmel on our way to Megiddo, the Armageddon battlefield.

Destruction has visited this land many times. Archaeologists have unearthed twenty levels of civilization and speculate this to be the site of the final battle referenced in Revelation 16:16. In the distance was Mt. Gilboa, where King Saul died. My mind drifted to King David.

He knew the hills and caves well from the many times he ran and hid from Saul fearing for his life. I wondered if the flat land was where he had tended sheep as a boy. Wandering this ground, the only light came from the sun, moon, and stars. He learned to listen and be on guard in the darkness. He came to sense the attacks coming on from lions and bears. In those attacks, he gained strength as he defeated them.

I could hear him singing songs of praise to God while he breathed in the stillness. He came to know and trust the Lord as he walked the pastures with him. His trust was such a foundation he declared victory before facing the giant Philistine. First Samuel 17:37, "The Lord who rescued me from the claws of the lion and bear will rescue me from this Philistine."

I borrowed David faith so many times. It was his strength in declaring victory over Goliath that strengthened me in facing my risen giant. Like David, I claimed God's victory over the giant that repeatedly sought me. The small stones in my small hands became powerful weapons in the name of the Lord of Heaven's Armies.

David meant so much to me. He was sought by the Lord as a man after his own heart, but he was not perfect. I love that about David. He did not claim to be above the touch of sin. Above anything else, he had an unwavering belief in the faithful and forgiving nature of God. He sinned but was quick to confess and his repentance was deeply genuine. Even in the middle of living out the consequences of his sin, his gratitude for forgiveness gave him a zest for living.

He taught me to humble myself to God's call. Although I sin and mess things up, God's power is above my mistakes. He called David long before his strength emerged. Just as in my darkness, God's power could not be choked out by the lack of light, but formed out of nothing, until all I could see was his light.

During Saul's repeated pursuit of David, David stayed encouraged, standing strong in his faith of God. His songs of praise shrunk seemingly powerful enemies. He declared who God is: my rock, fortress, savior, refuge, lamp. David's allegiance helped form my commitment to being a woman after God's own heart despite my imperfections. I looked fondly over the pastures and hills as I remembered my moments with David.

Leaving Megido, we drove into the hills we had seen in the distance and came upon Nazareth. Nazareth was busy with life's hustle and bustle like the rest of the world, but in the center was Nazareth village. Two thousand years after Jesus's birth, this farm and village remains untouched by change. Setting foot on these grounds whisks you away to a time of Jesus's youth.

This establishment recreates life in the times as Jesus grew. Looking around, life was simple. The function of the atmosphere was survival. In his daily activities, God strengthened him in the spirit and filled him with wisdom. The Holy Spirit had not yet descended upon Jesus. My curiosity wondered about his revelation. He had to know he was different. He had to feel the Father course through his veins.

He was set apart undoubtedly. Scholars recognized his enchanting wisdom as he taught in the temple at only the age of twelve. I wonder if in the moments God set him aside from the world in order to be filled with such wisdom, did Jesus feel alone? He knew he was not alone, but did he feel left out?

There have been numerous times in my wilderness that I was excluded from events, parties, and dinners. That hurt and felt lonely. I had to grasp hold of the fact that God was recreating a better version of myself during those alone times. I wasn't alone.

76

Our next stop and lodging the following two nights was on the Sea of Galilee. This area was another of my most anticipated, the atmosphere of most of Jesus's teaching and miracles. Oh, to breathe it all in! God had released so many miracles in my life. To stand in the space where it all began was another.

The rain had followed us all day but could not flood the enchantment of Galilee. I had my own private bungalow. It was beautiful, with a view of the Sea from my window. After unloading my luggage, I put on my rain poncho and walked down toward the Sea. I stood in unbelief that my feet were at the water's edge. So many Bible stories took place touching these waters. I had read, reread, and soaked up the stories into my heart. They were more than stories. They were real-life moments that skipped through time and brought me back to life. The miracles of ancient time are timeless. God released them into existence thousands of years ago with an endless power. Their power had found me.

Reflecting on the person I had been and the person now as God had resuscitated me back to life, my tears began to fall in line with the raindrops. So many times I wanted to be drained of life and give up my ability to breathe. I tried numerous times to drown myself in alcohol. But God, God drowned me in his love. As I lifted my hands in praise, he handed me scripture: Psalm 34.

Not being gifted with a good memory, upon returning to my room, I looked up Psalm 34. It is titled "The Happiness of Those Who Trust in God."

Line after line I connected with David's words. Like David, my enemies sought to destroy me. God's chase for me ran more wild and deeper than any effort evil could bring forth. Seeking God's truth foiled the evil one's attack. I was living smack in the middle of that final verse: "The Lord redeems the soul of his servants, and none of those who trust in him shall be condemned."

Our Israeli adventures this day started at the mouth of the Jordan River and Caesarea Philippi, the site of Peter's confession.

Jesus asked the disciples, "Who do you say I am?"

Peter answered, "You are the Messiah, the Son of the living God."

This was revealed to him through the Father, Jesus's identity had not been defined at that time.

Jesus, in return, revealed Peter's true identity: "You are Peter, and upon this rock I will build my church."

The profoundness of this event set in as I reflected on my journey. When I confessed Jesus as my savior, he gave me my new identify. I thought back to the moment we shared when he came to my happy place and sat beside me. He looked at me and called me his disciple. He declared me worthy and capable.

I was fully enthralled into the life of Jesus. We travelled to Capernaum where most of his miracles were performed. I viewed the ruins of an ancient synagogue and what was believed to be Peter's house. They had become very close friends, and Jesus often stayed with Peter. What an incredible opportunity Peter had to walk daily with the Messiah.

Capernaum was a seaside town. I stepped away from the group and toward the water's edge. The rain was falling briskly, winds blew with such force the waters were white capping. I imagined the disciples in their boat as they were attempting to cross to the other side. I often thought how frail Peter's faith was when he walked toward Jesus and then began to sink.

If that were me, I would walk boldly toward Jesus, I had thought during my many readings of the account. Standing here now with the strong winds smacking my face with the rain, the waves rolling violently in front of me, I felt Peter's fear.

I had thought how easy it was for him to believe; he had witnessed miracles countless times. He walked beside him, ate meals with him, had him as a guest many, many times.

"Peter, how could you doubt? How could you take your eyes off Jesus in the storm and allow yourself to sink?"

Watching the waves thrash upon the rocks, I recalled storms in my life when my eyes were on anything but Jesus. My faith had been "Peter faith." I sunk too.

Yes, Peter walked in the same time period on earth as Jesus. But the spirit of Jesus is stronger than any bounds of time and space. His death freed his spirit to walk daily with me too. I have seen Jesus perform miracles in front of my very eyes. How could I ever doubt?

Despite his failures, Peter went on to be a voice of the Gospel. He showed me that God is looking for real people. He was an example to how God's love and acceptance can create true change in a person. Peter sunk, but he got back up. He took Jesus's hand. Having fear doesn't make you faithless; pressing on in spite of fear makes you faithful.

Traveling to Tiberius for lunch, we passed Bethsaida, the site of multiplication of loaves and fish. I could see the scene through my window, like looking through time. The crowd so thick it covered the landscape. Jesus had been performing miracles and attempted to get away, but the people followed. He continued to teach and heal despite his weariness. The long day brought hunger, so the disciples asked Jesus to send them away. Jesus had been feeding their spiritual hunger. Which would have been enough, but not to Jesus. He cared about all of their needs. So he fed them. The miracle he performed is impressive, but his actions display the golden rule, which is at the heart of this miracle and his ministry.

Tiberius presented us with an old-style fish lunch. I opted for chicken. We were seated with a seascape view on the edge of Galilee. The storms had calmed, some leaving a haze of allurement over the waters. Our boat ride had been canceled due to the weather. That was disappointing, but as we sat eating lunch, an unexpected image appeared: a full rainbow over the Sea of Galilee. I captured the most beautiful photo. The full rainbow over the sea and under the arch of its beauty, a single fishing boat was anchored.

I would much rather have the rainbow than that boat ride. I didn't want the significance to slip by me. This stood for promise. In Genesis 9:12–17, God releases the rainbow as his covenant to never flood the earth again. It is even deeper than it appears. His promise is for all people, across all time. That colorful rainbow in the sky is the stamp of God's unwavering faithfulness. Whatever he speaks forth, he will bring to fruition. My heart hugged that rainbow.

The rain did not ease as we toured more interesting sites that afternoon. I was looking forward to returning to my bungalow on Galilee. I was craving intimate time with Jesus. The entire drive back, I prayed God would vanish the rain. I wanted to walk and talk with Jesus as the sun set over Galilee.

Rain or not, I was going down to the water. We parked and unloaded in the rain. It continued on my walk to my bungalow. Disappointment began to set in; I may not get my sunset on Galilee. As soon as I opened my door, I knelt down in prayer.

"Please, God, stop the rain only for a moment. I want to see the sunset by the sea."

I took ten minutes to clean myself up to start down to the water. I said another quick prayer, then opened my door. Clouds were moving, the sun began to peek out, and the raindrops were gone. I squealed with girlish excitement! I'm getting my sunset on the Sea of Galilee!

I may never have breathed in such fresh air. The stillness released a vibrancy of quiet excitement. A presence of familiarity walked me to the water. Part of my desire to come to Israel was to return my broken heart to its Maker. Looking across the sea, I could see the reflection of clouds and sunlight in the ripples. A soft breeze brushed my skin. I could feel God as he met me here.

He erupted the brokenness within me. My teardrops fell into the Sea of Galilee. I imagined God swirling them into his heart as he took them from me. I bent down to touch the waters that held miracles, washing believers into freedom. He released his saving into me that day I reached up to heaven. He breathed new oxygen into the lifeless shell of me. God birthed a warrior. Although life on earth would never be perfect, it would forever be different. I was different.

Praying over my broken heart, I set it upon the water and softly pushed it out of my hands. I knew it was safe with God, and he would restore it from pain. Sunset began releasing colors of gold across the waters. I thought back to the vision I had of Jesus walking on the water toward me.

"Come near now, Jesus," I whispered.

I needed revival to rush inside me. *Shed* needed to come forward with a fierce fire to show people freedom. My life circumstances had scarred me with that scarlet *R* of rejection. It once burned deep crimson, searing into my worth. When God entered my life, he began washing it. With the deep-crimson blood of Jesus, I was washed clean. He deemed me worthy of the sacrifice of his beloved, innocent lamb.

I had been set free, but looking down into my hands, I still had a hold of that *R*. It was no longer red and burning my soul, but it was still in my grip.

"God, I want to be your disciple like Peter. I want to be your warrior like David. I want to be your leader like Moses," I uttered along with my tears.

"Then release to me what was never meant to be yours."

Kneeling to God, like I had come to do, I bent toward the waters again. Even though it was destructive, that *R* had become a part of me. In order to be the woman God created me to be, I had to let go. I looked up as I released my *R*. I was in absolute awe of the gift God delivered to me. The sky still held some dark clouds mixed in with the sun performing its bow for the night. Set between the clouds of change was another rainbow. God sealed his promise to me. My fire for *Shed* was renewed.

How significantly God had ordered the events of my trip. My day began at Yardenit, the Jordan River baptismal site. The waters were not deemed holy; and Jesus is the only one that ever touched the earth, never sinned, and did not need to be cleansed. He was giving an example of obedience. "Let it be done, for we must carry out all that God requires" (Matthew 3:15). Jesus wanted to be an example of every step necessary. Any person looking into his life could mimic every choice and be counted righteous.

The water was so cold, my breath quickened. I was dipped into the same waters as my savior. He joined me in baptism, so I could join him in death. After coming out of the water, I wrapped myself in a dry towel and sat to observe the magnificence around me.

Looking at the river, God reminded me of the passage he gave me right after my move to Balston. Psalm 1:1–3 states, "Blessed is the one who does not walk in step with the wicked or stand in the way that sinners take or sit in the company of mockers, but whose delight is in the law of the Lord, and who meditates on his law day and night. That person is like a tree planted by streams of water, which yields his fruit in season and whose leaf does not wither-whatever they do prospers."

I had no idea at the time that God was prophesying over me. He removed me from the company of Jared to a place of safety. Ironically, Balston is located on the river. It was there I began to meditate on his law day and night. Like streams of water, he replenished my withering soul.

My life stood as proof to God's character. He is still the same God today. He fulfilled the prophecy he spoke over me. As I drank in his living water, he released prosperity over me. He reversed the withering away of my life. I did not come up out of the Jordan River the same woman as the one that had gone down. I was not the same woman that stepped the last step behind me. Every movement forward, I was a new creature. My change of direction created a change of heart.

After leaving the Jordan River, we stopped for lunch in Jericho, visited the Qumran caves where some of the Dead Sea Scrolls were found, saw Ein Gedi, and spent the night at the Dead Sea. It had been a long day. Floating in the Dead Sea with no effort was relaxing. I looked at tomorrow so eager to be in Jerusalem. Another of my most anticipated places was Gethsemane.

Sunrise over the sea gradually released its light over the mountains and water. It was a soft, hazy morning. I walked the beach and prayed before going to breakfast. Our first stop of the day was at Masada, Herod the Great's fortress on the mountain plateau.

SHED

The fortress was incredible, mighty. It boasted of the king's power. After spending several hours at the site, we drove the hour and a half to Jerusalem. The first stop to be the Mount of Olives, hotel check-in, and then the Temple Mount. I spent the drive studying to refresh my memory.

The city the Lord had chosen in which to put his name, Jerusalem. Stepping off the bus, onto the Mount of Olives, I opened the door to ancient times. Standing on the Mount, I could see so many events in history. Years of prophecy collided among these hills. Jesus wept over Jerusalem, for the salvation of the people. Yet in the end, this land held his crucifixion and burial. On the very ground underneath my feet, he ascended into heaven, forever breaking the capsule of his identity.

I wept here too. Mine were tears of gratitude that Jesus had stood here, wept here, prayed here, ascended from his captivity to freedom here. He took me with him, breaking my chains of bondage. His obedience gifted me with a freedom I had never known. Standing on the Mount of my freedom, the view of Jerusalem was spectacular.

Coming down the Mount of Olives, we walked a portion of the temple grounds. Our guide read from the Bible and also shared some history with us. Walking the stones beneath my feet, I tried to imagine what some of Jesus's thoughts must have been. The steps he took as a boy would lead to steps of his death. He grew here, taught here, and died here.

77

God had been leading me into Jesus's steps. He filled my path with irony and symbolism, like his parables, full of hidden meaning that brought revelation with deep study. Glancing down to my feet, they stood upon a stone of the temple. My small feet in strappy sandals, similar to what Jesus wore. He had become my foundation; his path was now my path. His death was my death; his resurrection, my rebirth.

After returning to the hotel and my room, I swung my curtains open to see what my view would be. The sky was a soft blue; the sun was beginning to slip behind the buildings of Jerusalem. It cast out reflections of yellows and oranges across the clouds that swept through the sky. In the distance were silhouettes of the olive trees. I prayed over tomorrow, for tomorrow, I would pray in the garden.

I awoke to the morning with a heavy heart. I had walked Galilee, felt the hope Jesus poured out of his heart for the people, then standing on the Mount of Olives, I could feel his weeping. I could not wait to reach Gethsemane to see what he would reveal to me.

Our first site of the day was the Wailing Wall, where hundreds of Jews lamented. We traveled through the hidden tunnels of the temple, then to the pool of Bethesda. At the side of this pool, Jesus healed a man by simply speaking over him. While our group stood among the temple and pool, our guide prepared us for Gethsemane.

We encircled our guide as he opened his Bible to read about Jesus praying in the garden. I always knew it was hard, but I never understood his anguish. I thought being Jesus, he had a special guard over his pain. I had never considered him human because he was

Christ, but when he left heaven, he left his protection and became fully human. He walked the earth with the same equipment each of us have, access to the Father through his spirit and a fleshly body.

He knew his mission his entire life. I thought that made the doing easy. He was sent for this. His disciples even gave him the opportunity to flee, and Jesus could have, but he chose not to run. No human has ever been put through the type of physical, mental, and spiritual torture Jesus endured. He felt it so deeply as he prayed, the intensity produced blood.

Walking the path to the garden, I hoped to walk into Jesus's anguish. I know I could never bear what he did, but I wanted to relate. My heart became heavier and heavier as I saw the olive grove come into my view. People were everywhere, and like Jesus, I needed solitude to pray. Walking past the ancient trees, my tears flowed unashamed.

Jesus came here having a glimpse of the pain he was about to endure. How terrifying to know his body was about to be pierced, whipped, and completely tortured. He had no Band-Aid for the pain; his body was fully flesh.

His heart was being crucified along with his body. The people he tried so desperately to save turned against him. He prayed with such force that his love poured out through his sweat with drops of blood. Not only was he denied by the present people, he felt the denial of those to come. He felt the denial from me.

For the first time since his creation, he would be separated from God's spirit. His foundation, his love, his creator would be polar opposite from him. Taking on sin from history to the present and into the future would knock him into a realm out of God's sphere. He would enter absolute isolation for generations of sin, none being his own.

The physical, emotional, and spiritual pain inflicted onto him was compounded to an enormity of generations so magnified that I can only grasp a portion of its meaning. And that breaks me. It is beyond my ability to behold what Jesus felt. That small piece that I could feel that broke me was quite unbearable.

He felt anguish so piercing even before the cross that he pleaded to his Father for another way. Putting aside his desire, he declared the desire for God's will to be his greatest desire. In order to die on the cross for humanity, he died to himself in this garden.

Walking the garden with the presence of his pain upon me, I searched for a quiet place. I walked and walked, looking for somewhere. I came to a church. People were walking in and out, standing around. I went around to the side and found an open door. Above the door was written: Gethsemane. The room stepped down into a rocky cave. Inside were a few chairs facing a cross and candles lit along the sides of the little room. To the left of the entry was a bowl of olive branches. I picked one up and found a chair.

I sat looking at the cross with Jesus hanging upon it. I cried for my portion of responsibility that put him there and asked for forgiveness. Slipping into the floor, I turned and knelt over the seat of the chair, crying out. I had so much pain to release. Pain and unknowing.

"God, what do I do with all of this? On top of Mt. Sinai, you told me this trip is my rebirth. At the Sea of Galilee, I handed you my *R* and my broken-again heart. What are you telling me?"

He started revealing his point to my heart.

"This is where you completely die to yourself. You must have death to have your rebirth. I asked for your *R* because it was never intended to be yours. The rejection, the shame, unworthiness, pain, and doubt, I drowned them in that Sea. They are gone. I asked for your heart because I wanted to cleanse it. It is now mine and forever protected. You are my bride. You must die to your concern of what people will think when your life becomes an open book with *Shed*. I birthed this story from you. This is my will."

Right here in Gethsemane where Jesus died to himself, I died to myself with him. Only through him was I able to die and live. My tears met with his tears. He chose God's will, and so do I.

In this garden, God planted assurance in me. Unveiling *Shed* would unveil deep, personal pains, but he wanted to use them. Within the lines of my pain, he infused empowerment. His power to save me reached into a dark, lowly pit. His power to save is stronger than any depth of despair sin can create. Shed exemplifies the magnitude of his ability.

Leaving Gethsemane, I was drained and revitalized. I knew I would face even more hard things, but pressing into God's will, I could overcome them too. We drove to Caiaphas where Jesus was arrested, and then we went into Bethlehem.

A church had been built over the supposed caves of Jesus's birth. We entered into the church and then stepped down into the cave system. The cave had been adorned to commemorate his birth. We circled around to an empty cave to gather. Christmas was a little over a week away. We sang several Christmas songs that vibrated their beauty in the echo of the cave.

The day had been long, full of impactful events. Tomorrow I would walk the Via Dolorosa, the path of suffering, and see Golgotha. It would be my final day in Israel. My heart was already missing this place.

I woke with excitement to complete my path in Jerusalem with Jesus. The path of suffering was exciting because the resurrection came with it. My feet set out on the stone path. I carried with me the glimpse of Jesus's pain I had received in the garden. He had the additional weights of dragging that heavy wooden cross.

When I reached Golgotha or Calvary, I expected sadness. I was surprised that that was not what I felt. I had felt Jesus die in the Garden. Standing here, facing Calvary, I felt life. When he took his last breath, he bestowed me with the gift of life. This was a location of joy and fulfilled prophecy.

Before going to the tomb, our group was taken to a cave. One of the pastors with our group gave us a sermon, and we partook in communion. Our worship session closed by singing "Amazing Grace," the very song I had sung to my babies. That was before the destruction of me.

Singing "Amazing Grace" now came from a heart of gratitude as I stood across the canyon of my destruction. He saved a wretch like me. I once was lost but now am found. How precious is his amazing grace to me.

Going down the hill, the empty tomb was the completion of Jesus's assignment. He left earth to release his spirit to dwell in us. He adopted us into sonship. Without the power of the spirit, we have no connection to heaven.

Following dinner, a group I had gotten close to decided to go into downtown Jerusalem. I felt so alive following these powerful past few days. The city at night offered an invigorating energy. I drank in the atmosphere all the way down to my soul. I was still in such disbelief of all I had experienced the past three weeks. I was not ready to say goodbye to Israel. My walk here was ending, but my walk with Christ had been strengthened.

We walked down to the Wailing Wall, then up a hill just beyond it. We stood on a portion of the Wall that surrounded Jerusalem. The night sky was full of shining stars and the city full of lights. Looking over the stunning view, I whispered my goodbye. Jerusalem said goodbye back to me as I saw a falling star. I squealed with excitement and two of my friends caught the sight with me. Before leaving, my tears fell upon the wall of the city.

My driver was arriving at 3:00 a.m. to take me to the airport. There was no point to sleeping. Entering the quietness of my room, I fell to the floor. I cried out to God in thankfulness for me being here physically, but more importantly, so far removed from Satan's creation.

Knowing all I had done, I just couldn't understand why God would be so good to me. I didn't even say that out loud, and I didn't have to. He answered my thought.

"Love, my child. You can only know in part the depth of my love. It is stronger, deeper, and wider than you realize. But one day you will see."

As the plane took off, I smiled. Not just with my lips but with my heart. I had found the love of my life. I had found the one whom my soul loves. He loves me fiercely, unparalleled, across time and space—from the beginning, beyond eternity, and without limits. I gently put my life in his hands. He cherishes and adores me. Rainbows and falling stars seal his promises to me. Through the shedding of his divine blood, he shed the broken woman that was to unveil the beauty of life within.

About the Author

Author photo by Danielle Arcilesi

Michelle is a native of Arkansas, now living in Maryland. She is married to Aaron, has four adult children, one teenage stepdaughter, two dogs, and one granddog. After leaving her twenty-five-year career in physical therapy, she became a real estate agent in Virginia and Maryland, thinking that would be her last career change. God boldly closed those doors, redirecting her to the vision he delivered many years prior: to publish her book and minister to women. She admits trying to run from the purpose God whispered during one of her most broken moments, but meeting powerfully with the Holy Spirit, the task was something her heart was unable to escape. She has an intense passion for freedom ministry and mission work. She loves travel, nature, exercise, and reading. All revitalize her spirit and quench her adventurous fire. Aaron and Michelle serve at Freedom Church in Bel Air, Maryland.

Printed in the USA
CPSIA information can be obtained
at www.ICGtesting.com
CBHW031525101024
15669CB00034B/311